Frontier Military Series
VIII

TENTH CAVALRY "BUFFALO SOLDIERS" ON THE PARADE GROUND
The Tenth Cavalry came to Fort Custer on May 5, 1892.
View to the northwest, with officer's quarters buildings in the background.
Courtesy, The National Archives.

FORT CUSTER
ON THE BIG HORN
1877-1898

its history and personalities
as told and pictured by
its contemporaries

compiled and edited by
RICHARD UPTON

917.8638
U71f

THE ARTHUR H. CLARK COMPANY
Glendale, California
1973

144469

Copyright ©, 1973, by
THE ARTHUR H. CLARK COMPANY

All rights reserved including the rights to
translate or reproduce this work or parts
thereof in any form or by any media.

LIBRARY OF CONGRESS CATALOG CARD NUMBER 72-90519

ISBN 0-87062-101-7

Dedicated to My Wife, Frankie,
and our two boys, Kip and Jim
all of whom it might be said
"served" at Fort Custer

Contents

ACKNOWLEDGMENTS	13
INTRODUCTION	15
PART ONE - THE EARLY YEARS, 1877-1884	
Captain Erasmus Corwin Gilbreath's Story	27
From Texas to Fort Custer	28
The Camp at Terry's Landing	36
At Fort Custer	42
The Bannock Campaign, 1878	48
Henry A. Frith's Bannock Trip	50
Duty and Pleasure in Montana	54
Rolando B. Moffett's Letter	60
Off for Fort Buford	66
PART TWO - THE MIDDLE YEARS, 1885-1892	
Private James O. Purvis	71
"Fort Custer News"	73
Comments by "Judge"	90
Tenth Anniversary of the Custer Fight	100
Captain Godfrey's Story	103
Sioux Chief Gall's Story	106
A Grand Ball at Fort Custer	113
Crow Indians and the Swordbearer Incident, 1887	117
The Death of Swordbearer	155
An Agency to be Vacant	166
Custer and Junction City	169
The Fort Custer Stage	173
Wovoka and the Lame Deer Episode, 1890	179
Crow Celebrations at the Custer Battlefield	191
H. L. Knight's Account	192

Part Three – The Twilight Years, 1893–1898

The Tenth Cavalry "Buffalo Soldiers" Arrive . . 201
    Captain Horace Bivins, by George Beebe . . . 205
Crow Scouts at Fort Custer, by W. H. Banfill . . 211
The Final Exodus and Fort Custer's Last Stand . 217
Dismantling the Fort: Major Reynolds' Account . 229

Part Four – Pioneer Rememberings

Charles F. Schneider's Recollections . . . 241
Trumpeter Olsen's Recollections 248
Sarah Thompson's Recollections 250

Epilogue

The Search for Fort Custer 261

Appendices

A: The Fort Custer History Document 273
B: Post Commanders of Fort Custer 289
C: Units Stationed at Fort Custer 291
D: Henry Klenck, Indian War Veteran 293

Bibliography 297

Index 303

Illustrations

Tenth Cavalry on the Parade Ground	*frontispiece*
Thomas Leforge with Dr. Thomas M. Marquis	19
Lieutenant Gustavus Cheney Doane	19
Map of the Fort Custer Area, 1877–1898	26
Second Cavalry Officers at Fort Ellis	31
Lieutenant Colonel George A. Custer	31
"Diamond R" Ox Teams in Miles City, 1880	33
The Steamboat "Rosebud"	33
Bones on the Custer Battlefield	43
First Monument on the Custer Hill	43
Eleventh Infantry at the Custer Battlefield	45
General Store Personnel, Fort Custer, 1880	47
Bannock Warriors Captured in 1878	51
The Stage Station, Fort Custer	63
Officers' Quarters at Fort Custer	63
Crow Indian Chiefs and Treaty Commissioners, 1879	67
The Fort Custer Band and Bandmaster Walker	77
Ice Detail Working on the Big Horn River	83
Fort Custer Commissary Building	83
A Picnic at Fort Custer	97
The Davey Milk Ranch	99
Interior View of the Enlisted Men's Barracks	99
General Godfrey, Major Reno, and Sioux Chief Gall	108
Tenth Anniversary of the Custer Fight	109
Company K, Fifth Infantry, at the Custer Battlefield	109
Survivors of the Custer Fight in 1886	111
Paul McCormick and "Liver-Eating" Johnson	115
Crows Firing at the Agency Building	119

Colonel N.A.M. Dudley and Staff, 1887	136
Mess Tables in the Field	136
Parade Ground and Fort Buildings	137
First Cavalry on the Parade Ground	139
Deaf Bull, Chief Crazy Head, and Chief Plenty Coups	145
Followers of Swordbearer in 1887	153
Plat of Swordbearer's Death	157
Fire Bear, Slayer of Swordbearer	157
Custer Forwarding Company	175
The Fort Custer Stage	175
Troop G, First Cavalry	187
Plat of the Lame Deer Episode	187
Forgotten Faces of Fort Custer	195
View of Fort Custer on the Bluffs of the Big Horn	200
Snow Scene at Fort Custer, 1897	203
Captain Robert D. Read, Tenth Cavalry	203
Sergeant of the Crow Scouts and Two Whistle	207
Horace Bivins, Tenth Cavalry	207
Crow Scouts at Fort Custer	213
Interior View of the Infantry Barracks	213
Abandoned Buildings at Fort Custer	230
The Fort Water Tower and Bar	231
Officers' Quarters and one of the Barns	233
The Ferry between Hardin and Fort Custer	235
Enlisted Men's Barracks	235
Trumpeter Kaiser	249
Monument on the Custer Battlefield	249
The Steamer "Batchelor"	253
Livery Stable at the Fort	253
Marker at the Site of the Parade Ground	257
Denny Burns, Fort Custer Forage Master	257
Aerial View of the Site of Fort Custer	263
Lillian Klenck Maynard and Mabel Klenck Nelson	268
Plat of Fort Custer, 1892	281
Henry Klenck	292

Acknowledgments

The contribution to *Fort Custer on the Big Horn* made by my wife, Frankie, is incalculable. Her ideas and suggestions provided a constant environment of creative stimuli. Without this help and encouragement the book could never have been written.

A special nod of appreciation is given to the staff of the old *Billings* (Montana) *Gazette* and the talented writers that graced the pages of that newspaper during those exciting early days, especially: Thomas B. Marquis, George H. Beebe, W.H. Banfill and H.L. Knight.

Two Montana librarians, Myrtle Cooper, reference librarian at the Parmly Billings Memorial Library in Billings, Montana, and Josephine Self, serials librarian at Eastern Montana College, also in Billings, were particularly helpful locating elusive manuscripts and providing microfilm of fragile early newspapers.

My special thanks to the late Lillian Klenck Maynard, May Klenck, both of Billings, Montana, and Mabel Klenck Nelson of Lake Park, Minnesota, all daughters of Henry Carl Klenck, Fort Custer soldier, for their kind hospitality at the Klenck farm.

I will always be grateful to Hugh Shick of North Hollywood, California, for the encouragement that he and his lovely wife, Penny, gave me on this Fort Custer project.

In addition to those whose help is acknowledged in the chapter entitled, "The Search for Fort Custer," I am pleased to recognize the following people whose help was greatly appreciated: Hank Maynard, Esther Stewart, Calvin Cumin, Fred Krieg, George Osten, the late Don Foote, Stella Foote, Peter Yegen, Jr., Ken Roahen and J.K. Ralston, all of Billings, Montana; James King, Lame Deer, Montana; Captain H. Kenneth Davidson, U.S.N. (Ret.), Long Beach, California; P.J. Walsh, Casper, Wyoming; Floyd Warren and sons, Hardin, Montana; Mike Reynolds, Hamilton, Montana; Cliff Soubier, Historian, Custer Battlefield, Montana; Alys Freeze, Head, Western History Department, Denver Public Library; Harriett C. Meloy, Librarian, Montana Historical Society, Helena; Harry Clifford, Crow Agency, Montana; Patricia Nurre, Librarian, Big Horn County Library, Hardin, Montana; Rudy and Dennis Boettger, both of Milwaukee, Wisconsin; Maurice Frink, Boulder, Colorado; Casey Barthelmess, Miles City, Montana; Jim Willert, Glendora, California; and B. William Henry, Jr., Historian, Fort Laramie, Wyoming.

To all the others who lent a helping hand please accept my sincere thanks.

And finally, thanks to my mother and father, George and Hazel Upton, of Cuesta-by-the-Sea, California, who never quite believed that this book would ever come to pass.

For whatever shortcomings this book may have, I, Richard Upton, am solely responsible.

El Segundo, California
September, 1972

Introduction

It's what you bring to something or someplace that makes the experience more meaningful. It can be just a house, or the house where Beethoven lived and worked; it can be just a barren hill, or the hill where Christ was crucified; it can be a rolling, broken countryside baking under a relentless summer sun, or a battlefield where a national hero and over two hundred soldiers died serving their country; it can be just a flat, open field atop a bluff overlooking two relatively unimportant rivers in Montana, or the one-time site of what some had called the "finest military post in the world." This is the story of Fort Custer and its people – by its people.

The need for a military post or posts in the Yellowstone Valley was quite obvious when the news of the Custer fight of June 25-26, 1876, was learned. As a matter of fact, Lieutenant-General Philip H. Sheridan and Brigadier General Alfred H. Terry, in their reports to the Secretary of War for the year 1875 stressed the great need for at least two military posts in the area. Their recommendations were acted on in July of 1876, and money was set aside for these forts.

Perhaps the most intriguing aspect of old Fort Custer is the remarkable number of men associated with the fort who have had written or have themselves written full length books of and about their western adventures. Among these were Lieutenant Gustavus Doane,[1] famous Yellowstone Park explorer; Tom Leforge,[2] Indian scout; Yellowstone Kelly,[3] scout and explorer; Liver-Eating Johnson,[4] mountain man; army leaders General Sheridan[5] and General Sherman;[6] Grant Marsh,[7] famous steamboat master; the famous Buffalo Soldiers,[8] and the 10th Cavalry; and frontier photographers F. Jay Haynes,[9] Christian Barthelmess,[10] and Stanley Morrow.[11]

Other photographers who had studios at the fort were David F. Barry, O. S. Goff, and from nearby Crow Agency, Fred E. Miller. A frustrating sidelight regarding these famous picture takers is that the author has been able to locate only a few samples of each one's pictorial record of the old fort. Among the glass-plate files of L. A. Huffman, frontier photographer long associated with Miles City and Fort Keogh, only one photo of Fort Custer could be located. One reason might be that the old glass plates could be wiped clean and used over again. Also the

---

[1] Orrin H. and Lorraine Bonney, *Battle Drums and Geysers: The Life and Journals of Lieutenant Gustavus Cheyney Doane*. (See bibliography for complete citations of footnote-cited works.)

[2] Thomas B. Marquis, *Memoirs of a White Crow Indian*.

[3] M. M. Quaife, *Yellowstone Kelly*.

[4] Raymond W. Thorpe, and Robert Bunker, *Crow Killer: The Saga of Liver-Eating Johnson*.

[5] Gen. Philip H. Sheridan, *Personal Memoirs*.

[6] Gen. William T. *Sherman, Memoirs*.

[7] Joseph Mills Hanson, *The Conquest of the Missouri*.

[8] William H. Leckie, *The Buffalo Soldiers: . . . Negro Cavalry in the West*.

[9] Freeman Tilden, *Following the Frontier with F. Jay Haynes*.

[10] Maurice Frink, with Casey Barthelmess, *Photographer on an Army Mule*.

[11] Wesley R. Hurt, and William E. Lass, *Frontier Photographer: Stanley J. Morrow's Dakota Years*.

glass plates would be broken quite easily. It is possible, but unlikely, that there were simply not many pictures taken.

Other legendary figures of the American West who are easily recognizable and who played parts in Fort Custer's history include Western artist and 10th Cavalry illustrator Frederic Remington,[12] General Nelson Miles,[13] General E. S. Godfrey, Reno Hill veteran, who formulated his famous *Century Magazine* article[14] at Fort Custer; and General Hugh Scott,[15] then a young lieutenant in the 7th Cavalry.

General John J. (Black Jack) Pershing, while carried in each of the Monthly Post Returns and Record of Events of Fort Custer, actually was on detached service at Fort Assinniboine, M.T. Pershing derived his nickname while serving as a white officer in the all-black 10th Cavalry.[16]

Military leaders of Civil War times such as General George P. Buell, Colonel John P. Hatch, Colonel Nathan A. M. Dudley, Colonel John W. Davidson and Colonel James S. Brisbin served as officers in command of the old post.

Indian fighters Major Eugene Baker,[17] Billy Hamilton,[18] Major Henry Carroll and Major-General Frank D. Baldwin[19] are among Fort Custer's alumni.

The names and deeds of Indian leaders Plenty

---

[12] Harold McCracken, *The Frederic Remington Book.*
[13] Gen. Nelson A. Miles, *Personal Recollections.*
[14] Gen. Edward Settle Godfrey, "Custer's Last Battle," in *Century Mag.*, vol. 43, no. 3 (Jan. 1892), pp. 358–87.
[15] Hugh Lenox Scott, *Some Memories of a Soldier.*
[16] Richard Wormser, *Yellowlegs: The Story of the United States Cavalry,* p. 452.
[17] Robert Ege, *Tell Baker to Strike Them Hard.*
[18] W. T. Hamilton, *My Sixty Years on the Plains.*
[19] Alice Blackwood Baldwin, *Memoirs of the Late Frank D. Baldwin.*

Coups,[20] Two Leggings,[21] Sitting Bull, Gall, and Swordbearer occupy places of special interest in the history of Fort Custer and its vicinity.

The remarkable thing about all of these men is that, in the thousands of words written about them and their adventures, seldom is there much, if any, mention of their experiences at the place, which for a time, was a dominant factor in their lives.

If it were not for the contemporary newspapers, a few diaries, a limited number of pictures, an articulate 1st Cavalry private and the memories of a diminishing number of old timers, our history of Fort Custer would be limited to twenty feet of records in the National Archives that record the facts but not the feelings of that marvelous old fort.

Tom Leforge, in Thomas B. Marquis' excellent book, *Memoirs of a White Crow Indian,* tells us of the selecting of the site of Big Horn Post #2 that later was to become Fort Custer.

In the spring of 1877, he and Lieutenant Gustavus Doane, went up the Big Horn River from the Yellowstone River by canoe to select the site of the new fort. Leforge says, "We set out some marker stakes for the guidance of the coming pioneer corps of workers. Not long afterward, I guided General Buell to the place, which was on a bench hill near the junction of the Little Big Horn and the Big Horn rivers, about fifteen miles down the valley from the site of the last stand of General Custer, after whom the post was to be named. I pointed out to the soldier workmen the stakes Lieutenant Doane had set for the road building."[22]

---

[20] Frank B. Linderman, *American: The Life Story of a Great Indian.*
[21] Peter Nabokov, *Two Leggings: The Making of a Crow Warrior.*
[22] Marquis, *op. cit.,* p. 281.

THOMAS LEFORGE AND
DR. THOMAS B. MARQUIS
"I guided General Buell
to this place . . ."
Courtesy, Custer Battlefield Museum.

LT. GUSTAVUS CHENEY DOANE
went up the Big Horn by canoe
to select the site of the fort.
Courtesy, Denver Public Library,
Western Collection.

Thus the story of old Fort Custer begins.

Using newspaper accounts, eye-witness accounts of events, letters and personal diaries, biographies, autobiographies and memoirs, examining archaeological and geological remains and through a selection of old photos, most never before published, we will follow, in a chronological fashion, the history of old Fort Custer.

Occasionally, because of a faltering memory, or simply because no two people view an event exactly alike, certain discrepancies in the tales will appear. The author's opinion will usually be stated on the basis of what evidence he has gathered over a period of ten years research.

The official records of the fort may be found in the appendices of the book. Those interested in the fort facts will not be disappointed, as there are twenty linear feet of these documental records in the National Archives in Washington, D.C., covering all twenty-one years of the fort's existence.[23] I just might warn anyone who is contemplating reading these, that an equivalent twenty-one years might be needed for a detailed reading – the records are all handwritten and fading.

We were especially pleased to discover the writings of Private James O. Purvis, 1st Cavalry, in issues of the *Billings* (Montana) *Gazette* of 1886. Writing under the heading "Fort Custer News," and some-

---

[23] U.S. National Archives. Record Group 98: Records of United States Army Commands, Preliminary Inventory of Records of Army Posts, 1813–1942. The entire period of existence of the fort is covered, including copies of letters sent, registers of letters received, and copies of orders. Other records include various rosters of commissioned and non-commissioned officers, summary court records, and records of post chaplain, post recruiting officer, and various post quartermasters.

times using his nickname "Coo," Purvis not only reported the news, but reflected, in a perceptive and intelligent manner, the feelings and attitudes of the enlisted men of 1886 at Fort Custer.

Many of the soldiers of that period were from other lands. Many did not speak English when they enlisted, a large number could not read and write, and many had no trade or occupation. The thirteen dollars a month that the privates received, considering the times in which they lived, actually was quite adequate.

James Purvis was an exception. He served in the cavalry for twenty years and was discharged a private whose character was determined by his commanding officer, Colonel N. A. Dudley, as "good." The designation GOOD is revealing in that a soldier could earn the character rating VERY GOOD or EXCELLENT. Of course, he may also have no comment on the discharge and he may receive a dishonorable discharge.

After reading his comments, which really are, in places, quite literary and even might be philosophical in nature, the reader, considering the times in which Purvis lived, can't help but be impressed by the outspokenness of Private Purvis. His criticism of his superiors and the living conditions, especially the canteen, are quite revolutionary for the day.

His comments and observations regarding the Custer fight during the 10th Anniversary of the battle reveal intellectual curiosity.

Perhaps the fact that Private Purvis received his discharge on October 10 of the same year stimulated this bravado. I think not. James Purvis was a man who lived a hundred years before his time.

I think that we all realize that no matter how many

famous soldiers, mountain men, scouts, Indians or Buffalo Soldiers lived at Fort Custer, the enigma of the man whose name the fort bears dominates in death the events of old Fort Custer as he dominated in life the people with whom he served.

The fort was named, of course, after Lieutenant Colonel George Armstrong Custer and was built as a direct result of the famous Custer fight of 1876.

Visitors to the fort were automatically attracted to the battlefield some twelve miles distant. Anniversaries of the Custer fight brought Indians and soldiers together at the field of battle and stimulated the fact and fancy about the fight and its white leader that continues to this day.

It has been said that Fort Custer was great in name only. This conclusion, of course, is not borne out by the facts. The delegations of military men from various parts of the world (Russia, France, Japan) pronounced the fort the finest cavalry post in the world.

Recorded in the Monthly Post Returns of the fort, we learn that certain of the post's officers served on detached service as instructors at West Point, Cornell University and Virginia Military Institute.

The commanding officers were, for the most part, outstanding men with spectacular credentials for leading men in battle during the Civil War.

The fort stimulated all activity in the Yellowstone Valley, towns were established, farms settled on the fertile soil, and steamboats were challenged to establish new records of speed and distance.

Fort Custer was a success. It helped neutralize the hostile Indians of the area, something that the Forts

Reno, Phil Kearny and C. F. Smith, guarding the Bozeman Trail, were never able to do. Fort Custer brought peace, security and a new civilization to the Yellowstone Valley.

In the main body of the text (Part One through Part Four) the contemporary accounts appear in Roman type, and *the introductory matter and comments by this editor are identified in italic type.*

PART ONE

The Early Years
1877–1884

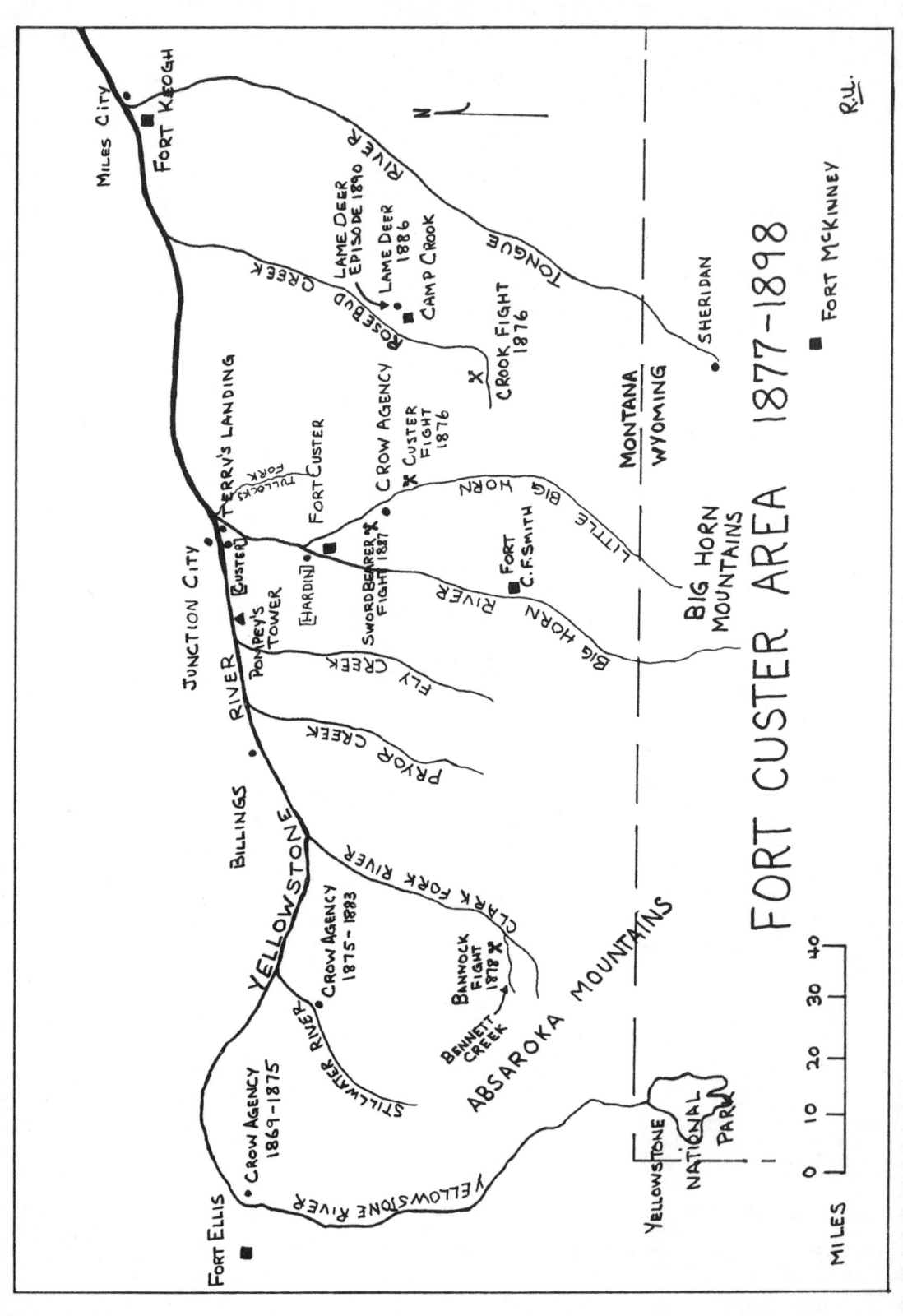

Captain Gilbreath's Story

The account of Captain Erasmus Corwin Gilbreath's adventures at and around Fort Custer was compiled by a journalist of the Billings Gazette *named W. H. Banfill. Banfill's work appears often in the newspapers of Montana during the 1920s and 1930s. His sensitive literary style and perceptive sense of history will appear from time to time to help tell the story of old Fort Custer.*

The account of the establishment of Terry's Landing, river trips up the Big Horn and life during the early years at Fort Custer contribute magnificently to the telling of the old fort's history.

Captain E. C. Gilbreath commanded Company H of the Eleventh Infantry at Fort Custer from 1877 to 1882, and was later for several years in command at Fort Buford at the junction of the Missouri and Yellowstone rivers.

The following story appeared serially in Montana newspapers: the Rocky Mountain Husbandman *of Great Falls (July 2, 1931), the* Fallon County Times *of Baker (July 10, 1931), and the* Hardin Tribune-Herald *(July 17 and 24, 1931). Captain Gilbreath writes:*

FROM TEXAS TO FORT CUSTER

In 1876 I was stationed at Fort Concho in Texas when news came of the massacre of Custer and his companies of the Seventh Cavalry. We were ordered to Dakota as part of the reinforcements that were sent into the northwest following the loss of Custer and his men. I left Concho with my company, marching to the railway at Denison which was as far as the Missouri, Kansas and Texas Railway had built from St. Louis at that time. The company marched the 260 miles from Fort Concho to Denison in 18 days.

The route through Brownville [?Brownwood] to Denison was very sparsely settled at that time and there were no railroads in the country. From Denison on it was necessary to change cars seven times to get to the end of railway transportation at Yankton in the territory of Dakota. My company went into camp there with others of the regiment. After a few days we went up the Missouri River on the steamer "Nellie Peck," arriving at Standing Rock, afterward called Fort Yates, on September 10, 1876.

In May 1877, our companies were ordered to join those of Sultz and Bennett and to rendezvous at Fort Abraham Lincoln near Bismarck, where we were to take transportation for the country around the Yellowstone River. We had a very good camp with General George P. Buell in command. He was ordered to send two companies to General Miles at Fort Keogh and to take the rest of his command up the Yellowstone and Big Horn rivers to build a fort to be called Fort Custer.

A and H companies, the latter my company, were selected for field service and placed under the command of Major [Charles G.] Bartlett. The companies embarked as steamboats were loaded for the upper country so that each boat would have a guard. The reasons for selecting A and H companies for service with General [Nelson] Miles was that there were but 60 men in the two companies, and General Buell wanted the strongest with him. My company was left to the last and I felt, as did the other officers, that we were being left in the cold. There were a great many steamboats on the Missouri then as the amount of supplies to be taken up from Bismarck was very great. In addition to the men in the regiment, about 500 mechanics were being taken up the river to help with construction work at both Keogh and Custer.

I was pretty much disgusted as the various outfits left and especially when I was told to take what boat I could get. Finally, I got notice that there would be room on the "Ashland" for my men. I went over to Bismarck on a ferry boat expecting to see some little bit of an uncomfortable affair and was consequently surprised to find the "Ashland" the largest and finest boat I had seen come up the river. This was a boat that had been used for transporting cotton out of the Arkansas River to New Orleans and was very finely outfitted. She was built very high to accommodate large quantities of cotton and her cabin was handsome. I concluded I was decidedly in luck to get my company on such a craft.

The "Ashland" was built so that she caught more wind than most boats and was consequently slow in her progress up the river. The distance from Bismarck to Fort Keogh was more than 700 miles by the river. We arrived at Fort Keogh on June 22, having been almost a month making that distance by boat. On the way, however, we had passed a number of smaller boats, especially in the Yellowstone River, which was a very rapid stream and required the most powerful machinery to stem the current. We overtook the "Dugan," which was carrying A and G companies and about 250 mechanics for Fort Custer. Major Bartlett was in command and he was glad enough to bring himself, Captain [George Louis] Choisey and the whole of company A on board the "Ashland."

Arriving at Fort Keogh, which was then called Cantonment or Post No. 1, we were placed in tents nearby and our little battalion of 60 men prepared to take the field. Fort Keogh, named after Captain Keogh, Custer's second in command who was killed with him,[24] was a busy place at that time with all of the Fifth Infantry of which 10 companies were mounted on Oregon horses; four troops of the Second Cavalry, four companies of the Twenty-second Infantry, four companies of the First Infantry, and two companies of the Eleventh Infantry.

Although we did not finally go into the field, I saw at this place the last hostile shots fired against troops of the United States.[25] There was a stage station on the north side of the Yellowstone, while our camp was on lower ground on the south side of the stream. There was a guard at the station to protect the men and animals from a prospective raid by the Indians. After sunset as we were strolling about shots were fired at the station and soon there was a regular fusillade of firing from the top of the hills back of the stage station. The Indians rushed in and tried to drive off the herds at the station. They got a few

---

[24] Maj. Marcus Reno was second in command at the Little Big Horn fight. Capt. Myles Keogh was in command of Troop I. Perhaps the responsibility of command evolved to Keogh during the fight, but this will never be known. (R.U.)

[25] Subsequent events proved this false, as we shall soon see. (R.U.)

SECOND CAVALRY OFFICERS AT FORT ELLIS IN 1871
Several of these men played important roles in the history of Fort Custer.
l. to r.: Lt. Grugan, Capt. Thompson, Lts. Wright and Doane, Capt. Forsyth, Asst. Surgeon Campbell, Physician Whitewood, Lt. Hamilton, Col. Lt. Jerome, Capt. Tyler, Lts. McClernand, Schofield.
W. H. Jackson photo.
Courtesy, Montana Historical Society, Helena.

LIEUT. COL. GEORGE A. CUSTER
The enigma of the man whose name the fort bears dominates in death the events of old Fort Custer as he dominated in life the people with whom he served.
Courtesy, Custer Battlefield Museum.

animals and then rode off, firing more than a hundred shots as they passed along the top of the bluff. The shots showed very distinctly in the distance. I have never seen a hostile shot since.

While we were at Fort Keogh, General [William T.] Sherman and General [Alfred] Terry came to the post, making the trip up the river by boat as there were no railroads beyond Bismarck. General Terry was going to Fort Custer, and Sherman, then commanding general of the United States armies, was crossing the continent to the Pacific coast. Sherman intended to take an ambulance and troop of cavalry and go west from the mouth of the Big Horn near Fort Custer.

After their visit to Fort Keogh was over, it was decided that Major Bartlett and our two companies should go on up the river on the same boat with them to report for duty at Fort Custer. The boat was the "Rosebud," of which the famous Captain Grant Marsh was the commander.

The trip up the Big Horn was a slow one and took six days. The Big Horn was a regular mountain torrent and we were obliged to do a great deal of cordelling or warping to get over some of the rapids. A long cable was run out from the bow of the boat and made fast to trees or logs and the machinery of the boat was then used to pull the boat over the difficulty. If no tree was available, it was attached to what the boatmen called a "dead man," a large log placed in a trench and held down by stakes driven in a slanting way over the log. The small engine used to draw in the cable and thus pull the boat along was called the "nigger" or "stop the nigger."

We had on board Colonel Broadwater, who was

"DIAMOND R" OX TEAMS AT MILES CITY IN 1880
Lumber for the construction of Fort Custer was hauled by these teams
the thirty-three miles from Terry's Landing.
L. A. Huffman photo. Courtesy, Montana Historical Society.

IT WAS A NOTABLE GATHERING ON THE "ROSEBUD," JULY 23, 1877
David F. Barry photo. Courtesy, Denver Public Library, Western Collection.

the contractor for wagon transportation. The mark of his trains was the Diamond R. He used oxen principally and the frontier word for ox train was bull train. Once when we were stuck in a bad place on the Big Horn Captain Marsh said: "General Broadwater, we're stuck. How much will you charge to haul this freight up to the fort with your bulls?" Broadwater said, "Oh, not very much, Captain."

As soon as the rope was made fast, and the boat began to move, the captain said, "Colonel Broadwater, I think I will take your bulls to haul this freight." Broadwater said, "All right." But as soon as the boat was moving smoothly again, Marsh said: "Broady, you shan't carry a pound of this freight if I have to carry it all up in a yawlboat." It had been General when we were stuck fast, Colonel as the prospects began to brighten, and when the boat was moving along serenely it was just "Broady."

The living on the boats was usually very good and one could get a cup of coffee or a lunch at any hour by going to the pantry. There was usually rice and hominy at every meal and this usually fell to the lot of the wharf men who got their food after our people were through. The life of a roustabout, called for short "rooster," was anything but a happy one and their fare was not good as a rule. We had excellent appetites. Mrs. Gilbreath once said, "Captain Marsh, I can't understand it, but I always have fine appetite and enjoy your food." He replied, "Well, Mrs. Gilbreath, I don't understand it either, for I pledge you my word, I have been sitting down with them rice cakes and hominy balls in front of me for 20 years and I have never put a tooth in them."

There was a very congenial party on the "Rosebud"

with Generals Sherman, Terry and Miles and their staffs as well as a good many other officers. It was very interesting to listen to them talk. Sherman told us of an officer who was in great trouble and went to his commanding officer, a gruff old fellow, with his difficulties. Not receiving much comfort, he said, "Colonel, if I don't get help in this matter, from you, I shall commit suicide." "I don't see any objection to that," the colonel replied.

On the way up the Big Horn River, we met the steamboat "Silver City" coming downstream. As she had General [Philip H.] Sheridan and a party on board, we tied up to the bank, both boats, and General Sheridan came on board our boat for a talk with General Sherman. It was a notable gathering for on board the "Rosebud" that day, July 23, 1877, every grade in the army was represented except that of major-general. There were: General [William T.] Sherman, Lieutenant-General [Philip H.] Sheridan, Brigadier-General [Alfred H.] Terry, Brigadier-General [George] Crook, Colonel [Orlando M.] Poe of the engineers, Colonel [Nelson A.] Miles, Fifth infantry, Colonel [John M.] Bacon, Seventh cavalry, Major [Charles G.] Bartlett, Captain Gilbreath and Lieutenants [James E.] Macklin, [John] Whitney and Reva.

After a long pow-wow to which we were all admitted without regard to rank, the boats separated and we went on our way. Boats going up or down on the Big Horn or Yellowstone never ran at night on account of the current so that we were six full days reaching Custer from Keogh, a distance of 200 miles or more by river.

I did not take my company off the boat at Custer

as I was ordered by General Buell to go back on the boat to the mouth of the Big Horn and find a place to land stores for Fort Custer. It was not practicable to navigate the Big Horn although I saw 15 boats at one time at the bank near Fort Custer.[26]

THE CAMP AT TERRY'S LANDING

We started back on the afternoon of July 24 and ran out of the river in a few hours and then up the Yellowstone River about two miles. General Sherman went with us. He left the boat at the mouth of the river to go with Captain [Randolph] Norwood, Troop L, Second Cavalry, up the Yellowstone River and on across the continent.

After taking my men off the boat we camped for the night in a cottonwood grove. Next day, I rode up and down the stream for some distance selecting a camping site. We then soon pitched our tents and got into good shape. In clearing off the beach for the camp, the men killed 16 rattlesnakes in one day. The sage brush was very thick and heavy. We framed our

---

[26] This is a remarkable statement considering the difficulty of navigating the Big Horn River even during the spring and early summer when the river would be at its highest. It is even more remarkable since, according to a privately printed work by Agnes L. Jones of Billings, Montana, entitled *Crow Country*, this represented one-half of the steamboats active on the entire Yellowstone River in 1877. These were:

Far West	Savanah	Rosebud
Western	Kendall	Big Horn
Tiger	Weaver	Fontanelle
Yellowstone	Victory	General Custer
General Meade	Arkansas	Josephine
Peninah	Fanchin (?)	Ashland
General Sherman	J. C. Fletcher	Dugan
Florence	Tidal Wave	E. H. Durfee
Meyer	Silver City	F. Y. Batchelor
Osceola*	J. H. Rankin**	Nellie Peck

*Blown to pieces in storm at mouth of Powder River.
**Sunk at mouth of O'Fallon Creek.

tents, using the lumber at hand for that purpose. For myself and Lieutenant [Ogden B.] Read, I had three large hospital tents while for the men there was a tent for each two.

The camp which I established at the mouth of the Big Horn as a forwarding point for the supplies going to Fort Custer was soon a busy place. Boats began to arrive and I received millions of pounds of all kinds of stores – lumber, grain, hay, provisions, and all sorts of material to be used in building the new post, which was to accommodate 10 companies. All the lumber for its construction except the main timbers of cottonwood cut about the post, was delivered at my camp and hauled by Diamond R trains 33 miles to the post.

I fixed on the name of Terry's Landing for my camp. Lieutenant Read and I went for our wives, who had remained at Fort Yates [Standing Rock, in southern North Dakota] and they joined us after a beautiful trip up the Yellowstone. We enjoyed the life of the camp very much and had a better time than the people who came up the river first. The country was alive with game and we always had several different kinds in our larder at once – elk, deer, buffalo and mountain sheep. Fish were very plentiful and delicious so we had no end of sport.[27]

We could see the road from the camp as it passed from the ferry above us down the other side of the river so that we always had timely warning of the coming of strangers. On sight of them we got everything in shape for a lunch in case the visitors needed one, which they usually did. There were no settle-

---

[27] Today, in 1971, the Yellowstone River from Billings to Custer is polluted by industrial waste and the fish must not be eaten. The fishing is still great above Billings toward Yellowstone Park.

ments along the Yellowstone in 1877 and our camp became a regular stopping place for all officers going to and from Fort Custer. Everyone getting off the boat came there and we were never without company. There were all classes of visitors and we thoroughly enjoyed having everybody.

Occasionally some of the visitors would think of us and bring a surprise. Once Colonel Broadwater came in covered with dust and getting out of his light wagon, started in his cheery way to bring Mrs. Gilbreath a watermelon. As he reached the door, his foot slipped and away went the melon, which he had carefully carried 120 miles. As it was thoroughly ripe, it broke into a dozen very small pieces. Another friend sent us a dozen chickens which were the very first in that part of the country.

The ferry established for crossing the Yellowstone had been built before we came up the river. The boat was of cottonwood, cut down with an axe alone to a thickness of about nine inches. It was a heavy affair and had been used before we came only occasionally. The mail used to cross over only now and then as Indians were too bad to trifle with. When we first went into the Yellowstone country our mail was sent to Bismarck and then up the river on any boat which would carry it.

Often we received 20 or 30 sacks of mail without locks, so that anyone thinking he might have a letter could look over the mail and take anything marked for him. I used to take out the mail for my camp and then send the bags on my trains to Fort Custer. Soon a stage line was established along the Yellowstone and then our mail came to Fort Custer by way of Ogden, Utah, and Helena, Montana, and then down the Yellowstone. We were often 16 or 18 days hearing from New York. Letter mail was always packed separately so that in any emergency the papers could be thrown away. Later lines were extended to Rock Creek on the Union Pacific Railway, going south from Fort Custer and from Fort Keogh east to Bismarck across the country. In a few months after we arrived at Terry's Landing, mail was being received regularly.

My daughter Nan was born in a tent at Terry's Landing on October 31, 1877. I was worried enough that day. I had sent for a doctor at the post and as none arrived, I could do nothing but walk up and down in front of the tent and look for him. He did not come and we had to depend on the services of our cook, who happened to be a very skillful nurse. On the second day the doctor came and after staying for a short time returned to the post.

One day I saw a boat come down the river and tie up on the opposite side near the ferry. As soon as a tent went up, I went to see what was up. I found that a Jew named Batzinski [Basinski] had put up a store tent.[28] In it was everything imaginable, from fish hooks and calico to grain and provisions – there was even reading matter, in fact about everything but pianos. Instead of one boat, he had three or four mackinaws with which he had brought his store from Bozeman or Helena. He had come down the river looking for a likely place to start a store somewhere. That was the beginning of Junction City.

I built a blockhouse for the protection of our families and men as the Indians were still very bad. The

---

[28] Mark H. Brown, *The Plainsman of the Yellowstone.*

Sioux were always lounging about and in August the Nez Perces had passed through the country about 12 miles above where I was. General Howard had followed them for miles and General Sturgis of the Seventh Cavalry had a fight with them at Canyon Creek about 40 miles above me.

At the time of this fight some men were coming down the Yellowstone on their way to Fort Keogh or Miles City, a town which had just been started near that post. General Sturgis put his wounded men on these boats and they came up to my landing. One man of L troop died before he got to the landing. I took him off the boat and buried him. The others I provided with canvas to shelter them from rough weather and they continued on to Fort Keogh. These mackinaws were flat bottom boats with a square stern and, being wide, could carry a large load. The potato and onion supply for the two posts, Keogh and Custer, was purchased in Montana and sent by mackinaws down the Yellowstone.

The teams hauling stores from our landing to the post were interesting. Oxen generally were used to draw the wagons which were placed with one large vehicle in the lead and two smaller ones hitched as trails to the first with short tongues and chains. Often there were from 18 to 20 oxen on one wagon with its trails and they carried a very heavy load.

The teamsters were a novelty and a study. One I remember had Henry Ward Beecher and Theodore Tilton on the tongue and Hayes and Tilden, Webster and Calhoun, Lincoln and Douglas, and other celebrities paired in an amusing way. The oxen knew their names too. For to impress it upon the mind of each for all time, the driver hurled out an oath and with a great swing of his whip, cracked it loudly and so close as to make the fur fly.

The teamsters, or bull whackers in their vernacular, came from all walks of life. Many were well educated – one I recall had been a superintendent of education in the state of Kansas. Most of them had drifted from one thing to another for years on the frontier. Their pay was 40 gold dollars a month and rations.

Once I went in the evening to the camp of a very large train. As usual the camp was in a corral form with the wagons almost touching in two lines which inclosed an open space where the cooking was done and into which the cattle could be driven. The men slept under the wagons. This form of corral was used by all trains, both government and citizen, as a guard against Indians, as the men could fight from the inside while the animals were protected by the wagons.

On the evening of this particular visit, the herd was out grazing and the teamsters were just finishing their supper. As each completed his meal, he rubbed off his tin plate with anything at hand. As soon as all had finished, a very large man with beard all over his face and with a very coarse voice, got up from his seat on an oxyoke and said, "Who killed cock robin?" A very small man with a thin, weak voice arose and said, "I, said the sparrow, with my bow and arrow." One by one they followed through the whole story of Cock Robin, carrying it out in the soberest fashion imaginable. One of these teamsters called himself "Calamity Bill." He was educated to a certain degree, but having been followed as he thought by continued bad luck, he had dropped his correct name and all connections with the past and was trying to lose himself in "Calamity Bill."

In 1877 the whole country about the Big Horn and Yellowstone rivers was overrun by prospectors who were looking for gold. Most of them came on foot although a few had ponies. They were living on what they could kill or pick up. They came begging almost every day to Terry's Landing. If no food could be furnished, they would borrow a fish line and go whistling off to try their luck angling or they would slip out and kill game of some kind. No matter what came up, they were always cheerful and good humored.

The surveyors of the Northern Pacific Railway passed through the country fixing a line near Terry's Landing in 1877. I remained in command there until December 27, 1877, when I went with my company to Fort Custer. During the time I had been at the landing, my company cared for and shipped out to Fort Custer something close to 6,000,000 pounds of freight.

AT FORT CUSTER

At Fort Custer, Lieut. Colonel George P. Buell was in command and he had under him companies B, C, F and H of the Eleventh Infantry and the headquarters and four troops of the Second Cavalry. The quarters were very good, although not entirely finished and the post as a whole was not completed.

I visited the battlefield where Custer and his men were massacred, soon after January 1, 1878, in company with Lieutenant Charles F. Roe, Second Cavalry, who was with the Terry command and had gone over the ground two days after the massacre. My visit to the scene was a year and a half after the battle but the trail of the Indians to the great camp where Custer

The First Monument on Custer Hill, 1879

"The Hill on which Custer Died was still Covered with Bones of Horses and Men"

Both photos by Stanley J. Morrow.
Courtesy, W. H. Over Dakota Museum, University of South Dakota, Vermillion.

found them was still very plain. The hill on which Custer and his command lost their lives was still covered with the bones of horses and men. The bodies of the men had been buried but they had been washed out or uncovered by animals. Lieutenant Roe pointed out to me the places where the bodies of the officers were found and the mutilation of each was described.

The winter of 1877 and 1878 was quite severe at Fort Custer and the snow was deep. Game was plentiful and the men brought wagon loads of frozen trout, freshly caught, to the post. Of all the game, I liked blacktail deer the best with the back strop of the buffalo a close second. This "back strop" consisted of a long piece of flesh running above the backbone and along the spine. It was sometimes three feet long and of a diameter of six or eight inches. When cut across, it furnished fine, good-sized steaks.

In the spring of 1878, all of the quarters were completed and many of the walks. Trees were planted in front of our houses. That year the post was greatly broken up on account of a quarrel between several officers and the commanding officer.[29] This resulted in a trial of the juniors at Fort Keogh and to that trial all the officers and many of the men were summoned. I was left in command of the post for a month and had only one officer with men, Lieutenant [Joshua L.] Fowler, of the Second Cavalry. We got out the men and built a new road from the steamboat landing on the Big Horn to the top of the bluff on which the post stood.

---

[29] The present editor has been unable to determine the nature of the problem. The commanding officer was Lieutenant Colonel George Buell of the 11th Infantry. It seems that for an infantry officer to command a post composed of mostly cavalry troops caused some resentment on the part of the cavalry. Perhaps this was at the root of the problem.

Capt. George K. Sanderson, Eleventh Infantry, from Fort Custer made camp at the Indian village site while his men re-buried the Custer dead in the spring of 1879. Stanley J. Morrow photo. Courtesy, W. H. Over Dakota Museum, University of South Dakota, Vermilion.

We had an officer at Fort Custer, a genial whole-souled sort of a man who was always getting into funny situations. He drank a great deal and one night had stayed out very late at the post tender's store, drinking. He had placed a light in the window to steer by when he left the store. When he started home, the night was dark and he was near-sighted. A pit had been dug near his path and as he was straggling along toward the light, he fell into it. He struggled out on the same side he fell in, and starting toward the light, again tumbled in. This time he got out on the other side but facing the store lights, and supposing they were his own, he promptly went into the hole again. This time he lost his glasses, so he sat down on the side of the excavation and began to call lustily for help, until the sergeant of the guard ran over and got him home.

Another time he was showing a stranger about the post on a winter day. In trying to point out something, he got too near the edge of the steep bluff on the Big Horn side, his feet slipped, and away he went sliding, tumbling and rolling to the bottom where he soon found himself sitting on the ice, 145 feet below. Fortunately enough snow had lodged along the sides of the bluff to break the force of the fall and he was not seriously hurt. His glasses were lost, of course, and he had to be led home again.

Once he came to see me while I was at Terry's Landing. He had been down the river with six large wagons to get nails for the post. Each wagon was filled with one course of kegs so that he could travel fast with a light load. He rode up to my tent, covered with dust, and in a terrible hurry. He had ridden for miles, sitting on a bag of straw on top of the nail

GENERAL STORE PERSONNEL, FORT CUSTER, 1880
l. to r: Chinese cook; Harman, clerk; Van Squall, general roustabout, and dog; Jack Colonel; Burry, proprietor; unknown; Irvin A. Richardson; housekeeper; Bartender in Officers' mess.
Courtesy, Montana Historical Society, Helena.

kegs and as he was driving at a trot, it was a most uncomfortable position. He wanted a lunch but could not wait to eat it there. Mrs. Gilbreath gave him, among other things, a hot blackberry pie. It was amusing to see him go off in a cloud of dust with a hot pie in his hand.

In September 1878, while I was stationed at Fort Custer, the Bannock Indians living on the west side of the Rocky Mountains had broken out and were endeavoring to force their way through the mountains, following about the same line of march as the Nez Perces the year before in an effort, like them, to get to British America. The Nez Perces got as far north as the Bear Paw Mountains but the Bannocks were slower and not so well provisioned and they only succeeded in getting to the north side of the Big Horn Mountains.

THE BANNOCK CAMPAIGN, 1878

Troops from Fort Custer were ordered out against the Bannocks. There were eight troops of cavalry under Buell while I was ordered to accompany them with 50 infantrymen of my own company and of others about the post. I was first ordered to go mounted on such horses as I could pick up from the quartermaster department and from the extra cavalry horses but after a vigorous protest, I got the order changed so that I could have my men march. I was ordered to take a pack train across the country to the mouth of Clark's Fork, to meet the cavalry there and take charge of the wagon train. The cavalry was to go to the Yellowstone and crossing that stream to go up on the north side of it and cross again at Clark's Fork, and then move up that stream. The object was to reach Clark's Fork canyon before the Bannocks came out of the mountains.

I had 250 pack mules loaded with about 350 pounds each. I left the post at the same time as the cavalry on September 7, and we camped together at Fly Creek that night. The cavalry started out across the hills the next morning, giving up the idea of crossing to the north of the Yellowstone. I was ordered to follow so as to camp with them that night. We stopped for lunch and coffee at noon and it was after dark, nearly 10 o'clock before we reached camp.

The next day we reached the Clark's Fork near where it emptied into the Yellowstone. I had had a good deal of difficulty all the way out and the loads became unfixed very often. General Buell took the cavalry and the packs and marched up Clark's Fork. I was to follow with the wagons of which I had about 40. It rained terribly and was slow going. I had to cross the Clark's Fork 16 times with my train but finally reached the camp of the cavalry near the canyon where Clark's Fork comes out of the mountains. I was soon filled up with mountain trout which Lieutenant Read had caught and cooked beside the stream.

We found that General Miles had got in ahead of Buell and had killed or captured all the Bannocks before his arrival. General Miles had arrived at the mouth of the Stillwater with his party on the way to the park when a half-breed called Little Rock, who had been with the Bannocks, came to him and reported that the Indians would come out of the mountains on a certain day. Miles only had a small escort of the Fifth Infantry, consisting mainly of members of his band, who, however, were armed, and some

Crows. He had started out at once, however, marching through the night. Surrounding the Bannock camp at daylight, he attacked them, killing 15 and capturing 30 or 40; Captain [Andrew S.] Bennett, of the Fifth Infantry, was killed, being shot through the heart, and a few of the soldiers were wounded.

Little Rock, who betrayed the Bannocks, was one of the first killed by them. He had lived with them for years and taken his wife from amongst them. After coming through the mountains with them, he had become displeased about something, and had slipped off and reported their coming at the Crow Agency just as General Miles arrived in that vicinity. Miles crept around the mountains in time to surprise them in their first camp after getting through. Little Rock was buried on top of a solitary conical hill which stood out in the valley of Clark's Fork. Captain Bennett's body was taken to Fort Keogh.

FRITH'S BANNOCK TRIP OF 1878

Henry A. Frith, an enlisted man in Captain Gilbreath's Company H, 11th Infantry recounts the fight from the enlisted man's point of view. His speculation on the confrontation between Miles and Buell is particularly interesting in that Gilbreath makes no mention of the stormy meeting. Mr. Frith's account of the fight appeared in the compilation of Pioneer Biographies *by I. D. O'Donnell, of Billings, Montana, and published privately in 1928-29. Mr. Henry A. Frith records what he called his Bannock Trip in 1878:*

At the time of the Bannock fight I was an enlisted man stationed at Fort Custer with my Co. H. of the

BANNOCK WARRIORS CAPTURED
IN THE BANNOCK FIGHT, 1878
"We took these Indians with us
when we returned to Fort Custer."

BANNOCK WARRIOR TAKEN
PRISONER BY GEN. MILES
Both photos by Stanley J. Morrow.
Courtesy, W. H. Over Dakota Museum,
University of South Dakota, Vermillion.

11th Infantry under General Buell who was Lieutenant Colonel and Post Commander. In accordance with orders my company was detailed on, what we always afterwards designated the "Bannock Trip." We struck out across the country to what is now known as "Bennett Creek," named after Captain Bennett, who was killed on this fight, the wagons belonging to the outfit going around by the ferry at Huntley and up Clark's Fork of the Yellowstone.

The last leg of the distance we marched half of the night, and in the morning, which was the morning of the fight, being close to Bennett Creek, we discovered a courier off a mile or more on the side of a mountain riding at a lope coming from Bennett Creek and going in the direction of Fort Custer. We did everything possible to attract his attention in order to discover the whereabouts of General Miles; we fixed small arms and halooed to little purpose; we finally fired off a piece of artillery we had with us, but although he must have heard the racket, he kept up his lope and even seemed to increase it. Evidently he had his orders to stop for nothing. I afterwards discovered that the courier was my friend Joe Hart of the 2nd Cavalry with a dispatch from General Miles to telegraph the fight. As we neared the scene of the fight we met one and two Indians, evidently "Crows," each driving small bands of captured horses. They too kept going and didn't want any familiarity.

When we arrived at the battleground everything was necessarily hear-say except what I could see for myself. A soldier told me of a stormy meeting between General Buell and General Miles. Buell complained that couriers from General Miles, that morning and the evening before especially, studiously kept away from his command, and that if the Bannocks had "taken in" Miles' small command, that he felt sure that he would have been blamed for not getting in in time for the fight; that in justice to his command he would make an official report of all the circumstances of the affair. Buell said that he had sent Miles a courier the evening before and that it was his opinion that the whole Indian camp could have been captured without firing a shot and that he would hold General Miles responsible for the death of Captain Bennett.

The fight took place before daylight on the creek probably a mile or more from the butte, behind which General Miles and his command of 30 soldiers and some scouts had hid all night and that from the top of the butte the Indian camp could be counted. My own recollection is, and I had it from a captured squaw, that there were at least one hundred bucks with the camp. I examined the creek and remember that the near side of the creek was lined with almost inpenetrable brush from six to ten feet high. This was the ground selected before the fight from which to surprise the Indians, who were camped on the other side of the creek.

The soldiers were instructed that when they arrived at their station on the creek, they were to fire as quickly as possible and not to take aim, so as to deceive the Indians as to their strength, which they did, and I found Captain Bennett lying where he had fallen on the near side of the bushes. He was shot through the heart and his orderly was attending him, wiping with a sponge the froth that would gather on his lips. I thought as I looked down at him I had never seen such soldierly appearance or finer looking officer anywhere.

From time to time the cavalry brought in some captured Indians, until there were 35 mostly squaws and children. I spoke to a young white squaw who spoke fairly good English, and she said that had the Indians known that Miles had only 30 men, (she didn't consider the Crow scouts) the Indians could have killed them all. I noticed among the captives a civilized looking oldish Indian, dressed in a velvet vest and a gold watch and chain on his person. We took these 35 Indians back with us when we returned to Fort Custer. How many Crow scouts General Miles had with him I did not learn, but there could not be many, only a few, and I probably saw all of them driving horses; their functions being evidently – the horse thieves of the outfit. I understood that they did but little fighting – those who were on the line, but decamped for the main chance – the horses. This jeopardized the commander. I saw only one soldier who had been wounded. He was walking about with his arm in a sling. One other citizen had been killed, a Frenchman I was told, besides Captain Bennett. A squaw had been killed, who was buried by the soldiers, and dug up by a Crow, who had probably missed the main chance – the horses; I was told his "heart was bad," and he dug up the dead squaw and dragged her around by a rope at the tail of his horse. The soldiers buried her again.

We continue now with Captain Gilbreath's story of the early years at Fort Custer.

DUTY AND PLEASURE IN MONTANA

We went into camp in a park at the edge of the mountains and were feasted on the most beautiful scenery that I have ever seen. The park in which we were camped was 7,000 feet above the sea, about 1,200 acres in extent with mountain spurs all about it. The stream running through it we called Bennett Creek. We had no end of trout and game and so thoroughly enjoyed our stay. After remaining in camp a week, we moved off for Fort Custer, going back by a different route, one which took us around the northeast end of the Big Horn Mountains through Pryor Gap and to old Fort C. F. Smith, which was built near where the Big Horn River comes through the mountains.

On the way in as we crossed the plains, we ran into a drove of migrating winged ants. These little pests are large red ants with wings which they shed late in life. They lodged on and crept down our necks and when pinched would sting in a very disagreeable manner. We had a wealthy man with us from Boston, a tenderfoot as such people are called. When we got in the midst of the ants, he rode as hard as he could in a great wide circle to get rid of them but as he simply rode around in the line of their movement, he only caught more of them while we old stagers only quickened our pace and passed through the line on which the ants were moving. This Mr. Booth wore a fancy leather suit of English make, of which he was very proud. The suit got very wet and we had to peel it off him and keep it wet so he could get into it for the rest of the trip. The officers, in wearing buckskin or any leather garments, usually wore other clothing outside of it to prevent its getting wet or stiff.

We got back to the fort from our Bannock campaign about September 20, 1878, after about as pleasant a campaign as I was ever in.

While stationed at Fort Custer, one of our favorite amusements was a trip each fall to the Big Horn Mountains about 45 or 50 miles away. One year, we got up a party consisting of my family, two young ladies who were daughters of the commanding officer, a lieutenant and Dr. Terry. We went up the Big Horn River to Fort C. F. Smith which had been abandoned at the demand of the Sioux Indians.

From there the ascent was gradual and easy to the top of the mountains, where there was a fine camping place near a spring which came out of a small ravine. The river comes through the mountains in a canyon about 64 miles long, a square cut, narrow and deep gorge. The Big Horn before it enters the gorge is known as Wind River. On the east side of the river and entering the Big Horn canyon from the south is another canyon known as Black Canyon. We could drive within two or three feet of the bluff at the junction of these canyons and from an ambulance look down to the river about 2,000 feet below.

The Big Horn canyon was entirely devoid of verdure and the different colors of the various strata of rock were always interesting. Black Canyon was filled with all sorts of wild growth and the little stream at the bottom gave good fishing as trout were there in great plenty. The camp was on the side of Black Canyon and an easy path led to the bottom. After camping there a few days we followed a trail on the east side of the mountains and camped as the fancy suited us as there were numerous small streams running out of the mountains. Our road finally led us to the Little Horn down which we went to the post. Our course formed a triangle and we sometimes went up one side and sometimes the other to the mountains. . .

In the summer of 1880 I was sent to survey a road from Fort Custer to Fort Keogh on the south side of the Yellowstone. I went out with a sergeant and five cavalry privates and a pack train of six mules. We crossed the Little Horn about two and a half miles from the post and then across the hills to Tullock's Fork and on to the Rosebud, a stream which empties into the Yellowstone about 40 miles above Fort Keogh. I then went back cutting off distances wherever I could from my first trail and then reported that the trail was not practical on account of the lack of water. The route was gone over next year again and was staked out for a road but was never used by a single train.

I was ordered to Poplar River on a court martial at the time when the Northern Pacific had been built as far as Forsyth which was then a typical frontier town, mostly composed of canvas houses and tents. The gambling and drinking were something terrible. Of 89 houses, 69 were said to be gambling places. I took cars at Forsyth and rode to Glendive where I stayed all night at the Glendive hotel. It was much the same type of place as Forsyth. From Glendive, I was to cross the Yellowstone and go north to Fort Buford at the mouth of the Yellowstone by buckboard, from whence I was to go up the north side of the Missouri River 60 miles to Poplar River.

I was rowed across the Yellowstone by the mail carrier as there was no ferry. He left me in charge of his packages while he returned for another passenger and more mail. I was in citizen's clothes and was seated in the shade of a cottonwood tree when a man came out of an old shack nearby which I had not known was inhabited. He wanted to know if I was going down on the stage and I told him that I was. "Armed, I spose?" he queried. I replied that I never carried any. "My God, man, you had better get a gun before you go. It's awful dangerous right here, now, not mentioning down the road. Stage was chased by the Indians yesterday and they killed six, just 14 miles below here." He went on telling me blood thirsty details of the killing of men, women and children, and gave me particulars of how to look out for Indians and how to fight them.

He wanted to know if I came from the east. I told him, "Some time ago," but added that I had just got in the night before from up the river on the train. "How far have you been anyway travelling without arms?" he asked. I said that I had been up on the Big Horn. He said: "You're takin' lots of chances. How long was you up there?" I told him three years. He asked if I was a rancher. When I told him I was an army officer he slapped his hand on his leg and said: "By God, I took you for a tenderfoot from the east – have a seegar."

The driver came back with his other passenger who was as drunk as a lord. As we started off, the other passenger began telling me his story at once. He was from New York City and his father was wealthy. He had gotten into bad company and taken up drinking habits and the father had bought him a ranch in Montana and stocked it and placed the son in charge to reform him.

The young man showed me a letter from his girl in which she begged him to reform and return to New York. As we stopped at the ranch, he said: "Now, I am reforming, and you can bet your life, I shall

DUTY AND PLEASURE

get out of this soon." He invited me in and I was amazed at the lavish waste of money in such a place. He was good picking for all the wild fellows.

On my arrival at Fort Buford, I found the post commanded by Lieut. Colonel H. R. Chipman of the Seventh Infantry who was formerly a captain in the 15th and 11th Infantry regiments. He received me with an old-time courtesy that was very pleasant. He sent a fine ambulance out to meet and bring me into the post, and kept me at his house. After being called upon by all the officers of the post, Colonel Chipman went with me in full uniform to call on everybody and he made me enjoy myself.

After resting a day, Colonel Chipman sent me to Poplar River in his ambulance. I found my old first lieutenant, now Captain O. B. Read, in command at Poplar River, and the post a rather pretty one, situated near an Indian agency for the Assiniboines. The court was not of long duration and I returned to Fort Custer by the same route that I had come over.

On the ride from Fort Buford to Glendive I saw the last herd of buffalo. They had been pretty generally killed off by skin hunters and where formerly the hills had been black with them, we now saw only one small herd of six or eight. There was still some other game in the country and we saw large bands of antelope.

We insert here a rare view of life at Fort Custer by an enlisted man. Rolando B. Moffett, as fate would have it, was with Company H, Eleventh U.S. Infantry, the very unit commanded by Captain Gilbreath whose interesting account of fort life we are following.

The letter was written to and printed by the Winners of the West *monthly communication. It was the official publication of the National Indian War Veterans, from the organization's National Headquarters, St. Joseph, Missouri. The letter appeared during April of 1933 and is partially reprinted below.*

ROLANDO B. MOFFETT'S LETTER

. . . When I arrived at Fort Custer, September 15, 1879, it was far from being built.

I was assigned to Co. H. 11th U. S. Infantry and was one of the many soldiers who helped build that fort on soldier's pay of thirteen dollars per month. I drove a mule to grind the clay to make the bricks with which that fort was built, and soldiers dug the clay, moulded the bricks and set them in the kilns, and tended the fires that burned the bricks.

I enlisted as a potter. I knew clay thoroughly, and was the soldier who selected the clay out of which to make the bricks. I guess that was why I was sent from David's Island, New York, to Fort Custer. I helped to burn the lime at Fort C. F. Smith, thirty-five miles from Fort Custer.

I carried a hod for the plasterer who plastered all of the buildings at Fort Custer, officers quarters, soldiers' quarters, hospital, headquarters building and all. I worked at the sawmill getting out lumber from the logs brought to Fort Custer by log trains.

The drivers of those six-mule teams composing the log trains were soldiers. The logs were cut in the timber by soldiers. The doors and shutters were made by soldiers, and so on all down the line. I therefore fail to understand how Fort Custer could have cost one million dollars to build. . .

It seems that Private Moffett failed to value his own time. We continue with the Gilbreath narrative.

While I was stationed at Fort Custer, I was appointed in 1879, inspector of supplies for the Crow Agency and much of my duties during the remaining years of my stay there were concerned with this work. My duties required that I weigh all cattle and flour as well as other goods received on contract as well as to examine all the goods received. During the first year particularly of the three years I filled this position, I had to go to the agency once a month and I saw a great deal of the Crows.

The Crow Agency was then situated about 140 miles by the road and about 100 miles west of the post of Fort Custer. I had to go north to the Yellowstone River and crossing to the north side, followed up that bank to the mouth of the Stillwater and then south 13 miles up the Stillwater River to the agency.

In passing to and from Fort Custer to the agency, I sometimes went by government transportation and sometimes by the stage. If with the former, I camped out at favorable points while if I went by stage, I took meals at the various stopping points of the stage. In most of these places the fare was anything but good, and I rode day and night having transportation sent me from the agency to meet me at the mouth of the Stillwater.

At Stillwater [now Columbus] I sometimes had to stay all night and stopped with an old man named Countryman, who kept the stage station with his two sons. He lived in the rudest way. All of his guests, himself and sons slept on the floor with their heads to the wall. Countryman himself slept in the center of the room with his head against a fine large post which supported the dirt roof of the house. He changed his position as the fancy struck him and sometimes his feet pointed north, south, east or west.

It was a motley crowd that was usually assembled there, sometimes consisting of cowboys, stage drivers and Indians. On the arrival of any in the night, the old man got up and after stirring the fire, swept the floor. He seemed to be always sweeping the floor and keeping the place filled with dust. I never saw the like of bedbugs – the walls of logs were filled with them. The old man and his sons were great spinners of yarns – they were the greatest liars among the old frontiersmen that I ever knew, which is saying a great deal.

A winter trip in the stage was anything but agreeable. On one occasion I came down the Yellowstone on the stage to Huntley, where I was to cross to go to Custer. We arrived at 12:00 o'clock at night, and the only thing I could get to eat was some stale bread and pickled beaver tail. The last did not taste badly resembling pigs feet to a certain extent except that it was much more oily. At any rate, I ate a good deal of it.

On going to the river, we found that the ice had broken up and had formed a great ice gorge where the ferry wire was stretched across the stream, which was about 400 feet across. The mail had to cross and I decided to go on, as I was anxious to get back to the post to attend the wedding of Lieutenant [Curtis B.] Hoppin [30] of the Second Cavalry. They rigged up a common hayrack attaching it to two iron wheels

---

[30] Lieut. Curtis B. Hoppin married the daughter of Col. John W. Davidson. Davidson became commanding officer of Fort Custer on Dec. 4, 1879. – Interview with Capt. H. K. Davidson, U.S.N. (Ret.), grandson of the colonel, Feb. 6, 1971.

THE STAGE STATION, FORT CUSTER
Courtesy, Billings Public Library, Montana.

THE OFFICERS' QUARTERS BUILDINGS, FORT CUSTER
"In the spring of 1878, all of the quarters were completed."
L. A. Huffman photo. Courtesy, Jack Coffrin, agent "Huffman Pictures," Miles City, Montana.

or travellers which ran on the wire. It was fixed by ropes so that a wheel was at each end of the rack. Then a board was placed on the rack in the center and the mail and express was placed on the board. The mail driver sat at the back end.

When we were all ready, men on the ground gave a strong pull on the rope attached under the rack and ran as hard as they could down the bank to the edge of the stream. The idea was to send us down the slack of the wire with such force that the impetus would send us well up on the slope of the wire on the other side of the stream. I shall never forget that ride. The water was roaring and foaming about the ice gorge and we rushed down within two feet of the top of the gorge. The moon was shining dimly and the situation was trying on one's nerves.

On reaching the end of the slope and as soon as we began to go up the slack from the other side, we both seized hold of the cable and began pulling for dear life. The weight was heavy and as we were sitting down with the wire passing close over our shoulders, we had all the strain on the upper parts of our bodies alone. The thing almost stopped, but we kept tugging away for dear life and crawling up at the last inch by inch, we finally reached the post and made fast to it. We threw off the mail and climbed down the post. I think I never was so tired and exhausted as at the end of that trip. I then had 40 miles to go to reach the fort and had to ride on the high seat of a common dead-axle wagon, such as farmers use for light hauling.

While I was inspector, I superintended the issue of annuities each year, and counted the entire tribe.

I also aided in the making of a treaty with the Crows by which they sold 3,000,000 acres of their reservation to the government. The part that was bought was the southwest and west river, and south of a line along foothills of mountains south of the agency.

The treaty was made out in Washington, but the Indians wouldn't agree to it. So I rewrote it, making some modifications which they wanted, and after a month of hard labor, I got the treaty adopted by three-fourths of the men of the tribe. The agent was a man from Ohio. The Indians did not have much confidence in him, so that he could not have gotten the treaty adopted without my help. We held the council in one of the buildings at the agency and after a good many speeches, succeeded in winning the assembled Indians over. It was then proposed for the department that a delegation go to Washington to see the president. The intention was to let some of the men who had no idea how many white people there were in the United States see something of the cities and towns in the east to impresss them with the white man's numbers and progress.

We selected those most inclined to be discontented among them one who was called Crazy Head. I asked him to go and he slowly got up on a bench and made a short speech. He said, as it was interpreted to us, that he had seen Indians who had been at Washington and all of them said that the Great Father lived in a beautiful White House, a house on top of a house (that is, two-storied), and that whenever anyone wanted to see the Great Father they went to the house to see him. Crazy Head did not want anything from the Great Father, but to be let alone. His lodge was right down there by the creek and if the Great Father wanted to see him, he could easily find his lodge.

The Indians were very superstitious. One of them said in a speech to a crowd that the night before he stepped out of his lodge and that he heard a dead Crow on the hill, call to one by the stream: "Hello, Crow, you tell Bear-in-the-Water, he must move his camp six miles away as where he is is in bad medicine, and his people will die." Bear-in-the-Water moved his camp at once although it was storming and we tried to prevent him from doing so.

In the spring of 1881 I was with my company again at Terry's Landing, receiving supplies and shipping them. I took leave of absence in September and went east. My wife had gone east in July, going down on the boat which carried "Rain-in-the-Face" and his band of Sioux who had surrendered that summer.

The regular passenger trains only ran west as far as Glendive, and I had to go by boat as far as that place. Boats then ran regularly from Glendive to Terry's Landing although their number was considerably reduced. We spent the winter in Baltimore where the children went to school. I had intended to retire from the army but as I found nothing to do, I got tired of my leave and went back to my company in May 1882. The company was again at Fort Custer. In July, I was ordered to go to Fort Buford for a station.

OFF FOR FORT BUFORD

I left Fort Custer on July 31, 1882, having served there five years and one week. It was a delightful station and I have never served at any place that I remember with more pleasure than Fort Custer. On

Crow Indian Chiefs and the Treaty Commissioners, 1879
"I got the treaty adopted by three-fourths of the men of the tribe."
Second from right, front, is Plenty Coups. Courtesy, Montana Historical Society.

going out of the post, the band was turned out to escort us and all the ladies, officers and men came to see us off. The band played "Auld Lang Syne" there. We boarded the "Caro" at Forsyth, after marching to that point, and we disembarked at Glendive. We crossed the Yellowstone there and camped until the contractor furnished us wagons for transportation. After waiting three days, we got off and in six days reached Buford.

My old friend Colonel Chipman was still in command. He was very dignified and formal in everything, and turned over the post in the most precise way. He asked me to accompany him to the office at a few minutes before 12:00 o'clock noon. At precisely that hour, he sat down at his desk and signed the final papers including an order, announcing that he "hereby surrendered command of Fort Buford, Dakota." He arose after signing the order, shook hands with me and giving me the commanding officer's chair, sat down on the chair I had occupied. I signed an order "hereby assuming command of Fort Buford, Dakota". . . I remained on duty at Fort Buford until September 23, 1886.

It is no surprise to the author that Captain Gilbreath was given a command of his own. His clear, precise and informative accounts of what it was like at and around Fort Custer in those early days reveal a person with keen insight and perception.

Erasmus Corwin Gilbreath remained a captain until April 30, 1897, when he became a major of the 9th Infantry. He was transferred back to his old outfit, the 11th Infantry, on May 20, 1897. Major Gilbreath died on Aug. 22, 1898.

PART TWO

The Middle Years
1885–1892

Private James O. Purvis

The summer of 1886 was a memorable one at Fort Custer. Private James O. (Coo) Purvis, Company B, First Cavalry, recorded in his sometimes published column in the Billings Daily Gazette *entitled "Fort Custer News," an articulate and informative account of what life was like at the Fort.*

He captured the flavor of army life from the enlisted man's viewpoint. If one reads, chronologically, the seemingly Hollywood gossip type article, the reader soon finds that sandwiched between the social news, which had considerable historical value, Purvis is reflecting in a sensitive way, the plight of both the Indian and the soldier, who, at times, are subjected to unbending rules and regulations with common sense sometimes a stranger.

Consider the entry for April 8, 1886, where he points out in a rather perceptive way the "difference" between dogs and Indians. His comment regarding battalion drill on April 10, 1886, is an example of his outspokenness. On April 14, 1886, he editorializes regarding work and drill. Humor is not lacking in his April 16, 1886, column. His efforts at reducing the prices at Fort Custer restaurants did not go in vain. His reference to the kitchen belles "along the line" indicates that the soldiers didn't spend all their time on strictly military duties.

Probably his most poignant moment came in his June 18, 1886, column regarding Trumpeter Hicks' inconsiderate (from Purvis' point of view) discharge from the army.

On June 25, with an unusual sense of history, Purvis recorded the tenth anniversary re-union of survivors of the famous Custer fight of 1876. Almost the entire cast of characters was present from Gall, a major Sioux Chief, to Captain Fred Benteen and Captain E. S. Godfrey of the 7th Cavalry. Purvis had the presence of mind to record Captain Godfrey's speech, given at the Fort Custer officer's club, which may be the basis of Godfrey's famous Century Magazine article of 1892. Purvis' defense of Major Reno, while revealing a certain naïveté, was notable because it contrasted sharply with that of Captain Godfrey.

James Purvis was discharged on October 10, 1886, at Fort Custer, Montana Territory. His character was designated by his commanding officer Colonel N. A. M. Dudley as "good."

On November 8, 1886, Purvis re-enlisted in Chicago at the age of 30. He was discharged, still a private, from the Fourth Cavalry on December 16, 1887, with a disability, at Fort Lowell, Arizona Territory, with a character again described as "good."

James O. Purvis was a soldier whose comments indicate he lived ahead of his time.

We present now, in chronological order, excerpts from Private Purvis' "Fort Custer News."

FORT CUSTER NEWS

APRIL 8, 1886. . . . Yesterday about forty men left this post to go to Black Canyon to establish power to cut logs for our lumber supply. . .

Visitors here requiring a stylish turnout for a pleasure ride or to visit the Custer monument can be supplied by that prince of good fellows, Edward McHale.

Charley Borup's beautiful span of black horses are "wasting their sweetness upon the desert air." Their beauty and speed would attract attention in any city.

The appearance of Fort Custer is improving daily under a liberal application of paint which was preceded by a general and thorough "policing" of the garrison.

The old mill near McNutt's ranch, half-way between the post and Junction City is gone, but will not soon be forgotten as a landmark and because of its familiar associations with labor and life on the spot by many of our population.

Provost Sergeant Mickey Powers turned out this morning, with orders to shoot all the dogs found trespassing upon the "parade." The garrison parade at Fort Custer is the reservation within the reservation, and the difference between the dogs and the Indians seems to be that the former are run off the reservation and the latter are run on.

Last night Captain Garrety [Garretty] continued his lecture upon "Ireland." The effort was supremely interesting and enjoyable; a rich humor permeated the solid truths of his argument. A variety of subjects have been ably handled by the officers of the garrison at these weekly lectures, notably: First Lieutenant

James Pilcher's "An empty grave and a nameless man"; Captain Moses Harris' "In the Shenandoah Valley"; Lieutenant George P. Borden's "Gladstone." The course has not yet been discontinued.

The immense target ranges adjacent to the Fort are being rapidly placed in apple-pie order by Lieutenant A. L. Mills, 1st Cavalry. The perfect operation of forty targets and forty-eight skirmish figures in conjunction with the opportunity the men of nine companies have to shoot every day, besides performing all the other military duties of a post like this, demands both skill and attention. Last season under the supervision of Lieutenant Mills, who has earned the reputation of being one of the most talented efficient officers of the army, the ranges moved like clock work, hence the conclusion for the season is congratulatory.

The Fort Custer Comic Opera and Burlesque party reached here last Wednesday, jubilant over their trip to Bozeman via Billings and Livingston. An extension of one day was wired by General Dudley, 1st Cavalry, on the 29th [March], and it was spent at Fort Ellis where the boys were royally entertained by their comrades of that place. The generous welcome received in the places named above will not permit any discrimination. So we say thanks all along the line.

FORT CUSTER NEWS: APRIL 9, 1886. Nearly every troop and company in the garrison has a private library.

The debris has been removed and the old site of Troop "D" quarters which were burned last winter only await the arrival of lumber and material to be a better building than before.

Within a month 194 volumes were added to the post library. Eighty volumes arrived this morning. The selections were made by Lieutenant A. L. Mills, 1st Cavalry, and are fine.

Lieutenant James B. Aleshire, 1st Cavalry, owner of Modoc and Tattler, has just purchased a handsome young bay stallion, with a way down eastern record. Modoc ran on the course at Helena last summer. Tattler is a war horse.

The Fort Custer Comic Opera and Burlesque Co. will close the season by giving a personal performance next Tuesday evening, April 13. It first opened September 9th, '85, to a crowded house here; gave twelve entertainments during the winter besides their trip to Billings, Livingston, Bozeman and Ellis. The record is fair to look upon and an incentive to display earnestness and energy in whatever cause.

Bandmaster Walker produced Julius Eichborg's comic opera, "The Doctor of Alcantara" here on the 4th, 5th, and 6th of March. It caused a sensation and was repeated again on the 8th. The patronage went far towards rewarding Mr. Walker for over two month's labor on it. "The Pirates of Penzance" is talked of next and if as great a success as the "Doctor of Alcantara" it will go on the road next fall as far as Helena and Butte.

Our band will soon appear in new uniform, to consist of dark blue trousers and black dress coats. A gold stripe will complete the former and the Prussian Amgaratta in gold will adorn the coats. The helmets will be of brass. Altogether the dress will be handsome. In former years everything in the line of dress was chosen for serviceableness. Nowadays a more stylish uniform throughout the army would be appreciated.

It was well enough in pioneer days to wear jeans. Let us have a little more style. "A thing of beauty is a joy forever."

FORT CUSTER NEWS: APRIL 10, 1886. . . . Corporal Teeple and Private Cummings left here yesterday for Fort Snelling, Minn., having in charge a deserter from the Fourth Artillery. Despite the amendment of the old $30 reward for the capture of a deserter, very few get away in good shape. This is the season of unrest but we advise our soldier friends to stick to their contract with Uncle Sam. It don't pay to go back on him. . .

First Cavalry battalion drill began yesterday. No one was excused. The maneuveres must have been satisfactory to [Brevet] Major Jackson, but his keeping the battalion on the drill ground more than an hour after "Recall," was not agreeable to the men. We fail to see why the time for stopping drill should be designated and then disregarded, especially when every man did his level best, as was the case yesterday.

FORT CUSTER NEWS: APRIL 12, 1886. . . . A grand competitive drill, soon to take place, will determine some of the most proficient, and who will be awarded a furlough.

The lumber for "B" Troop's quarters is at Junction City. It comes from Minneapolis, Minn., all ready for erection. A large force of carpenters will be put on the job in a few days.

Our day school is in a flourishing condition. Joseph Henry is teacher. Frank J. Wills, Esq., gives instruction every evening to enlisted men. Penmanship and book-keeping are specialties.

There are quite a number of civic societies in the

FORT CUSTER BAND IN 1887
"The Band plays at Guard mount at 9 a.m. and in the afternoon discourses sweet music."
Courtesy, Custer Battlefield Museum.

MR. WALKER, BANDLEADER
"Bandmaster Walker produced Julius Eichborg's comic opera 'The Doctor of Alcantara.'"
O. S. Goff photo. Courtesy, Montana Historical Society, Helena.

garrison: The officer's Literary Club; a Masonic Lodge of Instruction; Maennerchor Club; Custer Social Club; Ancient Order of Hibernians; Walker's Opera Company; and the Fort Custer Comic Opera and Burlesque Company; also a very prosperous Lodge of the Independent Order of Good Templars.

FORT CUSTER NEWS: APRIL 14, 1886.

> In the Spring a deeper war paint
> comes upon the Indian breast.
> In the Spring upon the reservation
> Little Knife Blade will not rest.
> In the Spring the tribe will make faces
> at the Agent with great wrath.
> In the Spring they mount their ponies
> and go out on the war path.

. . . This evening our German friends will enjoy a little recreation in the shape of a ball and supper. The Maennerchor Club is doing it, which is sufficient to insure us to predict that it will be a success. "Der Verlonene Schirm" (The Lost Umbrella) will close the evening's festivities.

The regular target season opens May 1st and closes August 31st. The latter two months will be devoted to skirmish firing at body figures in the standing, wheeling, and lying down positions, each man judging his own distance. This is an apparently more valuable practice than at the old fixed distance targets.

An exhaustive quantity of work is going on here every day. The road to the ferry is being macadamized; two cellars 25 x 30 feet, 10 feet deep, are being dug; logs are being cut, wood sawed, houses painted, brickyards cleaned, and everything overhauled. In fact we are so busy every day in the week that we have to do our drilling on Sunday.

Sergeant Major Henry White, First Cavalry, who is highly recommended for a commission by officers of this post, underwent a preliminary examination today. The final examination will take place at Fortress Monroe. No one doubts the result. White is a way up soldier, and every way qualifies to fill the honorable position he is looking for.

All the army, like the world's a stage, and the soldiers are "supes." Each in his time plays many parts, and the engagement lasts 1825 nights, or five years. The plays are all written in Washington, D.C., and are entirely devoid of a suspicion of bloodshed or anything of an over-exciting nature. The spectacular scenes are failures, because the "supes" always look like laborers when they are supposed to represent soldiery. . .

. . . Work and drill, two prominent features in the routine of military duties are entirely antagonistic. Like fire and water they don't mix together without injury to one or another. Both are equally essential in a garrison as the elements to which we happen to compare the, but no amount of finesse, judgement, or ability on the part of post military administration can make a laborer and a soldier one. The authority for the employment of enough laborers to do all the work of a post would have to come from Washington of course, but we are sure it would be money well spent; better than hundreds of thousands that go annually for ten thousand times less value received. The objection to labor on the part of a soldier is not on account of laziness or a dislike to work, but simply because it is not his profession. A soldier who has been on fatigue duty all day during the summer, cuts a sorry figure in the streets at dress parade in the evening. He may have found time to wash his face, but the chances are that his toilet on the whole is incomplete. He is no credit to himself in such a condition, and none to his officers. As the thing continues he loses pride, and after a little he is neither soldier nor laborer. Samples of which are seen daily by Coo.

FORT CUSTER NEWS: APRIL 16, 1886. Perkins, of the band, acted as floor manager at the Maennerchor hop last evening. When he stepped on the stage to make an announcement some one cried out, "Down in front." Involuntarily Perkins' hand sought his mustache, where it lingered caressingly a moment; then he smiled and proceeded with his speech. Perkins is almost as sensitive as he is big-hearted. No one surely would insinuate his mustache was composed of "down." It was only a girl in a back seat who wanted to have a good look at him.

Our post hospital is a model institution; a credit to the medical department of the U. S. Army, and a godsend to many of its soldiers who have found there the oasis in the desert of their affliction and disease. James Carroll, hospital steward, is without a superior in the execution of his duties. Ever kind and patient with all classes, he has won the gratitude and esteem of every man in the post. Billy Moore of "M" troop, has proved a valuable and competent assistant to Mr. Carroll, and an all around gentleman.

The statue of military justice is never seen with a bandage upon its eyes. Sometime we have cases of importance to try, but there is never the temptation to travesty this high, almost sacred tribunal, as exists in the operation of civil courts. Take the ambitious lawyer whose future may depend upon the result of a single case; the itching palms of twelve jurors; the vision of what a thousand or two will do for the Judge's expensive family, and we have an idea of the cause which lead to verdicts in civil courts that open the eyes of communities daily. Happily courts martial are unencumbered by these impediments to justice.

FORT CUSTER NEWS: APRIL 20, 1886. The soldiers at Fort Custer wear knight caps – helmets. . .

. . . In the German army a soldier is obliged to write home to his wife once a month. This explains why so many Germans come to this country to escape military duty.

In the east, the annual invasion of the tramp is regarded as a sure harbinger of ethereal mildness. We can't adopt that plan here, as we have no tramps. We are however, on the lookout for a robin.

Our comrades at Fort Ellis will soon give an entertainment in the city of Bozeman, which will be repeated at the garrison for the benefit of their baseball nine. We look forward to a return visit from our Fort Ellis friends and will not be happy until it comes to pass.

In a few days we will begin to publish extracts from the diary of a soldier who "skipped by the light of the moon" from Fort Coeur d'Alene in the spring of 1884, to seek his fortune in the gold fields near that place. This journal fell into our hands, and as it contains a record of his life for over two years, kept in an ingenious manner, we are of the opinion that it will prove interesting to you readers.[31]

Fort Custer is a long way behind the times in a

---

[31] The present editor was unable to find any record of the soldier's journal mentioned by Purvis.

great many things that affect the enlisted men and make them dissatisfied, because they are as a consequence, deprived of many comforts of the age, which they know they would enjoy if they had been stationed even on the frontier. Our distance from the railroad is more an excuse for not having, than a reason why we should not have, some things at least much cheaper than they are. Particularly in summer, a drink of beer for instance is both healthful and refreshing, but the price charged for it here is so exorbitant, that, in spite of the contrary prediction of the old New England tavern-keeper, when he tasted "Adam's Ale" for the first time, water is the very "popular drink." During the winter, a cup of coffee or chocolate with a sandwich or a piece of pie, would prove a luxury at a reasonable price, but they cannot be obtained here on these terms. Why, Delmonico's is a regular free lunch alongside a Fort Custer restaurant. We don't get a cent more for soldiering here than is paid elsewhere, and for that reason we ought to have an equal show for our money. The price of beer here is 40 cents per bottle; a cup of coffee and a sandwich costs 25 cents; both are luxuries, we know, but that is no excuse for the unnecessarily extortionate price of them. Coffee, bread, sugar, and such things are almost as cheap here as anything or anywhere in the world. A cup of coffee and a sandwich can be sold at a profit, as low as 5 cents, and it is too bad we can not have such a restaurant at every post if they had to be run in co-operation with the commissary department of the army. In most cases, winter and summer, the desire for refreshment would be requited by their means, which is far preferable to beer or any other alcoholic beverages.

FORT CUSTER ICE DETAIL ON THE BIG HORN RIVER
". . . work and drill . . . are entirely antagonistic."
Courtesy, Custer Battlefield Museum, Col. W: H. Bowen slides.

THE FORT CUSTER COMMISSARY BUILDING
Commissary Sergeant Budds in white shirt with beard.
O. S. Goff photo. Courtesy Montana Historical Society, Helena.

FORT. CUSTER NEWS: APRIL 27, 1886. We have had just enough rain this month to give our parade ground and grass plats a lovely shade of green.

April showers bring forth not May flowers alone, their effect being profitable as well as pleasing. We should have an abundance of good grass and bountiful crops this coming summer.

The gardens belonging to the various companies stationed here are situated on the banks of the Little Horn River, about two miles from the post. Yesterday some of the gardeners made the raise of a small barrel of whisky, wherewith to drink prosperity to the crops of '86. After a liberal "irrigation" in honor of their new "spuds" etc., they started in to drink success to agriculture generally throughout the territory. The sentiment was good enough but the whisky was of that quality which usually incites its patrons to become sluggers. The effect it had upon our agricultural friends proved no exception. One of the party was badly hurt and the others not improved any. The greater portion of the liquor was seized by the guard last night.

During the past winter a sentry has been posted in the rear of our officers' quarters much to the terror and discomfort of the garrison dudes who pay attention to the kitchen belles "along the line," because they have had to resort to all kinds of strategy in order to see the girls without being caught. Recently however, this unpleasant barrier was removed and the dudes are again happy in the performance of nightly back-gate osculatory exercises.

FORT CUSTER NEWS: APRIL 30, 1886. Captain [Frank Dwight] Baldwin, Fifth Infantry, is at Junction City.

Dog-robber, is a term in very common use among soldiers, who pretend to have great aversion towards the person to whom it is applied, because he chooses to earn a little extra money by working for an officer in the capacity of servant or groom. In return for the services the soldier is always liberally paid and well treated, so that he can apply a very healing salve to his feelings if they become hurt perchance by any of the unmerited deals he receives from comrades who would, in most cases, be only too glad to change places with him if they had a chance. Abusing a "dog-robber" is the stalest thing we know of in the army.

> The target practice days have come,
>   and like a chanticleer
> At early dawn till day is done,
>   the rifle's bang we hear.
> So when the Scorer calls your name,
>   Quick answer back your "page."
> And sit down on a cactus plant
>   To adjust your weather gauge.
> Now to the shoulder bring the piece.
>   Be sure it isn't "canted,"
> Get your head between your knees
>   And both feet firmly planted.
> Draw in your breath as still as death.
>   And call out the white disc,
> "I've got a five as I'm alive,"
>   "No! Brown another miss."
>
> Pull brothers pull with care,
> Marksman's buttons you may wear;
> A plain white disc is a "bull's eye,"
> A stripe of black, you got too high;
> When a plain black it is too low,
> And a red flag, Lord, I don't know.

Tomorrow the regular bi-monthly muster and inspection of the troops at this station will take place.

Infantry companies will turn out in heavy marching order, cavalry with saddles packed and ready for the field. After muster the paymaster is looked for. He is always the most welcome visitor we have.

It seems that most people do not go to church to pray, so much as to hear or see something new. The attendance of the gentler sex always increases largely during the spring-bonnet months. Considering the slim attendance at chapel here on ordinary occasions, we are certain that a great many who helped swell the large congregation gathered at the Easter services held at the Post Chapel last evening, belong to the class we refer to. Anyway they were not disappointed in seeing something special last night and as they came very near showing the more habitual worshippers a new feature in religious ceremonies by applauding the singing with hands and feet; a timely "hush" alone prevented it. The orchestra music was good and the vocal efforts of an impromptu choir were well worth listening to. The naturally gloomy interior of the chapel room was something improved last evening by a lot of flowers tastefully arranged.

FORT CUSTER NEWS: MAY 21, 1886. Very warm. 87° in the shade. Wind velocity, one mile an hour. The price of beer has been reduced to 30 cents a bottle.

Master Mechanic William Heffner, who had been recorded long ago under the head of old bachelors, will "fool dem shoost once" by wedding, on next Saturday evening, a comely German girl employed in the garrison."

Private James Purvis had time, between deadlines

for the "Fort Custer News," to submit an interesting letter to the Utica *(N. Y.)* Sunday Tribune *during the month of May, 1886. It is not known why he submitted the letter to the Utica paper. The record shows that he enlisted in New York City in 1881. Perhaps he migrated from Utica. The letter appeared as follows:*

Perhaps no factor, real or pretentious, of the Regular Army, is so meanly understood as their rifle practice. Previous to the great struggle between the North and South, occasion often arose to applaud the deeds of our little army in the wild west, fighting Indians and exploring regions which today are mighty States, but anything accomplished since that great event of bloodshed has seemed so insignificant in comparison, as to hardly merit recognition.

If there have been no battles to fight of late years, no Indians to subdue, no wilds to explore, the soldiers of the Regular Army have not been idle. They have performed a vast amount of manual and clerical labor and are so well prepared for war, during these piping times of peace, as to be able to vanquish an enemy ten times their own strength, less skilled in the use of the rifle, as are the armies of every other nation of the world.

The American army has followed no old world fashions in respect to rifle practice, but adopted a genuine Yankee style of its own which has made nearly every soldier of two years service, as expert with the rifle as a backwoodsman.

It is more interesting to look over old records, to compare old and new methods, and to note the great growth and important improvement in everything connected with the American army of the period. For the past five years the attention of every officer has been devoted to making each soldier in the ranks an expert in the use of the rifle. Occasionally a man turns up who cannot shoot. After a fair trial, he is shipped without exactly knowing why. Five years ago only a few men in each company could make a respectable score at a greater distance than 100 or 200 yards. In fact, the very limited practice of those days was entirely confined to short distances, but year by year the allowance of ammunition for target practice has been increased to such an extent and so much time given to practice, that the result of late years has been almost wonderful. Take for instance the record of Troop B, 1st Cavalry, for the year 1885 under the following conditions: Those making 90 per cent are classed as sharpshooters; those making 80 per cent, classed as marksmen; those making 70 per cent, classed as first class; those making 60 per cent classed as second class; those making 50 per cent, classed as third class; shooting at 200, 300, 500, 600, 800, and 1,000 yards. Out of a troop 65 strong, 12 qualifies as sharpshooters, 48 as marksmen, 3 as first class and 2 as second class.

At the close of the season of 1885 the troops of the 10 companies stationed at this post, engaged in a new practice which created no small amount of rivalry among the men and tested their skill and judgment to the greatest extent, viz: Twenty-four shapes of men made of iron frames covered with target paper, were placed in the different positions presumed to be natural for an enemy to assume, either standing, lying or kneeling, about five yards apart.

At the command "commence firing" the exercise

assumed all the details of a genuine skirmish. The bugle sounded "Advance," "Retreat," until each trooper had fired 10 shots. Then the markers counted the holes in the figures and declared the total, when another troop arrived to beat the score if possible. B Troop, 1st Cavalry, made the highest score last year: 258 hits out of a possible 300. The excellence of this work will be plain to any person who understands the necessity of lowering then elevating the sights of a rifle as the distance from the object is diminished or increased.

This degree of proficiency pertains not to one troop alone, but the whole army of 25,000 men who, in the event of a war of magnitude, would prove an invaluable corps of sharpshooters.

I could write pages of the great progress of our army in every respect, including the many comforts provided for the men not thought of in the older day.

Who would have very well believed, four years ago that we would have spring mattresses, linen sheets and feather pillows today? No one, but it is true, and we are all the better for them in mind, body and allegiance to the giver of all these good things – our Uncle Sam.

Stimulated by Purvis' Utica Tribune *letter, which was reprinted in the* Billings Gazette, *a correspondent known only as "Judge," submitted the following article to the May 27, 1886 edition of the* Billings Daily Gazette *in which he teases about the superiority of everything from bullets to beer at Fort Keogh.*

Even though "Judge" indicates that he will do more writing, this is the only evidence of his work in the Gazette. *"Judge" writes from Fort Keogh:*

COMMENTS BY "JUDGE"

I observe that the Gazette has a real live correspondence at Fort Custer. The news he sends you is very interesting to the military residents of this part of the Yellowstone Valley, and I note that much of the matter he writes for your columns also creeps into the two representative army papers. When the spirit moves, I shall endeavor now and then to send you something to fill up any small space that you may have to spare at times. The principal occupation here at present, at least of nine tenths of the garrison, is target practice. We have bulls eyes for breakfast, dinner and supper, with an occasional magpie and blackbird. I see your correspondent from the forks of the two Horns has been giving the Custer boys a send off in the way of shooting, and that he compares the recent big record of "B" troop 1st Cavalry at 500 yards with one of ours at all ranges. The 70 qualifying scores made here in one day by "A" 5th Infantry was at all sharpshooters distances, including 200, 300, 500, 600, 800 and 1,000 yards. All marksmen know that 500 yards is the easiest of all the ranges and had our crack company been kept pegging away at that distance and no other, there is no telling how many scores of 80 per cent and over would have been made. As it happened, a few possibles were knocked out the best shots within the 600 yard limit, and at the longer ranges 22's, 23's and 24's [32] began to show up quite frequently when the sergeant of the guard called us off.

No doubt the riflemen of "B" troop are great shooters, but confidentially Mr. Editor, between our-

---
[32] Out of a possible 25.

selves and everybody else, they caught onto most of their pointers while here at Keogh. Please don't mention it though. Our daily routine is company drill every morning, battalion drill Tuesdays and Fridays P.M., dress parade seven days of the week, and target practice between times. But for all that, beer is cheaper in this part of Montana than at Custer. Notwithstanding the small cost of the article down this way, I think "ours" drink less of it than do your military neighbors up the Big Horn. . . "Judge"

We continue with Purvis' "Fort Custer News" of May 21:

B Troop, First Cavalry, leads the van this season for the number of excellent scores made in a single day's shooting on any one range. On the 17th inst. eighty-four marksmen scores were tallied at 500 yards. Equally good work has been done by this troop at all the other ranges, and the boys have not got warmed up yet. Let us have another marker from Fort Keogh.

Our Fourth of July celebration is already being discussed. The good old lemonade-firecracker holiday should not be shelved among the relics of a glorious past, neglected and forgotten. Nothing delights the heart of Young America equal to the events of this day, if it is half celebrated. When we are inclined to say the firing of guns and burning of rockets, the parades and the speeches, are all played out nonsense, let us remember the boys and how much fun we used to have when we were one of them.

Last Saturday afternoon our ears were greeted with notes of the now unaccustomed, but once familiar and stirring bugle call, "Boots and Saddles," which send a hundred troopers in response, scouring the hills in every direction for two prisoners who had escaped from their sentry while at work on the outskirts of the garrison. Up to dark no trace of them could be found. Both expected long sentences for desertion, and were willing to risk a shot or two for the sake of the liberty they are now enjoying.

FORT CUSTER NEWS: MAY 24, 1886. . . . Borup & Co., post traders, are kept very busy dispensing "German battery" this warm weather. Since the reduction in price, the sale of beer has increased vastly.

About thirty Crow Indians are in the post today petitioning for a return of their guns and saddles taken away from them last summer by Troop "G" 1st Cavalry. . .

Of three soldiers who were drowned in the Yellowstone River opposite the cantonment of the morning of the 11th inst., one body has been recovered in an unrecognizable and greatly swollen condition. Boots and spurs, and cavalry trousers worn by the deceased led to almost certain identification of the remains of Edward Morton, Troop "K," 1st Cavalry. The other men belonged to Infantry companies and have not yet been heard of.

FORT CUSTER NEWS: JUNE 5, 1886. Our latest important acquisition is a beer garden.

The growler is being worked with considerable life the past two weeks.

The orchestra recently got up by Professor Maow to play in the beer garden, are inclined to neglect their duties. They seem to think that they go there to drink instead of play as they should. Maow himself is all right but he is too easy with his men.

Corporal Schwerin, Troop "B" 1st Cavalry wedded Miss Kittie Barry, one of the handsomest girls in the post, last night. The affair was of the quiet kind, but both have many friends and well wishers, who will remain the same whether it is cards or cake or no. Al has invited the boys of his troop to visit the beer garden tonight; of course there is something in that.

The recent marriage of Mr. William H. Heffner and Miss Christine Standgrebe, both of this place, was a decidedly pleasant and successfully enacted ceremony. Nothing occurred to mar the arrangements made by Mr. Chas. W. Pugh in the capacity of best man. Charles has never been there himself yet, but has evidently observed closely how such things are conducted. A magnificent dinner which must have filled one of Marquis De Mores' refrigerator cars at least was partaken of by the guests as heartily as the generous-hearted hostess, Mrs. Frushman, at whose residence the event took place, could desire. The drinks were numerous – I mean the kinds were numerous, but as the natural literal conception would be quite true, let it go – and kept the marriage bells ringing until three in the morning. During the night several serenades were given; one by the band and one by the Beer Garden orchestra. The latter did not require torches to read their music and got no beer for playing, which was a great oversight on the part of Mr. Emil Herrman. The bridesmaids were Miss Kittie Gleason and Miss Annie Newman. Some of the presents were costly ones, others useful and handsome. . . Space forbids further indulgence in recalling the many pleasant speeches made, songs sung and toasts drank, but it must be admitted we know how to run a wedding and assure our Custer friends when they are making up their list of invited guests that we are excellent company and never refuse anything good.

Decoration Day was observed here in a manner surpassing anything of the kind we ever saw in large cities or at first-class military cemeteries. We do not include flowers nor quantity of work as perhaps we should, but outside of these the spectacle presented about our handful of graves on this day was varyingly beautiful, thrillingly touching. All the troops in the post escorted the veterans of the G. A. R. to the little cemetery on the bank of the Big Horn. Along the north one large field piece boomed a salute. Man and horse vied with each other in steadiness of gait and seriousness of behaviour as the band played well-chosen music for the escort. A painter would have been delighted with the prospect afforded for a picture when all had reached the graves, but would never succeed in an attempt to illustrate, as words cannot describe the beauty and grandeur of seeing that little band of veterans passing among the graves of their dead comrades bestowing upon each with reverent air the flowers gathered for the occasion, wild as the surroundings, and perhaps, most appropriate. General Dudley's military figure would seem the very ideal of a commander of cavalry, surrounded by his staff and the captains and lieutenants of all companies and troops, his salutations for the command were grand and for the moment stirred every heart with admiration for the General and his officers and filled them with a thousand thoughts of the glory of war. While we thought of the dead and their sacrifice, we could not help also admiring the living members of John

Buford Post, G. A. R. and the way they performed their duties yesterday.

FORT CUSTER NEWS: JUNE 11, 1886. The many friends of Sergeant Charles Abbott, who leaves here on the 15th inst. for Washington, D. C., had an opportunity to have a good look at him Sunday night at dress parade, acting in the absence of Sergeant Major White. . .

In our correspondence last week we found it necessary as true chroniclers of the news of the Post to mention the names of two well-known persons who are very indignant over it, especially Prof. Maow, of the band, who claims we did both himself and orchestra a great injustice "in dot baper." We said his orchestra "spent too much of the time drinking," and as it was true, we repeat it. When they choose to take a different course we shall be equally as happy to give them due credit and notify the public. If the other gentleman thinks his name too good for publication, or that there is any law to prevent us from having it published we shall undeceive him by using his name just as often as occasion demands, and no oftener.

It is to be hoped that the issue of some sort of summer uniform to soldiers serving in warm climates may not be delayed much longer. When that time arrives let it be distinctly understood that Fort Custer, Montana, comes just under that head, for if there is any warmer place than this at present we don't want to be there under an obligation wearing the same clothing as when the thermometer registered 20 below zero. The blue has become unsightly enough at all times to have a rest during the heated term. In their efforts to keep cool, soldiers are obliged to sacrifice their military appearance for the comfort of an old pair of overalls or stable pants, which does not produce results very pleasing to the eye, but which cannot be avoided until we are provided with "uniforms for summer wear."

What a picnic everybody had at the B. C. Club picnic Sunday. Sometimes it rains at picnics; or the weather is roasting hot; beer stale; or the musicians get drunk; but nothing of the kind happened last Sunday at the B. C. Club and their friends, who left the post intent upon having "more fun this summer than any summer yet," and in which, thanks to the attentive kindness of Quartermaster Sergeant Buchner and others, there was not much likelihood of their being disappointed. By the kindness of General Dudley, who seems to encourage every form of harmless enjoyment, two ambulances were furnished for the transportation of the party to the picnic grounds, where they arrived at 2:30 P.M. A beautiful spot had been chosen for occasion on the banks of the Little Horn River, and a space cleared for dancing. Time would not permit the erection of a platform, but the ground was so smooth and even that a large canvas tarpaulin stretched tightly across the green sward proved a delightful substitute. A few minutes after the arrival of the ambulances containing most of the ladies of the party, carriages of all descriptions began to make their appearance through the grove.

Among the earliest arrivals were Red McHale, accompanied by Mr. W. J. Dailey, of the Signal Corps and Mr. H. Ebert, telegraph operator at Custer City. In an incredibly short space of time preparations to extinguish thirst were in progress and willing hands

A Picnic at Fort Custer in the 1880s
"Sometimes it rains at picnics . . . or the musicians get drunk."
Courtesy, Montana Historical Society, Helena.

were found in plenty to spread the cloth for a bountiful repast. A large tub of ice cream in a swarthy bandage of glittering ice looked exceedingly tempting and tasted as good as it looked and better. Dancing began at half past three and continued until a few minutes before midnight. No happier party ever picnicked. For a short time in the afternoon the clouds were threatening, but old Prob was not cruel enough to spoil that merry party, and his threat was the signal for increased animation and happiness, until the entire party returned to the Post filled with pleasure enough to last until the B. C. picnic again.

FORT CUSTER NEWS: JUNE 18, 1886. Troop "B" will move into their new quarters about the last of the month.

Mr. LeMoy our new veterinarian surgeon has arrived and is already overhauling the nags.

Proposals for rebuilding "M" Troop's stables, burned last month, have been advertised. . .

Trumpeter George Hicks, Troop "M" First Cavalry, received his discharge yesterday quite unexpectedly, and in a manner not at all considerate, if just. Hicks had served about twenty-four years in the army, covering the period of the war, had the reputation of a brave and faithful soldier until lately, and as his future prospects are really painful to contemplate, a great many are of the opinion that he deserved better treatment. The fact of his being addicted to drink sufficiently to interfere with the proper performance of his duties seems to have been the sole cause of so summary an action. Old age, physical debility, war service, hardships and rebel prisons, all counted not one iota in his favor when the question to go or not to go arose. He went into a world that

THE DAVEY MILK RANCH SUPPLIED MILK PRODUCTS FOR FORT CUSTER
When this picture was taken the ranch was owned by Val Lechner.
O. S. Goff photo. Courtesy, Montana Historical Society, Helena.

INTERIOR VIEW OF ENLISTED MEN'S BARRACKS, FORT CUSTER, 1892
"Fort Custer is behind the times in many things that affect enlisted men."
Courtesy, Custer Battlefield Museum, and Maurice Frink.

after twenty odd years of a soldier's life will be very new to him and very cold indeed after the few dollars he received when he left here are spent; restricted from again enlisting, without health, which was sacrificed at the time he offered his life for his country, we surely do not envy him and many other old soldiers their probable fate. About as well retire soldiers after death as after thirty years' service. It is plain that some provision should be made for the old age of soldiers who have served say twenty years, either retirement as now applied to a service of thirty years, a pension or the soldier's home, for the number of wrecks turned out of the army under circumstances similar to the one in question is cruel and disgraceful. It is of course understood that military power is in no way to blame for these unfortunate cases, but rather our legislators who are notorious for not delaying to make provision for their own old age until the eleventh hour of mortality.

TENTH ANNIVERSARY OF THE CUSTER FIGHT REPORTED BY PRIVATE PURVIS

FORT CUSTER NEWS: JUNE 25, 1886. As a preface to the tenth anniversary ceremonies at Custer Battle ground, June 25th, at the hour of retreat last evening, Captain E. S. Godfrey, Seventh Cavalry, recited in the presence of a large assemblage of officers, soldiers, civilians and ladies of the garrison, from a rather voluminous collection, a few notes most pertinent to the Custer expedition of 1876.

The speaker, a tall, slim, dark man, displayed remarkable coolness in handling his notes and picking out the points most appropriate for the occasion, the whole having been, as the gentleman explained, collected for an entirely dissimilar purpose. Captain Godfrey also appeared under the additional disadvantage of being called upon to deliver the reading at twenty minutes notice; this, however, could not obliterate their value nor the most palpable fact that they were the result of careful work and thought. It was unmistakably the purpose of the speaker to present Major Reno in no enviable way, but we doubt the possibility of any attempt to attribute cowardice to this man ever succeeding. General Custer, brave and capable, with the larger portion of the regiment met with a fate which places a high premium on discretion, and is prima-facie evidence that Reno was acting wisely to retreat after his first encounter upon crossing the Little Big Horn and discovering the alarming and unexpected strength of the enemy, even though such movement did (as the speaker said he was recently informed by an Indian at Standing Rock was the case) cause the Indians to change their minds about moving camp. In his effort to make Reno's delay on the bluffs from 2 till 5 o'clock in the afternoon appear cowardly, the speaker did not succeed, owing to a previous statement that "they all thought Custer had been repulsed, crossed the river and would join Terry."

The presence of Chief Gall who threatens to wave his role of stoic and speak out on the subject may be regarded as likely to throw some light upon the manner and stubborness of Custer's defense.

FORT CUSTER NEWS: JUNE 26, 1886. . . . In introducing Captain E. S. Godfrey, Seventh Cavalry, who gave a recital of notes and personal recollection of events connected with Custer's famous battlefield on Wednesday evening last, General Dudley drew the line of distinction very markedly among the audience present. He said: "Ladies, gentlemen and men." Then followed a neat and graceful speech. Our commanding officer does not endorse the sentiment of Sir Charles Napier that "every soldier is of necessity a gentleman." . . .

Apropos of a comparison of notes by the survivors of the ill-fated Custer expedition and the elucidation on the obscure and sad reckonings of June 25th., 1876, by Chief Gall, leader of the hostile Indians, it might prove of interest to the public to hear the reason why the combined forces of General Terry and Major Reno did not upon coming together after the massacre make some effort to overtake the Indians and avenge the horrible mutilation of their comrades, if not to carry out the original purpose of the campaign.

FORT CUSTER NEWS: JUNE 28, 1886. After ten years the main facts of the Custer massacre, on the 25th of June, 1876, have been obtained. About one thousand persons visited the battlefields today (both Reno's and Custer's) including many officers of the Seventh Cavalry, who participated in the fight under Reno after a division of the regiment by Custer. Chief Gall had been known to have been the leading spirit of the fight on the Indians' side, and the killing of his two squaws by Reno may have been, as he says, the cause of his "bad heart" and fighting with the hatchet (meaning to mutilate the bodies after death).

Without comment we will give the narration of Captain E. S. Godfrey (then lieutenant), Seventh Cavalry, one of the survivors of the expedition who was with that portion of the regiment under Major Reno's command from the moment of separation at the divide until their discovery of Custer's last field of white dead.

CAPTAIN GODFREY'S STORY

The expedition against hostile Sioux Indians, composed of the entire strength of the Seventh Cavalry, left Fort Lincoln on the sixth day of June 1876.[33] On the morning of the 25th of June 1876, in the region of the valley of the Big Horn, the scouts reported to General Custer the discovery of a trail which indicated beyond a doubt their close proximity to the Indians; and to the subaltern officers of the command these scouts also said, "there were enough Indians to make three good day's fighting." Custer overheard the remark and replied in his quick, energetic, nervous manner: "I guess we will get through with it in one day." Ignorant of the multiplicity of the enemy and eager for the fray, Custer divided the regiment into three bodies for the purpose of striking the definite location of the enemy's village in the quickest possible time. That portion under command of Reno first discovered the Indians, and crossing the river, proceeded to charge their camp, which did not seem a formidable one, until hundreds of well-armed warriors rushed at him from the scattered lodges. After what was of necessity a feeble resistance on Reno's part, a retreat was made and the river recrossed with a loss of several killed and wounded, among the latter a lieutenant, who cried: "For God's sake don't leave me boys," and clinging to the stirrups was brought ashore by his horse to be shot on the other side of the river. Private Dahlgren's horse was shot under him, when he fired at an Indian, killed him, took his horse away, and joined the command, which was ascending the steep, clayey bluffs, minus eighteen of their number. (Captain Godfrey relates that Major Reno discharged his pistols in the retreat and then threw them away.)

Soon after this retreat Reno joined the other companies under Benteen, and both waited the return of Custer or

---

[33] Of course, this is inaccurate. The Terry-Custer expedition left Fort Abraham Lincoln on May 17, 1876. Quite possibly Private Purvis heard it wrong.

a dispatch from him, doing the best they could by lariating their horses down close in a coulee, and returning the fire of the Indians, which it was today ascertained, came from Sitting Bull's party of the older warriors, squaws, boys, and even papooses, while the ablest and greater body of Indians followed the direction taken by Custer. The part of the regiment not with Custer remained upon the bluffs, returning the fire of the Indians which came from every direction of the surrounding hills.

Eagerly they watched for signs of Custer, believing they were contending with the whole party and little dreaming of what was going on five miles away.

Shots were heard in the valley during the afternoon by Reno's party, but their infrequency and slight reports would not indicate that Custer was having so great a fight. Once a volley rang out loud and clear, but its significance was not comprehended at the time, as it is now believed to have been a signal of distress from Custer.

Towards evening the wind changed favorable to transmitting sounds in Reno's direction, and repeated shots heard at intervals, are now known to have been fired by the squaws and Indians while performing their atrocious work of mutilation. It was shown today that about 5 o'clock on the 25th of June, Colonel Benteen and Lieutenant Weir reached points within sight of Custer's field, but were driven back by the Indians.

At this time the inactive, restless, besieged Reno command were of the opinion, by reason of the shots heard that Custer had had a fight, met with a repulse, and would seek to join the command of Terry and Gibbons, shortly expected: therefore when dark came the men began to dig trenches in the hard earth. Everything capable of raising an ounce of soil was utilized: knives, spoons, tin plates, and even forks. Then follows the painful features of the position of the soldiers, without water all next day, the bold fire of a plainly re-enforced enemy, and the several attempts to drive the Indians back, made by the soldiers. Once a skirmish line succeeded in doing this without the loss of a single life except one, who had begged in piteous, whining tones to be left in the trenches. When Major Reno ordered the deployed company K back under cover he was found dead. Suddenly the firing ceased and no Indians were to be seen. This was regarded as a ruse to lure the soldiers from their thus-far successful protection. About the middle of the day a large column was seen moving in their direction. The appearance was at first likened to a drove of buffalo. Some one cried out, "It's Custer; look out for the gray company." Closer they came until they were recognized, not as Custer by the presence of the troop of gray horses, but as General Terry's command. Enough for these half famished men to know it meant deliverance from the awful rage of thirst, hunger and dread of torture; enough to stimulate their parched and weak throats to repeat many loud hurrahs.

Lieutenant [James] Bradley and a scout rode in advance of the new column; Captain Godfrey dashed forward to meet him saying eagerly, "Have you seen anything of Custer?" Then for the first time came the sad tidings in the timely awful reply, We counted 270 bodies, not one could have escaped. Back through the valley marched the whole command until suddenly upon reaching the crest of the hill they saw numerous white objects outlined upon the green earth; they were the naked bodies of one-half the troops and officers of the 7th Cavalry, horribly and shockingly mutilated, save Custer alone. Tom Custer's skull had been crushed in and several arrow heads found in it; his body was signally cut and dismembered, and the heart cut out.

The bodies were buried at once and remain until this day just where they fell.[34] General Custer, as it is well known, was buried at West Point, N. Y.

---

[34] Not quite true. Besides the original hurried burial in 1876, the bodies were re-buried in 1877 under the leadership of Major-General George A. Forsyth, in 1879 with Captain G. K. Sanderson in command, and finally in 1881 under Lieutenant C. F. Roe's direction. The officers' remains were dispersed as per next-of-kin requests in 1877 (Charles Kuhlman, *Legend into History*). Major Reno and 2nd Lt. John Crittenden were the only known officers buried on the Custer Battlefield; Reno was re-buried with full military honors in 1967 as a result of a finding by the Army Board for Correction of Military Records which declared him honorably discharged. His remains had been buried in Glenwood Cemetery in Washington, D.C., since his death on March 30, 1889. (R.U.)

Ever since the massacre, the Indians concerned in it have been reticent, to the extent of dumbness, on the subject. Even Sitting Bull who would be expected to repose enough confidence in his eastern patrons to tell how the battle was so fought, would never do so.

It has remained a sad, great unknown fact, until the arrangements by the survivors, for celebrating the tenth anniversary of the battle, included the presence of the great war chief, Gall, who went over the entire field today with an interpreter and officers related the following valuable historical narrative:

SIOUX CHIEF GALL'S STORY

We saw the soldiers early in the morning crossing the divide. When Reno and Custer separated we watched them until they came down into the valley. Our people cried: "The white soldiers are coming." Reno swept down so rapidly that the Indians were forced to fight. Sitting Bull and I were at the point where Reno attacked. Sitting Bull was big Medicine Man. The squaws and children we moved down where the Cheyennes were camped. The women and children caught the horses for the bucks to mount. The Sioux attacked Reno, and the Cheyennes Custer, then all mixed together. . . We crossed the river in many places; our lodges were all along it. When the bucks were mounted they drove Reno back. The soldiers were then in the timber and tied their horses to trees to fight on foot. Soon as Reno was driven back across river most of our force started in pursuit of Custer. Met him about three miles further up, half a mile up a ravine now called Reno Creek. Fought the soldiers and beat them back step by step until all were killed. To do this we sent a courier to the force fighting Reno, which came up in rear of Custer by the coulees, unseen. When Custer moved up to take a position on the hill, the Indians were behind and in front of him, many as the grass. The companies of Keogh and Calhoun were the first to dismount to fight on foot. They never grouped nor broke, but retired step by step to the ridge where they received fire from rear and front until all had perished. The Indians directed special fire upon the men who held horses while the others fought. When they were killed the squaws and old men shouted and waved blankets until the horses stampeded and were herded off the field by them. My two squaws were killed when Reno first attacked our village, and that made my heart so bad I fought with the hatchet (meaning to mutilate).

Custer's soldiers had the greater part of their ammunition in the saddle pockets. We scared their horses away and they had none, at the last they had to fight with small guns (pistols). When the soldiers were all dead the Indians ran up and butchered them with hatchets.

Fifty-four Indians were killed in the fight and many wounded ones came across the river and died in the rushes. We had Ogallalas, Minneconjous, Brule Sioux, Uncapapa, Sioux, Cheyennes, Arrapahoes and Gros Ventres.

When big dust came in the morning (meaning the approach of Terry and Gibbon's command), we struck our lodges and went up a creek to White Rain Mountains (Big Horn Range covered with snow in June), waited four days and went to Wolf Mountains.

With the conclusion of Chief Gall's narrative comes reflection as to the main cause of Custer's terrible defeat. He says the Indians were many as the grass. Every word and gesture of this noble looking specimen of his race today, betokened sincerity and no trace of contempt for his completely vanquished foes was visible, but instead a repeated affirmation from his lips of the universal belief that no one surrendered, but all fought desperately to the end.

FORT CUSTER NEWS, JUNE 28. Notes Taken on the Field and at Camp Crittenden:

Chief Gall was assigned a tent in the camp on the

GEN. E. S. GODFREY (above left)
"Have you seen anything of Custer?"
Courtesy, Montana Historical Society.

UNCPAPA SIOUX CHIEF GALL LED THE
ASSAULT ON CUSTER (above)
"No one surrendered, but fought
desperately to the end."
Courtesy, Montana Historical Society.

MAJOR MARCUS A. RENO (left)
"In his effort to make Reno appear
cowardly, Godfrey did not succeed."
David F. Barry photo. Courtesy, Denver Public
Library, Western Collection.

TENTH ANNIVERSARY OF THE CUSTER FIGHT, JUNE 25, 1886
At the monument, which blended with the sky and dropped out of this photo by David F. Barry. Courtesy, Denver Public Library, Western Collection. *l. to r.:* Corporal Hall, Dr. H. R. Porter, Capt. E. S. Godfrey, Capt. F. W. Benteen, Capt. W. S. Edgerly, Capt. T. M. McDougall, Trumpeter Penwell, White Swan.

**CAPTAIN FRANK D. BALDWIN'S COMPANY K, FIFTH INFANTRY
GIVES FIRING DEMONSTRATION WHERE CUSTER DISMOUNTED**
Both photos by David F. Barry; both courtesy, Denver Public Library, Western Collection.

night of the 24th. About midnight he picked up his blankets and moved under a wagon. It is believed he was afraid of a blow in the dark from Curley, Custer's famous scout.

Mr. A. H. Hersey took notes for the Helena Independent and helped to adorn Artist Berry's [Barry's] photographs in several cases.

Company K, 5th Infantry, extended the hospitality of their camp to the soldiers who visited the field. . .

Colonel [Frederick] Benteen pointed out the position of his men when he prescribed a very warm dose for the Indians.

Artist Berry [D. F. Barry] of Bismarck photographed the procession at many points; also the survivors and ladies of the party.

FORT CUSTER NEWS: JUNE 29, 1886. Chief Gall says Custer's scout, Curley, ran away too early in the fight to know anything about it. . .

Officers of the Seventh Cavalry were very much pleased to obtain a shell or bullet picked up on the field as a relic. A horse's hoof with an arrow shot into it a couple of inches was bought by one of the party for fifteen dollars. . .

Some of the reporters say: "Chief Gall was reticent and sullen until he saw the battlefield, then his eyes sparkled etc." It was a purse of money collected for him on the morning of the 25th, just before the procession moved, that made his eyes sparkle, and if that purse had not been forthcoming and another promised after his story was told, the chances are he would have resorted to the old subterfuge, "no sabe." [35]

---

[35] A. H. Hersey, through interpreter Cummings, interviewed Chief Gall during the 10th Anniversary gathering at the Custer Battlefield. Evidently the purse money that Purvis mentioned caused the old warrior's eyes to sparkle brilliantly. After almost 85 years' opportunity for reflection, the reader will recognize that

TENTH ANNIVERSARY – HONORED SURVIVORS AT FORT CUSTER
No. 1, Capt. McDougall; 2, Capt. Benteen; 3, Col. Dudley; 4, Lt. Brewer; 5, Dr. Porter; 6, Lt. Mann; 7, Tingell, St. Paul Globe; 8, Capt. Garety; 9, Baker, St. Paul Globe; 10, Capt. Godfrey; 11, Fred Benteen, Jr.; 12, Col. Slocum; 13, Col. Portello. David F. Barry photo. Courtesy, Custer Battlefield Museum.

The officers stationed at this post gave a reception and ball last Saturday evening, June 26. In spite of the unfavorable temperature the attendance of upwards of fifty officers and ladies marked it a pleasant and successful social event. [Brevet] Colonel F. W. Benteen, Major F. M. McDougall, Captain E. S. Godfrey, Captain W. S. Edgerly, Dr. H. R. Porter, survivors of the Custer Massacre, in whose honor the reception was given were all present.

FORT CUSTER NEWS: JUNE 29, 1886. At Camp Crittenden near Custer Battlefield, Company K, 5th Infantry (which has been stationed there since the night preceding the anniversary exercises) whiled away the time by practicing for the Fourth of July prizes at the post. Jack Kennard won the swimming match, Tom Pepper the foot race and Sergeant Titus deserved the purse in the horse race for the excellent horsemanship he displayed in riding the race through after the parting of the girth strap and turning of the saddle.

This represents the final contribution to the story of old Fort Custer by Private Purvis. Purvis was discharged from the Army on October 10, 1886. On November 8, 1886, he re-enlisted while in Chicago, Illinois, assigned to Company A, 4th Cavalry at Fort Lowell, Arizona Territory, he received a discharge on December 16, 1887 because of a disability. Private Purvis' ultimate fate is a mystery.

Gall simply realized the commercial value of his story and capitalized upon it. Hersey's interview appeared in the Helena, Montana, *Independent* in June 1886.

A Grand Ball at Fort Custer

The First Cavalry came to Fort Custer on July 15, 1884 from Fort Walla Walla. From the Winners of the West *(vol. VII, no. 11, October 1930) we get another enlisted man's view of yet another incident at the old fort. Maurice J. O'Leary, K Troop, First U.S. Cavalry remembers a Grand Ball at old Fort Custer:*

. . . I'm a-telling you right now, those were great days around those frontier Army posts, in particular Fort Custer. Did you ever hear of the biggest dance ever given by soldiers at any army post in Montana? No? Well, it was given at Old Fort Custer. I can tell you the names of some of the old-timers that were at that dance. There was old man Dana, a big livestock man; Jim McNutt, a contractor; Paul McCormick, of Billings; Theodore Borup, who later was with the old Pioneer Press for years, and old Liver-Eating Johnson. Those are just a few of the prominent ones I recall. . .

Well, we soldiers gave that dance at Fort Custer, and it cost us $500. We were getting $13 a month then – so just figure it out for yourself. One hundred of us gave $5 each. I will tell you how this thing came up.

At the fort there was a nice hall and a stage, with some scenery. But under the chaplain, in charge then, it was always used as a chapel. Then he organized a kind of a temperance society, enrolling all the girls and women at the fort – there were about seventy-five of them – and since none of the soldiers, or very very few of them joined, it was mighty lonesome for the buck private, and some of the officers. He would not let us use the hall for a dance. Well, there was a switch in commanding officers, and some of the boys got at him first, and the commanding officer said the building was to be used by all of the boys at the garrison, and that we could go ahead and give a dance if we wanted to.

We got together and organized what was known as the Rounders' Club. It cost five bucks to join, and to belong there were several qualifications that would not please Mr. Volstead now. We raised our $500 and bought turkey, and ordered lemons, oranges, grapes and other fruits from St. Paul. The dance was to be given on the evening of St. Patrick's Day. We sent an escort wagon over to the Junction, which was nothing but a cow town, and that day it got mighty cold. The men built a large fire, and threw in a lot of good-sized rocks. In the morning, when the fire cooled, they fished the hot rocks out, put them in the escort wagon, and packed in the fruit and covered it all up with a tarp. It arrived at the Fort all okay.

Well, the big night arrived. We had supper in the schoolroom, back of the stage. There were babies tied in chairs and lying on blankets all over the stage. Folks came for miles around. The officers and their ladies cast aside all formality. There was not enough room to seat them all at midnight, so the officers'

PAUL McCORMICK
One of the old timers at the dance, and a well-known man of the Fort Custer area.

JOHN "LIVER-EATING" JOHNSON
One of the men at the dance. "The only way to make a Piegan quit horse-stealing is to kill him. That's my plan."

wives and the laundresses, and nursemaids, and visiting ladies all sat down to the same table and had a good time. Later the men followed suit.

The old Cavalry Band played and the orchestra was made up of bandsmen who could also play stringed instruments. The orchestra played a lot of old Irish airs. Then Captain Garrity [Frank D. Garretty] of the 17th Infantry rose to his feet. He expressed a great desire to dance one of the old Irish reels, if he could only find an Irish girl from the old country who could dance it with him. Gosh, I wish I could remember her name. And how that Irish girl could dance! Well, they danced two or three Irish reels and then the fun was on.

Colonel N. A. M. Dudley of the 1st Cavalry was commanding officer. And I am sure Mr. Dana was there, as Lieutenant James B. Alyshire [Aleshire], who later became Quartermaster General of the USA, was then keeping company with Dana's daughter.

And we danced until morning –

And then what?

Well, we appointed a committee to check up the finances. We had $17 left in the treasury. We bought $17 worth of beer – closed the books, and the Rounders disbanded. And, oh heck, the next morning was just as it always is the morning after.

Crow Indians and the Swordbearer Incident

Through the back issues of the Billings Gazette *we follow, in chronological order, the origins, development and the inevitable conclusion to the little known, but significant encounter with a group of recalcitrant Crow Indians led by a young warrior whom we shall refer to as Swordbearer.*[36]

The significance of this fight lies not in the number of soldiers and Indians involved, although the Billings Gazette *reflects genuine concern, if not potential panic amongst its citizens. Rather the real importance of this action was one of the first recorded instances of Indian mythology mixed with the white man's Christianity that eventually reached a disastrous climax at Wounded Knee in December of 1890.*

We shall read that the great Indian chiefs Gall, Two Moon, and Sitting Bull played little-known but important roles in the story.

As background, we include accounts of the horse-stealing activities between the various Indian tribes, the political intrigues of Agent Henry E. Williamson and other events leading up to the confrontation with

---

[36] He is also referred to, according to the particular reporter, as Wraps-up-his-tail, Man-who-wraps-up-his-tail, Pah-ches-tab, Cheschapah, and Cheestapah.

the Fort Custer soldiers. In the contemporary accounts of the final action we failed to find a reliable account of the death of the Crow leader, Swordbearer.

During the summer of 1970, while in Billings, Montana, we were indeed fortunate to meet Mike Reynolds, the son of the former Superintendent of the Crow Agency, Major S. G. Reynolds. (Major Reynolds' account of the destruction of old Fort Custer is recounted further on in this volume.)

Mike Reynolds gives us an accurate version of Swordbearer's death at the hands of the Indian policeman, Fire Bear. Mr. Reynolds' account along with that of Miss Elizabeth W. Barstow, daughter of Major C. H. Barstow, a leading figure in the episode and that of Allie Stevenson gives us an accurate picture of the climax of those exciting days of the uprising.

Reprinted in the issues of the Billings Gazette *of 1887 were accounts taken from the* Pioneer Press, River Press, Yellowstone Journal, Miles City Journal, *and* Helena Independent. *We use all of these stories in telling the Swordbearer incident of 1887.*

TROUBLE ON THE RESERVE

FORT CUSTER: OCTOBER 3, 1887. On Friday morning a party of twenty-two young Crow Indians under the leadership of an Indian who has lately become famous as a medicine man, returned from a successful raid on the Piegan Indians, bringing back with them about 60 head of horses. The Crows were celebrating this event with great rejoicings when Agent Williamson ordered his police to arrest the entire party for horse stealing. This incensed the Indians so that they made an attack on the agency buildings. Fortunately no

CROW INDIANS FIRING INTO THE AGENCY BUILDINGS
"The houses and office of the agent were riddled with bullets."
An illustration by Frederic Remington, from Harper's Weekly, November 5, 1887.

one was hurt, though the houses and office of the agent were riddled with bullets. The agent immediately dispatched a scout to Fort Custer for troops. Four troops of cavalry arrived at the agency Saturday morning. On their arrival they found the Indians camped about the place threatening the life of the agent. Three of the troops returned Sunday morning, leaving one to protect the agent. The arrests were to be made by the civil authorities and the Indians, however, say that they do not want to fight the soldiers, but will resist to the utmost any attempt of the police to arrest them.

THE CROW INDIANS

The system of horse stealing between the Piegans and the Crows had been in existence ever since the Indians were placed on the reservations, and these roving bands of thieves have been the trouble of the ranchmen located between the Yellowstone and the Missouri rivers. Every fall the hostilities are carried on and in passing across the Judith Basin these Indians always take from one to a dozen horses belonging to ranchmen living in their line of march. A stop should have been put to it long ago, but that trouble sometime on account of this would be the inevitable result – was the opinion of all who were well informed. The time has come. General Williamson who has been endeavoring with a strict hand to restrain the evil proclivities of the Indians under his charge, determined to make a stand and punish the offenders who were unusually successful in their deviltry. In the midst of their rejoicings he orders their arrest and punishment. This new policy was such a surprise and disgrace to them that trouble results as a matter of course. What is needed now is a firm and fearless carrying out of the plan proposed and the severe punishment of the offenders. This will be most effectual, as the case is one over which the whole Crow nation is aroused and a successful break up of their band of horse thieves will be a lesson that will not be forgotten. We trust that this will be the policy pursued and the agent should receive every assist from those in authority elsewhere in the performance of his duty. The time for sentiment in these matters has gone by, and the stern hand of the law should never relax its hold on these Indians until the whole Crow tribe have a wholesome respect for its mandates inculcated into their rebellious hearts. We hope that no lives will be lost in carrying out the orders of arrest, but they should be carried out if necessary with force, as no other way is open without an admission on the part of the Indian Department that they cannot enforce their orders. This matter brings up the ever present question of throwing the reservation open and is but another strong argument in its favor.

THE CROW SITUATION

OCTOBER 8, 1887. As shown by a visit to Fort Custer and the Indian Agency and by interviews with those in authority the situation is serious, much more so than the authorities at Washington seem to consider it from word received from there. They say that the Interior Department agrees with General Terry in his endorsement on the news which was forwarded by him from the Crow Reservation, to the effect that the action of the agent had been hasty and that the disturbance had better be allowed to subside of its own accord. A visit to the scene of the disturbance and a careful inquiry into the state of feeling which now exists will quickly dispel any idea of that kind, and that a wide-spread and deep-seated dissatisfaction is prevalent among the Crows is a matter easily seen. The trouble in the first place is helped by the seeds of discontent sown by the Sioux braves during their visit last summer. A young chief, Sword Bearer or "Man Who-Wraps-His-Tail-Up," made a visit to one of the Sioux agencies some time this summer and went through their tortuous ceremonies with so much eclat that they convinced him that he was a prophet and conferred upon him the title of Sword Bearer; he returned to the Crow Agency filled with the idea of his importance, and thirsting for some adventure. Easily finding a number of young Crows anxious for deeds of daring he organized this horse-stealing raid. On his return from this most successful trip he was filled with the idea nothing was impossible to him. There is also a possibility that their young warriors had obtained some whisky on their way home, which had something to do with their attack on the agency. The attack was made about dark. Five of the returned thieves were the principal offenders, riding around the agency buildings, firing into the sutler's store, on his refusal to give them ammunition. One Indian pointed his gun at the breast of the interpreter then raising it, fired a few inches over his head.

In the meantime a courier had been dispatched for troops. They arrived just at dark, and it is claimed by some that they were openly defied by the Indians, who withdrew to the top of a hill west of the agency and prepared for an attack which they expected immediately from the soldiers. The troops however had strict orders not to arrest or not to use any violence, and when the Indians found such was the case they scattered to different places on the Big and Little Horn Rivers. . .

Sword Bearer is supposed to be in the mountains making medicine, the other Indians are holding war dances and the sound of the tom-toms can be heard in every camp. Word has come from the Blackfoot agency that five parties of raiding Piegans left the agency on an expedition against the Crows some days ago. The Crows are much excited over this prospective raid and are gathering together for mutual protection. There are about 50 lodges camped across the Big Horn from the Fort and over one hundred a short distance above the agency on the Little Horn. Some of the Indians claim that the Piegans are already on the reserve in hiding, waiting for a good opportunity to take a band of horses and leave for the north.

That the situation is undoubtedly serious, none of the officials deny. But that there is no danger to the whites in the surrounding country is true and there is no occasion for any alarm. It is an interesting question for the government to settle, however, and the result will be watched with intense interest by people in this territory and Wyoming. It is a question between the Indians and the government and its outcome will decide whether these Indians can pursue their formerly unchecked course of systematic horse stealing or whether they will finally be forced to come to the conclusion that the government means business and that its Indian policy is not a failure. In an interview with [Brevet] General N. A. M. Dudley,[37]

---

[37] Like almost all of Fort Custer's commanding officers, Colonel Nathan Augustus Monroe Dudley possessed impressive credentials. Not so well known is

the commandant at Fort Custer, he expressed himself as very sorry that the law did not allow him to make these arrests the first night this trouble occurred and if he received authority shortly, it would be but a short time before all would be under arrest or, as he expressed it, "A few would be killed." But under the present policy of the government and the laws as they stand today the heaviest penalties are attached to an officer using troops as a "posse comitatus." And they can do nothing without the authority of the president, which will probably be withheld if in accordance with the spirit shown by the dispatches from Washington. General Dudley has done everything that lies in his power to preserve peace and to protect property and life. He has done this with promptness and willingness and undoubtedly to his prompt action is due the fact that no further trouble resulted at the time. A massacre was probably averted, which taking place, would have been a second Meeker outrage. With General Williamson it is different. For two years he has been laboring with the Crow Indians to civilize and educate them. How far he has gone can only be realized by visiting the agency, inspecting the gardens, work shops, schools and various industries which are carried on there by the Indians and their children.

---

the story of Dudley's involvement in the famous Lincoln County War of 1878 in New Mexico. It was this incident that helped William H. Bonney, alias Billy the Kid, get started on his maniacal reign of terror, and brought about the removal of Dudley as commanding officer of Fort Stanton in New Mexico Territory. A brief but highly informative account of this interesting occurrence can be found in an article by Philip J. Rasch, published in the *1949 Brand Book* of the Los Angeles Corral of the Westerners. Rasch concludes his story by saying, "Dudley possessed in full measure both the failings and the virtues of his fellows. He was hard-drinking, prejudiced and obstinate, but he was also a competent officer and a first-class fighting man."

To a man that has labored in this way and who was beginning to think that much permanent good had been accomplished, this occurrence is a bitter disappointment and source of chagrin. Whatever mistakes General Williamson may have made in his policy and whatever tendency towards harshness he may have shown, as claimed by some, the fruits of his labor during these two years show that he must have labored hard and faithfully to regenerate the Indian. He feels deeply this bad break on the part of the Indians and his inability to enforce the arrest of the thieves. His Indian police are not sufficient and he stated in an interview that the greatest mistake, although unavoidable, was not arresting Sword Bearer and his followers the moment of their return. He says "The question as it now stands is an issue between the department and the Indians. If these arrests are not made, if the authorities give an inch in their purpose of punishing these offenders, all authority is at an end. The agent might as well leave the Indians to pursue their own way and to do as they please. It is a critical moment and any hesitancy shown in not punishing these Indians will lead to outrages of more magnitude."

The general opinion among the army officers is the same and immediate steps should be taken to that effect. Every day that intervenes sends more recruits to Sword Bearer's outfit. The number is estimated at from 150 to 200 young followers and there will be serious difficulty in executing these warrants of arrest at the best, and they will increase as time goes on. Today is issue day at the agency and rations for over 2,000 Indians will be issued. Trouble is anticipated by some, but the general opinion is that there will be no trouble of a serious nature. Troops are to be held in readiness and any disturbance will be promptly quelled.

We hope no trouble will occur and do not think that it will, as the Indians know too well that everyone is prepared. Arrangements have been made to use the school house at the agency as a garrison and block house. Water, provisions and ammunition have been arranged for, and these precautions are such that even in case of trouble no lives would probably be lost. The arrangements are most complete, efficient soldiers under experienced officers, many friendly Indians, and the extent of civilization among the Crows all tend to prevent any such outbreak, and if the government pursues the policy that it should and insists upon the immediate arrest and punishment of these thieves, even with the assistance of the military, everything will quiet down and kindly feeling will resume its sway. The older Indians are anxious to see this, and Sword Bearer can count on no assistance from them.

ALL QUIET

FORT CUSTER: OCTOBER 9, 1887. Special Agent Howard is now investigating the trouble at the agency, and informs your correspondent that the arrests will be attempted Saturday and that the troops will assist. Another special agent is en route from Washington to co-operate with General Howard. He may alter these arrangements. The order for the troops to assist in making the arrests has not yet arrived. Sword Bearer's party are camped near the agency and defy the troops to arrest them. The other Indians are quiet but sullen and rather inclined to submit.

The *Pioneer Press* says: The War and Interior departments are mystified over the Crow outbreak and undecided as to the proper steps to be taken. Secretary Lamar has not yet decided to send an inspector to the reservation, for the Indian bureau has advised against it; but he today telegraphed the alloting agents who are at work on the reservation, to ascertain if it is necessary to send an inspector. A government official from the West who understands the situation, says: "Much surprise is expressed at the hostility shown by the Crows toward Agent Williamson, who has been a good agent in looking after their interests. Three years ago Blake and Williamson offered the government $50,000 for the privilege of grazing on the Crow Reservation. The last Crow treaty gives the Secretary of the Interior the right to fix the amount for this privilege and to make the lease for the Indians. This contract was never consummated. Last year Agent Williamson wrote the department that five or six parties, one of them named Briggs, had offered $20,000 for the extra grazing on the Crow Reservation. He added that some of these parties were already grazing their cattle upon the reservation. The value of the privilege was so apparent that the secretary instructed Agent Williamson to advertise in the West that the extra grazing privilege on the reservation would be let to the highest bidder. After some delay Agent Williamson made the curious reply to the department that he did not understand its order about advertising, and that the Indians would allow no other persons than the five or six parties for whom he made the offer to graze the cattle upon the reservation. Nothing more has been done about the matter. No lease has been granted, but those parties still continue to graze their cattle at just what tolls the agent can collect. This matter, I think, has had something to do in aggravating the Indians, and may have given them cause for ill feeling toward Agent Williamson. The talk of putting this matter in the hands of the sheriff is nonsense. The allotment law does not make these Indians citizens or amenable to civil process until they have taken their land in severalty.[38]

FORT CUSTER: OCTOBER 17. General Dudley states that "Sword Bearer" has come down out of the mountains, where he has been fasting and "making medicine" or as the Indians express it, talking with the spirits of his grandfathers, and is now camped with his followers about six miles south of Fort Custer. General Dudley also states that if permission were granted by the authorities, the troops could capture these Indians in a few hours without serious difficulty.

The situation remains virtually unchanged up to present date. "Sword Bearer's" following has not materially increased in numbers but those that are with him are full of courage and the cause is gaining fresh impetus daily from the inaction of the government.

FORT CUSTER: OCTOBER 26. Everything is a scene of activity here. Two companies of infantry arrived tonight from Fort Keogh, two more from Keogh by way of Cheyenne Agency, which failed to overtake the Indians, will arrive tomorrow, one of the cavalry is now en route from Fort Maginnis and two from Fort McKinney. Two more mountain howitzers arrived today for the use of the troops. Great prepara-

---

[38] Land owned by individual right.

tions are being made for a thorough campaign. Sword Bearer and party are reported by Indian runners to have arrived this afternoon at the 40-mile ranch on the Little Horn which is close to the Custer Battleground. The weather is becoming much milder and the troops will take the field as soon as the snow melts, which will be in three or four days if there are no more storms. The impression among the officers is that this is no boys' play. No such preparations for war have been made since 1876. General Dudley will be in command, Brigadier-General [Thomas H.] Ruger directing operations. The Indians say that allies from other tribes are now on their way to join Sword Bearer. It is not known how many recruits were obtained at Cheyenne Agency, but it is supposed there were quite a number. The infantry now guarding the agency are engaged in throwing up earthworks and digging trenches about the buildings.

The Indian situation as has been held in the *Gazette* since the first disturbance is serious. We stated at that time that it was a vital question between the Indians and government. It has turned out to be so; not only do the special agent's reports note this fact, but the serious consideration and vast expense which is now required from the government upholds this. Troops are being called from four posts situated in two departments. The Department Commander Brigadier-General [Thomas H.] Ruger has come from St. Paul to give his personal attention to the matter and he finds plenty to do. The affair is now in the hands of the War Department alone, and vigorous measures are to be resorted to, to bring these "fools," as the peaceable Indians call them, to terms. A large force is to be put in the field, the same as though a war was in progress. No move will be made until a successful issue can be assured, and the number of troops will show the Indians their futility of resistance. These outcomes remain to be seen. Force may have to be used and it probably will be, the rebellious Indians will be handled without gloves. What a significant event and how far-reaching in effect would be a crushing defeat to the Indians on the scene of their former triumphs – the Custer Battleground.[39]

CROW AGENCY: OCTOBER 27. The Infantry are still guarding the agency. The weather here is fine and snow fast disappearing, and troops will be in motion in a day or two. Saturday was issue day and 101 families were missing, not drawing rations. Forty-six of these were from Pryor Creek and the balance from other points. It is not supposed that they are belligerent, but only scared. The whole Crow nation with few exceptions have left their farms and houses and are gathered in large camps on the Big and Little Horn rivers.

Inspector General Armstrong, through whose reports this affair has been placed in the hands of the War Department, is here and will stay until matters are settled. He says that prompt action and energetic methods will be used by General Ruger, but that he thinks little resistance will be made to the large body of troops now gathered here. Though it is impossible to tell, as some of the influential chiefs claim that they will support Sword Bearer if he is arrested. He

---

[39] At the time of the Custer Fight the Crow Indians fought on the side of the soldiers. The irony of the Crow uprising of 1887 seems to have escaped the *Billings Gazette* reporter. The Crows did not experience a triumph at the Custer Fight. The Sioux Chief, Gall, said in November of 1887, "The whites and Crows fought me at the Custer battle and tried to kill me."

thinks that there are only about forty who will actually fight; but that Sword Bearer is a smart man and can control a large number who unless guarded will join the belligerents. He says, also, that it is deplorable that these arrests should not have been the day after the first trouble on the 30th of September. All this that is following would have been saved. Trouble has undoubtedly been caused by the seeds of discontent sown by Sitting Bull, and the allotment question has nothing to do with this trouble. That visiting of Indians in war paint and feathers should be stopped and they should not be allowed to leave the reservations unless they dressed in white men's clothes and went without arms and on the railroad.

Sword Bearer is half Bannock or Snake and half Crow, and if any Indians join him it would be the Shoshones from that part of the country. . .

General Armstrong estimates the male Crows over 16 years of age at 650, among which are 400 fighting men. The Crows are estimated to have about 400 rifles, but a limited supply of ammunition.

The *Yellowstone Journal* of the 26th of October says that yesterday one of the head men of the Tongue river Cheyennes, Red Cherries by name, came to Fort Keogh direct from the Cheyenne Agency, which he had left on Monday last. He was closely interrogated by Colonel Gibson through H. C. Thompson, interpreter, and told the following story: On Saturday last a party of Crow Indians were seen approaching the Cheyenne Agency. At first they were taken to be a war party and preparations were made by the Cheyennes to receive them, but before coming within range runners were sent to the Cheyennes declaring the Crow party to be friendly visitors and they were so received. The Crow party consisted of about one hundred young bucks and sixty squaws. As soon as the preliminary greetings had been exchanged one of the chiefs of the Crow party – who was none other than the somewhat noted "Sword Bearer," of the Crow revolt – made a talk to the Cheyennes, professing friendship and the most pacific motives and asked permission to have a dance with the Cheyennes - a dance described by the interpreter as one in which both bucks and squaws joined and which is emblematic of social and friendly feelings. Two Moon, chief of the Cheyennes, knowing of the trouble at the Crow Agency and not wishing to be drawn into it with his tribe refused to join the Crows in the dance or even allow them to hold it at the Cheyenne camp. Being disappointed in this the Crows departed the next day. Further interrogation of Red Cherries in regard to the intentions of the Crows in visiting the Cheyennes led to the expressed belief on the part of Red Cherries, which he said was also the opinion of Two Moon and the other Cheyenne chiefs, that the intention of the Crows was to get the dance started and after the Cheyennes had got warmed up, to have a talk and to talk war. The Crows, he said, had no war paint on, but were so eager for the Cheyennes to join in the dance that it was evident there was a hidden motive for their visit beyond the very trivial one of friendly dance. Being asked what stand the Cheyennes would take in case of a war between the Crows and the whites, Red Cherries promptly replied that the Cheyennes, if permitted, would join the whites in fighting the Crows, and intimated that they were rather eager to do so. He said the Cheyennes could muster 156 warriors, all of whom would gladly take the trail against their life-long enemies the Crows. This, if true, is a very reassuring feature of the situation and completely does away with any apprehension of an Indian raid upon the unprotected settlers of the Tongue River and Rosebud.

The visit of the Crows was undoubtedly to secure some pledge of neutrality if not assistance from the Cheyennes in case they made a break, and failing in both they will undoubtedly see the futility of declaring war, knowing that so stealthy and fearless a foe as the Cheyennes can be loosed against them, backed by the military and the cowboys. . .

FORT CUSTER: OCTOBER 27. . . . Scout James Campbell, an interpreter, and two others went to the hostile camp yesterday 12 miles from the post on Big Horn. Sword Bearer has in camp about 200 braves, and on being asked to give himself up and come into Post – refused to consider the proposition. The weather is fine, snow all gone, mud rapidly drying. Four or five days will see the affair settled unless the campaign is prolonged by the Indians retreating. It is thought, however, that no resistance will be made. That on the appearance in the field of a large body of troops, Indians will come in of their own accord. Officers and men are anxious to take the field and have the affair settled. A humiliation of the Indians in this case will settle the question of raids among the Crows. The newspaper correspondents here have received transportation and will take the field with the troops, it is understood that Monday morning is the date set for the troops to leave. The other companies on their way are drawing nearer. The Missoula troops arrived tonight, and the McKinney troops will arrive on the Big Horn at the mouth of Grass Lodge, where they were ordered to, in a day or two. This is probably what the military are now waiting for. These troops will be there to intercept Sword Bearer's retreat to the mountains in case he wishes to run away. There are no signs of his giving in, a rumor was started by one of the Indian scouts last night that he was coming in, but it was found to be just the opposite to the truth of the matter. Although his following is not gaining in numbers, every day gives those who are with him fresh confidence. Pretty Eagle says that a large number of the Crow tribe other than those who are with him will go to his assistance if the arrests are attempted. The Indian most feared by the authorities is "Deaf Bull," who is a powerful chief in the tribe, and is one of Sword Bearer's strongest supporters. He has a large following, and if he wants to can make a great deal of trouble.

From the *Yellowstone Journal:* A gentleman just returned from Custer Station informs us that news of the Indian troubles brought in by yesterday's coach indicates that the Indians are still defiant and no attempts at arrest have been made as yet. Under the leadership of Sword Bearer a band of young Crow warriors numbering about 200 are camped on a hill in full sight of the agency and almost on the sight of the historical Custer Battleground. The latest demonstration made by the Crows was to fire into the agency buildings and they have made threats of burning the buildings. At Junction City, says our informant, the general opinion is that the Indians will not submit without bloodshed, and anticipating such an outcome, several of the old settlers from Junction will go up to the agency today to see the fun, among them being Paul McCormick. There has been a great deal of snow up in that country and melting during the past two days has left the roads in an almost impassable condition, so that quick movements of troops will be utterly impossible.

FORT CUSTER: OCTOBER 29. The actual appearance of this post at present is so much at variance with the sensational reports contained in some of the eastern papers and among the associated press telegrams that it is worthy of comment. Although in thirty minutes from the bugle call of "Boots and Saddles" five troops of cavalry and twelve companies of infantry could be in line ready to march, the regular duties of the post go on undisturbed. The band plays at guard mount at 9 A. M. and in the afternoon when pleasant it discourses sweet music to the officers and their families who are lounging about the quarters. But it is noticeable while on drill and when pursuing their ordinary duties the cavalry saddles are fully equipped for a ten days' trip. The officers are impatiently waiting orders to go into the field and eagerly snatch at any bit of news that is circulated around in regard to prospective movements of troops. There seems to be a strong feeling among them that this Man-Who-Wraps-His-Tail-Up, or Sword Bearer, should be killed, and if the occasion comes when the order is given to fire, many rifle bullets will seek him out exclusively.

This is a remarkably well ordered post. General Armstrong, the Indian inspector, says that in his extensive travels among the posts and reservations in

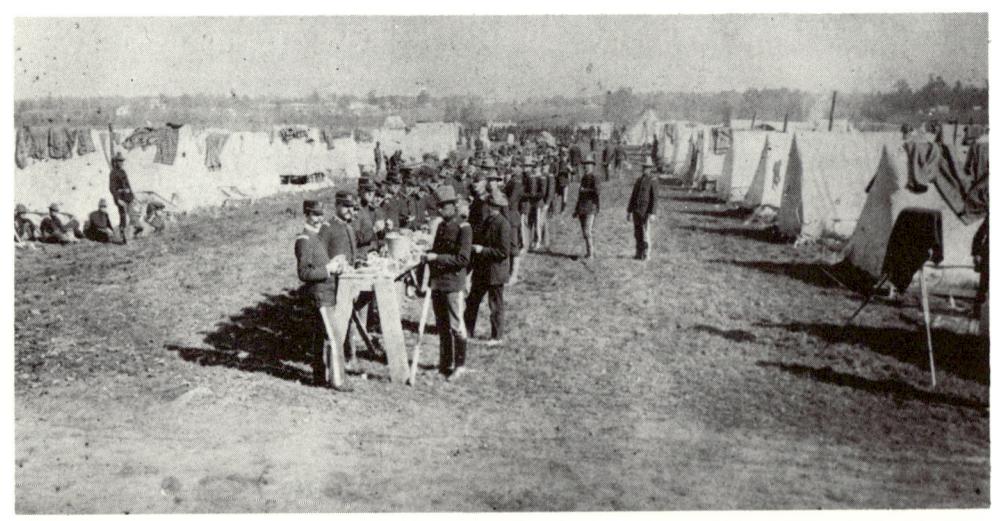

COLONEL NATHAN A. M. DUDLEY AND STAFF, FORT CUSTER, 1887
Dudley is seated second from right. Others are not identified.
"The officers are impatiently waiting orders to go into the field."
Courtesy, Custer Battlefield Museum.

AT THE MESS TABLES IN THE FIELD, 1887
"A large group of tents . . . shelter the soldiers who have arrived."
Courtesy, Custer Battlefield Museum.

The First Cavalry on the Parade Ground at Fort Custer, 1887
The hospital and barracks buildings in the background.
"A large force is to be put in the field. . ."
O. S. Goff photo. Courtesy, Custer Battlefield Museum.

none of them has the order, precision and thorough system prevailed to such an extent as it does here.

A very picturesque appearance is presented here now. The barracks, officers' quarters, etc. form a large circle, enclosing the parade ground. On this, every afternoon, the cavalry goes through its evolutions. Close to the barracks is a large group of tents which shelter the soldiers who have arrived from other posts. In another place not far removed are the four or five large teepees of the twenty wandering Gros Ventre Indians who were checked on their southward journey. During the cavalry drill there is generally a row of twenty or twenty-five Indians, mostly scouts, sitting on their horses gravely watching the proceedings. Their varied costumes and the brilliant colors which prevail lend a variety to the scene, which would otherwise be monotonous. The ordinance sergeant toward evening has a little target practice. The target is placed one mile away and the explosive balls of the Hotchkiss guns do great execution. It is a pity that Sword Bearer and his followers cannot be used instead of the target; it would soon settle a much vexed question and one which is now costing Uncle Sam large amounts of money for transportation of troops.

A remarkable feature of this Indian trouble is that this medicine man, Pah-Ches-tab, or Sword Bearer, is ruling these Indians by their superstitious fears. Even the well-disposed and quiet Indians say that there is no doubt but what he possesses some occult power, derived from supernatural sources. He predicts, and being a smart man, can predict many things.

CROW AGENCY: NOVEMBER 2. A *Yellowstone Journal* representative was agreeably entertained by an

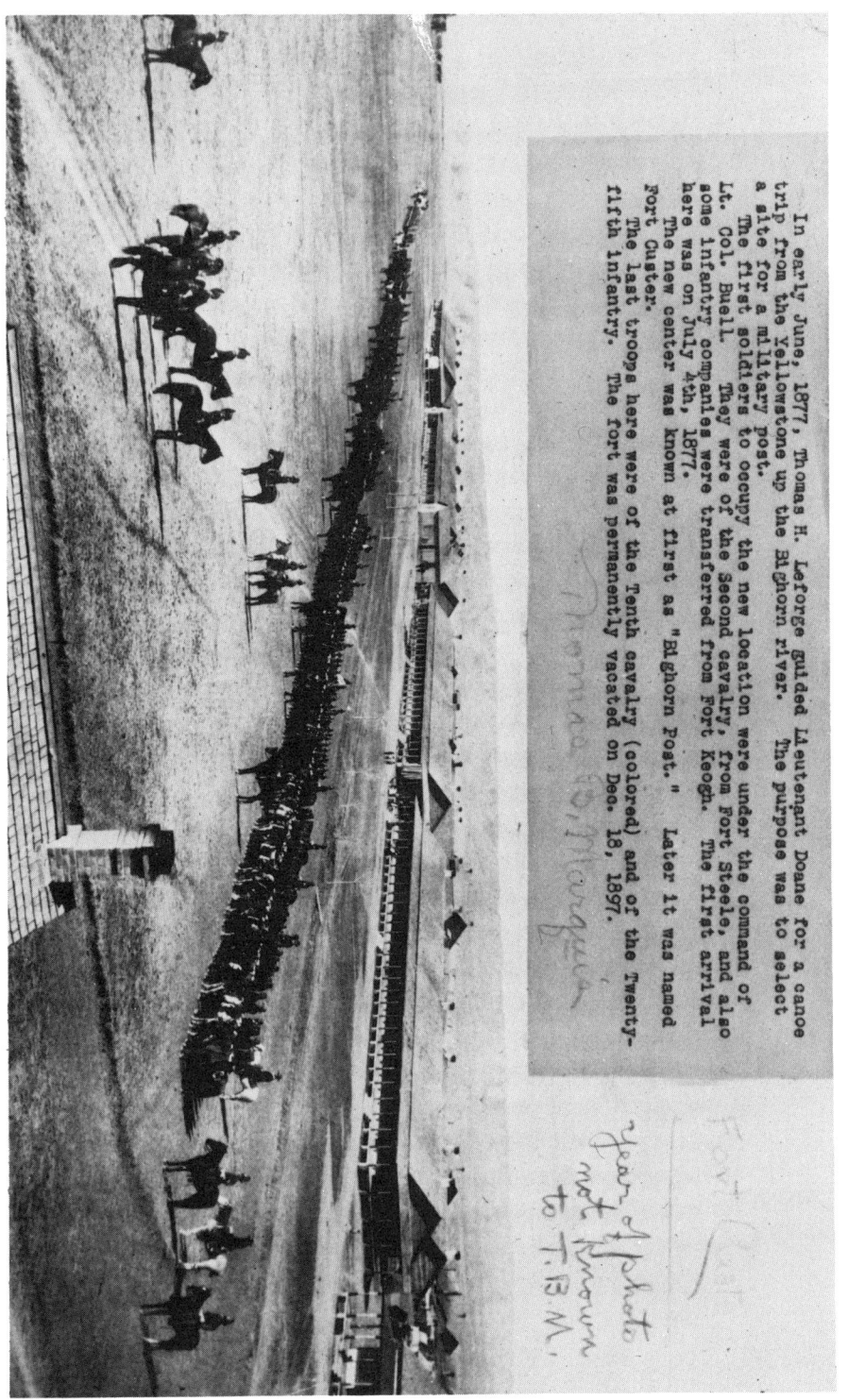

THE FIRST CAVALRY AT FORT CUSTER ABOUT 1887
"Every afternoon the cavalry goes through its evolutions."
O. S. Goff photo with note by Thomas B. Marquis. Courtesy, Big Horn County Library, Hardin.

account of the Crow troubles from the lips of Hugh S. Campbell, who for seven years was chief gardener at the agency and is now live-stock inspector, holding under the Montana board of stock commissioners, entirely distinct from the stock association. Mr. Campbell as before stated is as well posted on Indians, particularly Crow Indians, as any white man among them since 1879. His version of the trouble in effect coincides with former accounts and he does not consider that General Williamson is to be blamed in the matter, being tied down to department orders which he was obliged to enforce – or attempt to enforce. Two companies of soldiers could have captured the ringleaders and quelled the revolt if the move had been made at the proper time, but delay only strengthens the Indians in numerical strength and confidence in their importance.

When Mr. Campbell left the agency Monday the war cloud was thickening and it has now come to that pass that Wraps-His-Tail-Up must be arrested without bloodshed or the entire Crow tribe would take the war path. On the other hand if his nibs surrenders and without making a fight he will become the laughing stock of the tribe, who will make an old woman of him and he will be dressed like a squaw and shut out from the councils of the tribe forever, in other words ostracised. This Wraps-His-Tail-Up will never do; he lacks the moral courage (if such term may be used in connection with a Crow) to withstand the taunts and gibes of his nation. He has posed before them as a prophet, a big medicine man and is ruling the Crows by their superstitious fears. Being a shrewd cuss he takes advantage of every circumstance that comes his way and has so far been remarkably lucky in fulfillment of his predictions. One instance of the success of his ventures will suffice in this connection: the soldiers had one of the Hotchkiss guns getting it ready for use and the Crows were somewhat alarmed, not liking that kind of warfare, but the medicine man said that after that gun was once fired he would put a spell over it which would render it useless for many days. Mark the verification. The very next day the cannon was loaded and fired at a target and when the smoke cleared away it was seen dismounted and practically disabled. The recoil had burst the fastenings and the medicine man was triumphant. All these things give him great prestige among the Indians and in their blind obedience to his will lays the secret of the situation.

Wraps-His-Tail-Up is being used as a cat's paw by the old Chief Deaf Bull, and Crazy Head, the war chief of the Crows, stands in with the play. The statement that the hostiles had defied the soldiers at several times and dared them to take them is verified by Mr. Campbell, who has been on the ground, through the camp and among the warriors since the beginning of the revolt. He it was at whom Wraps-His-Tail-Up made a war-like demonstration on the first day of the trouble, pointing a gun at his breast and then raising it a little fired over his head. Mr. Campbell is positive in the statement that no encounter has yet taken place and that no soldiers had been fired upon. Though no other Indians had yet joined in the revolt Mr. Campbell thinks unless a decisive attack is made on the Crows and the matter settled at one blow a general Indian war will surely ensue: The Cheyennes will join if there is any show for the Crows after the first bloodshed and that will be the signal for a general uprising.

So far as the Crows are immediately concerned they will confine their movements to "fighting soldiers," but the cattlemen will not tamely submit to the sacrifice of their property in such an event and the cowboys of Pass Creek and the region adjacent to the reserve are ready for the signal to measure their strength with the hostiles. The camp of the Indians is now virtually surrounded. The time for making the final movement has been extended to Friday. Orders have been issued that all Indians who remain without the agency are to be dealt with as hostiles and this time General Ruger means business.

WHAT "BILL" HAMILTON SAYS

BILLINGS, MONTANA: NOVEMBER 4, 1887. Mr. William Hamilton called at the *Gazette* office today. He has been on the plains and amongst the Indians since 1844, and has had experience enough to perfectly understand the Indian characteristic and is acquainted with every tribe in Montana and has lived among the Crows. He has just come from the reservation and had talked with the hostile Indians who had just come from the camp. The Indians say that Sword Bearer does not wish to be arrested for stealing Piegan horses, but has no other animosity toward the whites. He says there are no Sioux but some Cheyennes with Sword Bearer and that there are more Indians leaving him than are being added to the number of the belligerents. The Indians say they do not want to fight the whites, and will not unless forced. The Indians will not break out in this valley, "too many whites," and Mr. Hamilton says he would stake his life that one-fourth of the 300 warriors are opposed to the fight and each Indian has not to exceed 50 cartridges and many of the guns are in poor order. The hostile Indians are 60 miles away and the friendly Indians say the hostile ones will surrender the moment they are surrounded. Bill Hamilton says that there is no danger whatever to Billings and his closing remark as he left the office was: "Tell the ladies for me that there is not the slightest danger for them."

GALL SPEAKS OUT

STANDING ROCK AGENCY: NOVEMBER 4. The much feared outbreak of the Sioux and Crow Indians against the government on account of the proposed enforcement of the land severalty law is not attracting the attention of the people and the press of the country and the *Tribune* is pleased to announce that the greatest of the Sioux says he is with the whites.

On Tuesday the chiefs of the Sioux tribe held a council at Standing Rock for the purpose of discussing the question and nearly all the noted chiefs delivered speeches. Among the number were Running Antelope, John Grass, Mad Deer, Red Fish, Cottonwood, and Gall. All save Gall stated that they had always felt friendly towards the whites and were lavish in their expressions of the long standing-affection for the pale face.

The commanding and intelligent Gall, who led the Indians in the Custer massacre and who has been their military leader for many years, arose with a scowl of contempt for the orators who had preceded him and said: "I have not always felt friendly to the whites. I fought them and tried to kill them. The whites and Crows fought me at the Custer battle and tried to kill me; after that they chased me from place to place. I always wished the Crows would have trouble with the whites, they professed to be so friendly with them. I am now a heavy man and cannot ride a horse like I used to but am ready to take my men and help the whites in settling this trouble with the Crows. I should like to show the whites my friendly feeling." . . . Gall's speech was listened to with the most profound respect and at the close of his remarks was loudly applauded.

Sitting Bull did not speak, and as he is jealous of the power which Gall holds in the tribe he was sullen and sulky over the attention which was paid him by the crowd. Sitting Bull has been visiting the Crows during the past summer, and it is believed he has had an understanding with them. He will advise war if he can get a following, but in that event he will have Gall and his followers against him.

CROW AGENCY: NOVEMBER 3. The Indians are now practically all in camp at the agency except Plenty Coups' band from Pryor Creek and Clarke's Fork. He would have been in tomorrow but his wife died last week and he was found by James Campbell away from home, mourning in the mountains for his loss. He consented very reluctantly to come into the agency claiming, however, that he does not sympathise in any manner whatever with the bad Indians in the Crow tribe. He will be in by Sunday noon with all his people. . .

The Indian camp is quiet today although they are

CHIEF PLENTY COUPS (above)
"Plenty Coups . . . does not sympathize with the bad Indians in the tribe."
Courtesy, K. F. Roahen, Billings, Montana.

CHIEF CRAZY HEAD (above right)
"The war chief of the Crows stands in with the play."
Richard Throssel photo.
Courtesy, Billings Public Library.

DEAF BULL (lower right)
"The bravest and most reckless of all the tribe."
Courtesy, Montana Historical Society.

much disturbed and fearful that some harm may be done them. They have an idea that the soldiers are going to round them up and that there will be a fight in their camp. Many are digging holes to crawl into near the teepees. Sword Bearer comes and goes at his own sweet will. The Indians are afraid of him and all acknowledge it, even the larger chiefs. A cordon of Indian police has been established about the agency buildings except on the side where the soldiers are. Sword Bearer has been telling the other Indians that he would ride through the agency and soldiers camp and show them that no one would touch or hurt him. The police have been ordered to allow him to ride inside the lines and then close in on and arrest him. They are given authority to shoot and kill him if resistance is offered, and at the first gun three companies of infantry will be instantly moved to his support. . .

. . . Sword Bearer would undoubtedly be killed if he comes in as he has promised to do. The probabilities are however, that he will not come until brought in by the soldiers. It will be the plan to try and bring enough pressure to bear to induce the Indians to give these fellows up themselves, but it is doubtful as there are nineteen of them wanted, Sword Bearer, Deaf Bull, and the seventeen original horse thieves who are all to be arrested or killed. Some of these do not expect this severity to be shown and there undoubtedly will be trouble before they will all be corralled. The Indians fear treachery and say that the whites have got them into a trap and if they want to can harm them seriously. If they are stampeded now come morning will show a lot of the teepees missing and it will be next to an impossibility to get them in again. But everything now depends on the methods pursued in making the arrests whether there is serious trouble or a peaceful solution of a very serious and important Indian situation.

THE FIGHT

CROW AGENCY: NOVEMBER 5. Today has been a memorable one in the history of the Crow nation and many a summer and winter will pass by before a medicine man will have the control and power over them which has been held by "Wraps-His-Tail-Up" or "Sword Bearer" as he has been variously called by Indians and whites. Early this morning it was evident that some important move was to be made, orderlies hurrying from headquarters to the various commands, and all the preparations incident to military movement were being made. The Indians themselves were conscious of it and were gathered in groups throughout their camp anxiously awaiting developments. About 10 A. M. James Campbell, the chief of scouts was sent to their camp by General Ruger to tell the chiefs to come for council to headquarters. After a short parley about a dozen Indians came up and rode in front of General Ruger's quarters. He was there waiting to receive them accompanied by Indian Inspector-General Frank Armstrong. Among the chiefs were Pretty Eagle, Crazy Head, Old Kearney, and others well known among the Crows. After shaking hands General Armstrong said, "I was sent here by the Great Father at Washington to see what was the trouble with the Crows and to settle it, but I find you have bad men among you who have made trouble, and I find that you will not give them up, so I now turn everything over to the great soldier chief (General Ruger) who will settle this matter with you. That is all I have to say." Pretty Eagle then said, "We will give up this medicine man but we cannot give up the others that are wanted." General Ruger replied by saying, "I want them all, and these are the men we must have brought to us. 'The Medicine Man,' 'Carries his Food,' 'Looks with his Ear,' 'The Rock,' 'The Bank,' 'He knows his Coups,' (Crazy Head's Son) and 'Big Hail.' These men must be brought to us in one hour and one-half or we will come and take them. That is all." Pretty Eagle then said, "We will go and talk to the Medicine Man (Sword Bearer) and see what he says." They then got on their ponies and galloped them across the bottom to the Indian camp.

During this time teepees had been tumbling down, and those Indians who were afraid of a fight had been rapidly moving up close to the agency, making a very small but thickly populated camp of squaws, papooses and old men. The young bucks could be seen rapidly returning to the council where the chiefs were assembled. The soldiers were in readiness and as no move was made by the Indians to return the order was given to mount, and the command of six troops of cavalry under General N. A. M. Dudley and three companies of infantry under Major [Simon] Snyder who had moved down from the camp above in the meantime, prepared themselves for action. The Hotchkiss battery of two guns under Lieutenant Miler was planted on the edge of the hill commanding the village. The troops then waited to see what the Indians intended to do. Sword Bearer was seen riding among them evidently urging war. Suddenly the Indians began to yell and, firing a few shots in the air to announce their intention to fight, scattered in every direction, but finally ranged themselves in a long line and commenced riding furiously down the valley of the Little Horn. Two troops of cavalry immediately charged down the valley to head them off, but they whirled and as is their custom in a fight rode back and forth at a distance of a half mile, yelling and shooting off their guns. The two troops K and E of the First Cavalry kept on until they reached the bottom land close to the river, there they were met by a volley from the river which killed Corporal Simpson of K Troop and wounded Private Maloy of the same troop. One man, Private Clark, was thrown from his horse and dislocated his shoulder. This troop saw the hottest of the fight and was commanded by Lieutenant F. A. Edwards, Second Lieutenant G. L. Ryan. Troop E was commanded by Captain Max Wesendorf. Both troops were then deployed in skirmishing line, and the fusilade was fast and furious for a few moments. The Indians then retreated to the brush and four or five were seen approaching the command with a white flag of truce. They said that some of the Indians did not want to fight and wanted a chance to go to the agency building and join the peaceful camp. A cessation of hostilities then followed for a short time, during which it was evident that although some of the Indians went to the agency the balance took advantage of the opportunity and retreated across the Little Horn River and into the brush. They then commenced firing from their ambush; the soldiers returned the fire and gradually moving down towards the river forced the Indians out of the bottom into the hills on the other side. Sword Bearer with a few followers made a final stand at a ford about a half mile below the agency and was there killed by a red hot skirmish fire which was kept up by Troop G, 1st Cavalry commanded by Captain F. K. Upham and 2nd Lieutenant J. B. Aleshire.[40] The balance of the Indians then broke and ran for the hills. Two troops of cavalry then crossed and followed them, having one quite lively skirmish on top of the first ridge. But the Indians with their reckless riding and tough ponies made good their escape.

These troops then returned to camp and one troop under Captain Moylan was sent up the Little Horn Valley with two days rations to drive them back.

During the attack before the troops reached the river bottom, three shots were fired from the Hotchkiss guns with explosive shells. One of the shells burst underneath an Indian on a horse blowing them into the air several feet and killing both of them.

It is not definitely known at present writing what the mortality among the Indians has been, but ten will cover it. It was supposed that there were only three at first, but new ones are constantly being heard of. Crazy Head, one of the most independent of the tribe has given up, and whereas he refused to give up his son before, after the fight he brought him in himself and gave him up to the soldiers and he is now a prisoner. This one and Sword Bearer who is dead makes two out of the seven who fired into the agency, which are secured, and unless some of them are among the unknown killed there are yet five to be secured. How many have taken to the hills it is impossible to tell. A great many young bucks are missing and good authorities estimate the number on

---

[40] This account of Swordbearer's death does not coincide with later facts revealed during the present editor's research.

the war path from 40 to 150. More can be told tomorrow when the excitement which is now intense, dies away. Several tragical incidents occurred this day which show to good advantage the Indian character. One Indian was covered by a six shooter in the hands of an officer and called upon to surrender and before he could be stopped he pulled his own gun and shot himself. Another while trying to shoot a soldier with his pistol, accidentally shot himself, shattering his arm so it had to be amputated.[41]

What the outcome of this will be it is impossible to tell. The "medicine man" is dead. His medicine did not destroy the troops as he claimed it would and the Indians no longer have him to encourage them. But one of the worst Indians in the tribe, "Deaf Bull," who is out and in command of these young bucks, is said to be really the instigator of the whole proceeding. A winter campaign in pursuit of these fellows is much dreaded by the officers, but unless they are caught before or come in, there is such a campaign before the troops.

Sword Bearer's body was put out on the prairie in plain view of the Indians still camped here to show them their bulletproof prophet. Hundreds have come and looked at him this afternoon since the battle was over, about three o'clock.

The troops behaved splendidly and the thoroughness of their ability was amply shown in their calmness during an exciting moment. The Crows made

---

[41] The Indian's name was Two Whistles. The soldier he was attempting to kill was Lieutenant Robert Powell Page Wainwright, father of General Jonathan M. Wainwright, hero of Bataan and Corregidor during World War II. Lieutenant Wainwright kept Two Whistles' Winchester rifle in the family, and on June 25, 1952, General Wainwright, standing with Art Bravo, a descendant of Two Whistles, presented the rifle to the National Park Service.

a bold stand, relying on the supernatural power of their leader to ward off disaster, but when they saw it fail they weakened and retreated to the brush in a hurry. It was one of the most remarkable incidents in the history of the northwestern Indians that nearly 200 of them should stand before 15 companies of soldiers and a battery of two Hotchkiss rifles on the strength of such a belief.

CROW AGENCY: NOVEMBER 7. The troops were sent after the Indians who escaped last night, but before they returned, the Indians who were wanted came into General Ruger's headquarters and gave themselves up. They were: Looks-With-His-Ears, The Rock, The Bank, Big Hail, and Deaf Bull, making all except Carries-His-Food, who is yet out. Most of the other Indians came in about daybreak. A few young bucks and a chief named Black Hawk, with his family are the only ones now out, and they will probably be in in a day or so. The troops will remain at the agency about one week. The annuities will be issued and the Indians sent to their homes. The trouble is now practically over and the Crows have been taught a lesson which will never be forgotten.

The Crow Indian war is over and all the Indians are either in camp eating their rations with a humble heart or else in the guard house meditating on the strength and power of the whites, and the weakness of the medicine by which young Sword Bearer was going to clean the whites from the face of the earth. All of the Indians have now come in who were wanted and several others who were arrested on later information of their participation in this last row. These chiefs such as Deaf Bull, Crazy Head, and Black Hawk,

FOLLOWERS OF SWORDBEARER IN 1887
While not individually identified, this group of Crow Indians includes: Carries His Food, Look With His Ear, The Bank, He Knows His Coups, Big Hail, and Deaf Bull.
Courtesy of Western History Collection, University of Oklahoma Library.

although not principals in the lawless proceedings on the thirtieth of September, have been urging on the young fellows to resist and make war on the whites. They have lied to them and lied to the whites and have been the real cause of all the trouble which has been had this fall. The intention now is to send them to Fort Snelling in Minnesota. . . The Indians are thoroughly cowed and are constantly inquiring when they will be allowed to return to their homes as they do not seem to know but what some harm will be done to them. They will be allowed to go as soon as the annuities are issued, which will probably be accomplished by Friday, and the Indians will then be allowed to disperse to their homes for the winter. . .

The Death of Swordbearer

In the summer of 1887 Chees-ta-pah had obtained a cavalry sword. Many soldier-Indian fights had taken place in years past in the area and the sword could have been picked up at almost any of them. It was not acquired at the Custer Fight of 1876 simply because there were no swords used in that action.

The young Crow leader told his gullible followers that in a vision the Great Spirit sent the sword and told him that nothing would harm him and that the white man's bullets would not kill them. After this event he was known as Swordbearer. An amazing chain of events that seemed to substantiate his claim of supernatural powers came to a dramatic showdown on the Little Big Horn River.

Mike Reynolds lived at Crow Agency while many of the major Indian participants were still alive. His father, Major S. G. Reynolds was the Crow Indian Superintendent around the turn of the century.

Mr. Reynolds, now living in Hamilton, Montana, is an articulate and energetic spokesman of the past and may often be found exploring Montana historic sites with other Montana pioneers.

In letters to the author, dated November 18, 1970, and December 23, 1970, Mike Reynolds records how

Swordbearer died as told to him by his father and the Indians who were there.

Fire Bear, Swordbearer's killer, was allowed to live by the Crow survivors because of their respect or fear of the Crow Indian Police.[42]

Mike Reynolds writes:

When we got to Crow Agency there were several employees on the payroll who were there during the Swordbearer fracas. Of course, Fire Bear and Bear Claw were there too. If they had ever been released as Indian policemen the Wraps-Up-His-Tail followers would have killed them. Both died of old age, still policemen.

For several days before Fire Bear got Wraps-Up-His-Tail, groups of young Indians would ride through the Agency shooting off firearms in an attempt to terrorize the inhabitants. They finally got so bold that they charged past the Agency office and fired into the front porch.

Williamson, the agent, who was scared spitless, sent Bear Claw, by a round-about way, to Fort Custer for assistance. Then he ordered Fire Bear to "Go get Wraps-Up-His-Tail." Fire Bear, garbed in the regulation hat and blue coat of the Indian Police, rode through the trenches the Indians had thrown up just south of their encampment, and through the encampment down to the banks of the Little Big Horn River where he encountered Wraps-Up-His-Tail. As he rode up to him Wraps-Up-His-Tail reached under his blanket for a gun and Fire Bear shot him right between the eyes with his service revolver. Fire Bear threw

---

[42] It is interesting to note that Sitting Bull was also killed by an Indian policeman, Red Tomahawk, on December 15, 1890.

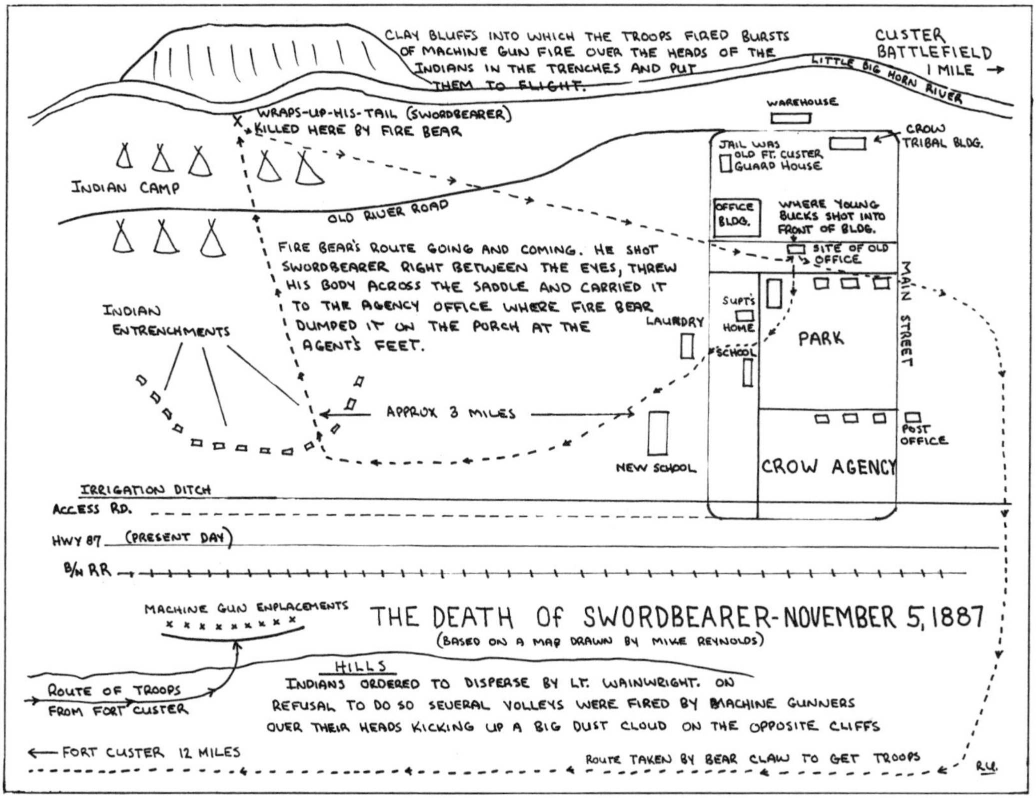

FIRE BEAR
SLAYER OF SWORDBEARER
Courtesy, Montana Historical Society.

the dead body across his saddle, jumped on behind, and took a shortcut along the river up to the agency office. As he rode up to the front porch, Williamson came out and Fire Bear flopped the body off at his feet. From that day until he died Fire Bear was kept on the Agency Police force to protect him from being killed by Wraps-Up-His-Tail followers.

This fine account by Mike Reynolds and the following excerpt of an interview of M. "Allie" Stevenson, who was present at the time of the Crow Indian riot at the agency in the autumn of 1887, agree on the essential facts of the death of Swordbearer. Mr. Stevenson's account of Swordbearer's death appeared in the November 18, 1934, edition of the Billings Gazette:

The stories I have read tell of Wraps-Up-His-Tail having been killed by the soldiers at the time Spotted Rabbit and Two Whistles were wounded or at a later time during the soldier advance and the firing of the Gatling gun and their rifles. But that is not true. His end came in this way: He was among those rushing to the river to wash off the personal paints. While he was doing this he was confronted by Fire Bear, an Indian policeman, who emerged suddenly from the brush nearby. Fire Bear said, "You have been the cause of all this trouble, and I am going to kill you." Wraps-Up-His-Tail asked that the killing be postponed until after all of his paint was washed off. He resumed the washing while Fire Bear waited. After a while Wraps-Up-His-Tail straightened up and announced: "I am ready now." Fire Bear standing close at hand, pulled the trigger of his level revolver and sent a bullet that instantly killed the victim. For that act, Fire Bear was held in social contempt ever afterward by the Crows in general. But he was kept in employment as a policeman as long as he lived. He was about 50 years old, I believe, at the time he killed that medicine man leader.

The report of the affair by Miss Elizabeth W. Barstow, daughter of Major C. H. Barstow, one of the figures in the exciting days of the uprising, climaxes the first authoritative account, from beginning to end, of the Swordbearer incident of 1887.

Other versions will be found in the literature that was inspired by this event, and while intensely interesting will be found inaccurate in most details. (Present day Western pulp magazines are notoriously guilty of this.)

We present Miss Barstow's story as it appeared in the Billings Gazette *on September 18, 1903:*

Although sullen and resentful because of their confinement to the reservation, little indication of serious trouble was given by the Crows on September 30, 1887, when the Indians discovered that Cheestapah[43] and some young braves were to be arrested on a recent horse-stealing expedition.

On that day Major Barstow and a confederate veteran Tom Steward were seated in an office at the Crow Agency when a volley of shots rang out.

Shooting at marks was so common among the Indians as to make the men far from apprehensive, and it was only when the second volley, deafening when compared with the first, and mingled with the thud of horses' hoofs, was heard that the attention of the

---

[43] This, of course, is Swordbearer.

two men was arrested. Twice again did this occur. They stepped out upon the veranda, just in time to see five young braves, among them Cheestapah, come up the road at a pace suggestive of disdainful adagio . . . they wheeled about facing the men, no words could portray the incessable contempt written in each ones crafty face. Certainly not a minute elapsed as each raised a Winchester first to the knees, to the waist, to the breast, then to the heads of the two men, and finally the bullets crash off the roof of the building.

The Indians then went on to each succeeding house, firing over the roof of each until they reached the Agent's quarters. Here they halted and waited a second for the agent to defy them. There is not the slightest doubt that had he stepped outside the gate he would have been shot outright, but as it was, he remained motionless. So firing over the roof the Indians continued their trek around the square, and after having fired 11 volleys in all made their way back to camp.

The agent immediately requested the added aid of troops from Fort Custer, and several hours later 100 men under Captain Max Wessendorf neared the agency. A detachment of eight men, led by Lieutenant Byram, preceded the main group and arrived at the agent's house, where officials had gathered. As soon as they arrived, however, a force of nearly 200 young braves began crowding the cavalrymen against a picket fence, apparently attempting to force a fight.

One bullet, one ill-timed gesture, one little fuse to the dynamite, would have resulted in a prompt massacre. Major Barstow, comprehending the danger in which all were involved, quietly crossed the lawn and spoke to Bull Nose and several others, Medicine Crow, Fringe, Bull-Goes-A-Hunting, and Bull Chief, telling them to go out and drive the enemy back . . . Calmly, deliberately, the chiefs walked out the gate, on one side of which the soldiers were still flattened, forcing themselves between the two lines and raising their quirts beat such a tatoo upon the foreheads of the ponies that for the space of half a minute the proceedings were suggestive of a hailstorm.

The desired result, however, was obtained. The braves fell back farther and farther and a few moments later the main body of troops came tearing up and fell into line with the remainder of the company who had so narrowly escaped the vengeance of the bloodthirsty, deluded young men, who shortly after returned to camp.

Excitement was not over for the evening, however, for a short time after the captain of Indian police, Boy-That-Grabs, rushed into the agency to inform the white men that the discontented element was gathering in preparation to killing the agent and those in his house before the soldiers could be awakened. The warning had scarcely been given when 400 warriors, hideously painted, barged into the agency and began firing over the agent's house.

But then, a dramatic move by Bull Nose again saved the white men. A warning hand was raised, a blanket was cast to the ground, and old Bull Nose in distinctly primitive attire, but never nobler than at this moment, drew himself up in solitary grandeur and spoke: "You kill one white man in this place, you kill me first." An incoherent murmur from the band without. Then something happened very quickly and quietly. Sports, the leader of the band, dismounted and joined the brave old chief. Why? That is one of the mysteries that will forever remain unanswered. The redskins without turned around and went back to their respective teepees.

Although danger was temporarily averted, the medicine man, Cheestapah, continued to stir up resentment and trouble. He went into the seclusion of the mountains to "dream" at frequent intervals. Once, while riding upon the outskirts of the agency, he stopped at a teepee and asked for a drink of water. He turned for a moment and slyly dropping some chemical in the cup, faced the astonished redskins with the water in a state of effervescence. Surely this was a great man who could make water boil without a fire?

Most remarkable, however, was the next feat of Cheestapah. One day when the Indians were short of rations, he said, "Tomorrow I will give you all the beef you want." The next morning a cattle train crossing the reservation encountered a severe storm and several cattle were struck by lightning. These were immediately appropriated by followers of the medicine man, and Cheestapah was held in great esteem.

A few days later Cheestapah informed his followers, I have made medicine. Tomorrow there come a rain, and the soldiers go away. The next morning there was a shower and the company was ordered back to Fort Custer. When the troop reached the fort, however, and the commandant received word of Cheestapah's medicine he ordered the men back to the Crow Agency. The marching soldiers were barely able to stumble back to the agency, and Cheestapah was given credit for great power.

Reinforcements were steadily sent to the agency during the next month before attempting to arrest the leaders of the belligerent Indians, until on November 4 there were 13 companies of soldiers present.

The presence of the soldiers did not dismay the Indians, however, as they were firmly convinced of the great power of Cheestapah's medicine. Their belief in this power was revealed by Chief Pretty Eagle, who warned Major Barstow against resistance. "You think you strong," he said. "You think your soldiers hurt us. You no much know our medicine. Why, if you had soldiers for every grass blade on hills not one would be finally left. Our medicine man he great, he strong. The Great Father give him bag of ashes, bag dirt. Tomorrow he throw them in the air and a dust storm will come no white man can see through, but we see. Then he wave his sword and the head of every white man roll on the ground. If you stay your head fall, too, and the head of your meacotti (wife). Our medicine strong – no white man know. You go and your head no roll off. You stand and you die in the dust storm."

The army commanders, however summoned chiefs of the tribe and informed them that they could be given until noon, November 5, to deliver the miscreants, and that troops would go after them if they were not surrendered. The chiefs flatly refused.

All that night barbaric drubbing of the tom-tom and the half-demoniacal chanting which always accompanies a war dance proclaimed that such was taking place, preparatory to the "heap fight" of the coming day.

Now Cheestapah possessed a most extraordinary intellect. His ambition to become a great man among his people had caused him to unconsciously lead himself into a trap, but he now realized his folly and doubtless knew that his doom was sealed. The beautiful morning of the fifth arrived and found the medicine man groveling upon the floor of his teepee and complaining of being "heap sick." Deaf Bull, the bravest and most reckless of all the tribe came to him saying, "You must get up and no say you sick. The whites are going to fight us. We believe in you, but you must get up and lead us."

Shortly after the bugles sounded preparatory to the advance, but before the troops could start, Cheestapah, at the head of the braves and conspicuous in a shirt of crimson, galloped around from the right flank of the camp. It was evident that the redskins wished to reach the hills, always advantageous to their peculiar style of warfare. Troops of the First, Seventh, and Ninth Cavalry were ordered to intercept them, which they did, at the same time returning the volley of musketry from the Indians. Cheestapah was almost immediately wounded. He turned back to the others and said "I can't do it, you will have to take care of yourselves."

Instantly there was the wildest confusion. Old Deaf Bull attempted to muster the band and reach the mountains, there to carry the battle to a finish. A number started for the hills, while others, realizing that they were beaten, stopped by the Little Big Horn River to wash off the war paint, hoping that in doing away with this evidence of their hostility, they might not be recognized by the whites as having been among those participating in the fray.

Cheestapah was just attempting to ford the river when Crazy Head, with true philosophy, went to him and said, "You no get away from the whites. They catch you some time, mebbe one week, mebbe one month away - they then punish you worse than now. You come with me and let me take you to them, then they punish you and it be over and you be one of us again." Cheestapah, seeing it was useless to resist, consented, suffering Crazy Head to take his horse by the bridle.

Now Fire Bear had, but a few moments before, heard the rumor that Medicine Tail, a most loyal friend of his and a great favorite throughout the tribe, had been killed by those under the medicine man.[44] Furious and embittered, however outwardly as calm and stoical as ever, he rode up to where the defeated brave was standing and said contemptuously: "You think you strong medicine, don't you?"

Cheestapah, who saw what was coming, replied, "My friend, I am thirsty. Let me get a drink."

He had not time to dismount when Fire Bear said, "I'll show you strong medicine," and raising a revolver, shot him through the forehead. A few minutes later the body of the great medicine man was brought into camp and literally thrown to the ground as the crowning thorn in his ignominy.

How did the followers of Cheestapah account for his death? Ah! You shall see with what consummate cunning did he leave a loophole for himself. "Away up in the mountains," he told them once, "There grows an herb. No one knows of it but me, but if

---

[44] The rumor of Medicine Tail's death proved to be false. According to Frank Grouard (Joe DeBarthe, *Life and Adventures of Frank Grouard*, p. 203) it was Medicine Tail who wounded Swordbearer in the arm while the medicine man was taunting the bluecoats. Swordbearer then fled the field to the spot on the Little Big Horn where Fire Bear eventually found him.

the white men find and rub a bullet with it, that bullet kill me." The Indians believe to this day that the two bullets, one wounding, the other killing their leader, were rubbed with this mysterious herb. It is owing to this that his memory is ever kept sacred by the non-enlightened of his own race.

Many of the old, old men will tell you, as they sit with furrowed cheeks and dimming eye, that when the Storm King rides over the barren prairie they can hear above the rush and roar of raging elements the shrill whistle of Cheestapah, and who knows but what he is again mustering his forces beyond the great divide.

AN AGENCY TO BE VACANT

WASHINGTON: DECEMBER 8. Crow Indian Agent Williamson has resigned to take effect December 31. The resignation, which was called for by the Secretary, is the result of Inspector Armstrong's visit. The latter is now here, but refuses to make public the result of his investigations. It is believed, however, that he found Williamson had neglected to comply with the Secretary's order to advertise the grazing privileges of the reservation, leaving the monopoly in the hands of one syndicate, who had simply a private agreement as to their occupancy. When directed to so lease the lands, Williamson wrote to the Secretary counseling delay, saying the Indians wanted the stockmen then on the lands to have the grazing. The secretary made no reply. Armstrong also found that Williamson had made a contract giving Paul McCormick and McNutt the right to cut hay on the reservation, though having no right to make such a contract. Armstrong tore their contract up and made them pay the Indians $2 per ton for the hay. Charges of a personal nature were also made, that Williamson is loud, profane and quick tempered.

Custer and Junction City

It might be interesting, at this point to contrast the account of the founding of Terry's Landing by Captain E. C. Gilbreath with the following account that appeared in the July 26, 1888 edition of the Billings Gazette.

The area around the junction of the Big Horn River and the Yellowstone River is rich in history. The fact that this was considered the practical head of navigation of the Yellowstone River made it a natural shipping center.

In 1806, William Clark returned from his famous expedition down the Yellowstone River towards the Missouri River and his reports of his adventures attracted others to the region.

The establishment of Fort Manuel Lisa in 1807, Fort Benton in 1822 and Fort Cass in 1832 were all located where the Big Horn and Yellowstone rivers join. Other establishments in the area were Fort Alexander around 1842, Fort Van Buren in 1835 and Fort Sarpy in 1840.[45]

Of course, the advent of the railroad brought to an end steamboating on the Yellowstone River and

---
[45] Brown, *Plainsman of the Yellowstone*, pp. 30–31.

the closing of old Fort Custer in 1898 finished off, for all practical purposes, all activity at and around this once exciting spot.

A comprehensive study is needed to fully document the rich history of this area.

CUSTER AND JUNCTION

Custer station is on the Northern Pacific 53 miles east of Billings and is a very important freight point. As it is on the Crow Reservation, there is no town there, but an enormous amount of merchandise is handled by the forwarding companies, this being the shipping point for Buffalo, Lander, Dayton, Fort Custer and a dozen other towns and supply points in Northern Wyoming and on the Crow Reservation. There are four warehouses, the railroad station, a store, two blacksmith's shops, a hotel and the residence of T. H. Youell, the agent.

The first warehouse east of the depot is the railroad freight house, through which passes nearly all freight that does not remain any length of time. Next to this is situated the government warehouse in charge of the U.S. Agent Mr. J. H. Brown. Into this goes all Uncle Sam's supplies for the boys in blue that are stationed at Fort Custer, and as it is a large post the business in the course of the year reaches large dimensions. Paul McCormick and Co.'s warehouse and store is the next building this firm representing the well known Custer Forwarding Company, and their operations embrace hay, grain and wood contracts as well as freighting and merchandizing. Mr. Aleshire, a brother of Lieutenant Aleshire of Fort Custer, is the representative of the company in their store at this point. The fourth and last warehouse is that of the Merchants' Forwarding Company which is managed by our genial County Commissioner, Frank S. Whitney, well known to fame and everybody in the country for his winning way and wholesome hospitality. He is a man of weight in the community – 265 pounds.

The blacksmith's shops are owned by Jerry Crimmins and J. S. Dewitt, respectively, well known Junctionites who also have shops across the river. The Server Hotel is well known to everyone who has ever had occasion to stop over for a meal at the station. Fred is an old timer and his house is a favorite stopping place for hundreds of travellers in the course of the season.

If one prefers riding the short half mile to the Junction Ferry, a conveyance makes several trips a day between here and Junction City, crossing the river on the McCormick Ferry, landing the traveller on the main street of the town. Junction is very pretty located on the banks of the Yellowstone under a bluff which protects the town from the northern storms in winter. Large cottonwood trees shade the streets, giving the town an appearance comparing very favorably with larger but barer and less attractive towns in the territory.

The principal business houses are Paul McCormick and Co., general store, of which C. H. McArthur is the manager, assisted by Charles Spear; D. A. Burr, general store, Mr. Burr is also the proprietor of the Empire Hotel, a first class house, and is interested in stock raising as well. T. Campbell is the postmaster and runs a notion store in connection therewith. The well known Junction Hotel is kept by Mr. DeLong who has bought the Yellowstone house at Glendive and will shortly move there. The Junction house will still remain in operation, however, though it is not known who will run it.

Among the saloons are those owned by Bertrand and Griffin, W. L. Williams, James McMannus and Jerry Crimmins. J. S. DeWitt and Jerry Crimmins also have blacksmith shops here as well as at Custer station.

A drug store owned by Dr. T. Martin, carries a remarkably complete stock of goods for a town of this size, and in an interview with the doctor he said that the trade was much larger than one would suppose for the size of the town. Several well-known stockmen and businessmen whose interests are elsewhere have residences in Junction, among them being County Commissioner Whitney. The town has a population of about 200 and the businessmen confidently expect a steady growth in size and prosperity in the near future. Your correspondent is confident of one thing however, and that is that a traveller would go many miles and stop in many towns before he would find one where he would be met with more cordiality, or meet a pleasanter lot of people than in Junction.

The Fort Custer Stage

Pompey's Pillar is a famous landmark of the Lewis and Clark expedition. On its side, carved in sandstone, is the only physical evidence of the epic adventure. William Clark carved his name and the date, July 25, 1806, to forever note the occasion of his visit.

It was on a hot Montana afternoon in August of 1967 that my trail led me to this historical site.

As things developed, the "guide" turned out to be Don Foote, the famous collector of Western Americana and the owner of Pompey's Pillar. When I realized who this very informed gentleman was, I offered to let him see my collection of Fort Custer pictures. Mr. Foote's wife, Stella, was present and together we looked at the pictorial record of the old fort.

Don Foote, realizing that I had more than a passing interest in the subject of Fort Custer, suggested that I hop in my car and follow him over to some barns located a short distance away. It seems that, in order to buy Pompey's Pillar, Don also had to purchase the adjoining farm and he used the barns to store his prolific collection of antique automobiles and wagons.

Upon reaching the building, he threw open the doors and our eyes rested on the original Fort Custer *stage coach. Talk about being in the right place at the right time!*

Well, during the following winter, Don Foote passed away with all Montana mourning the loss of this fine gentleman. His gracious wife, Stella, allowed us to use a picture of the Fort Custer stage along with other photos pertaining to the old fort, and we thank her for them.

We include the following colorful story, by a nameless writer, that gives a rare view of a trip on the Fort Custer stage. From the Billings Gazette *of July 18, 1889:*

GRUMPY STAGE DRIVERS

You reach Fort Custer by a stage which runs from Custer Station on the Northern Pacific to Rock Creek on the Union Pacific, a distance of 430 miles. This is one of the few important stage lines that have managed to survive the locomotives' raids. Its route takes in the mountainous districts of northern Wyoming, says the writer in the *New York Tribune,* where there are several large towns to which the railroads have not yet penetrated. It runs through Crow country, the richest agricultural region of all Montana. There are a dozen "bottoms" along the Big Horn and the Little Horn rivers, of from 60,000 to 100,000 acres in extent, rank with prairie vegetation, where the grain of a nation might be grown, now all vacant and useless. Every one of them could be irrigated at an expense of less than 50 cents an acre. The stage drivers say that there are just such fertile bottoms along the Yellowstone and along all the mountain streams that course through the reservation in all directions.

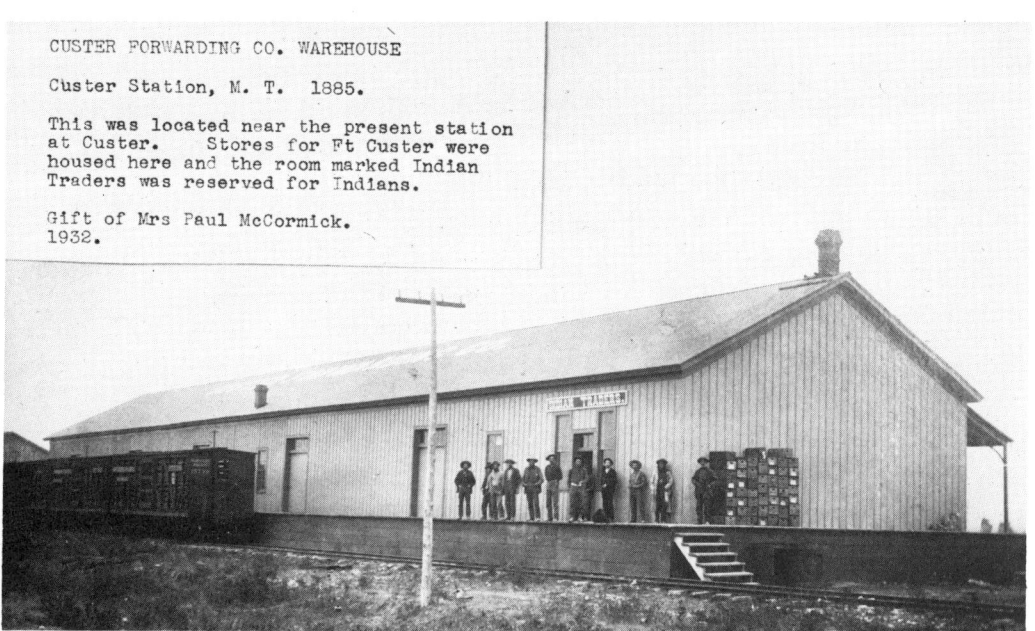

CUSTER FORWARDING CO. WAREHOUSE
Custer Station, M. T. 1885.
This was located near the present station at Custer. Stores for Ft Custer were housed here and the room marked Indian Traders was reserved for Indians.
Gift of Mrs Paul McCormick. 1932.

Courtesy, Billings Public Library.

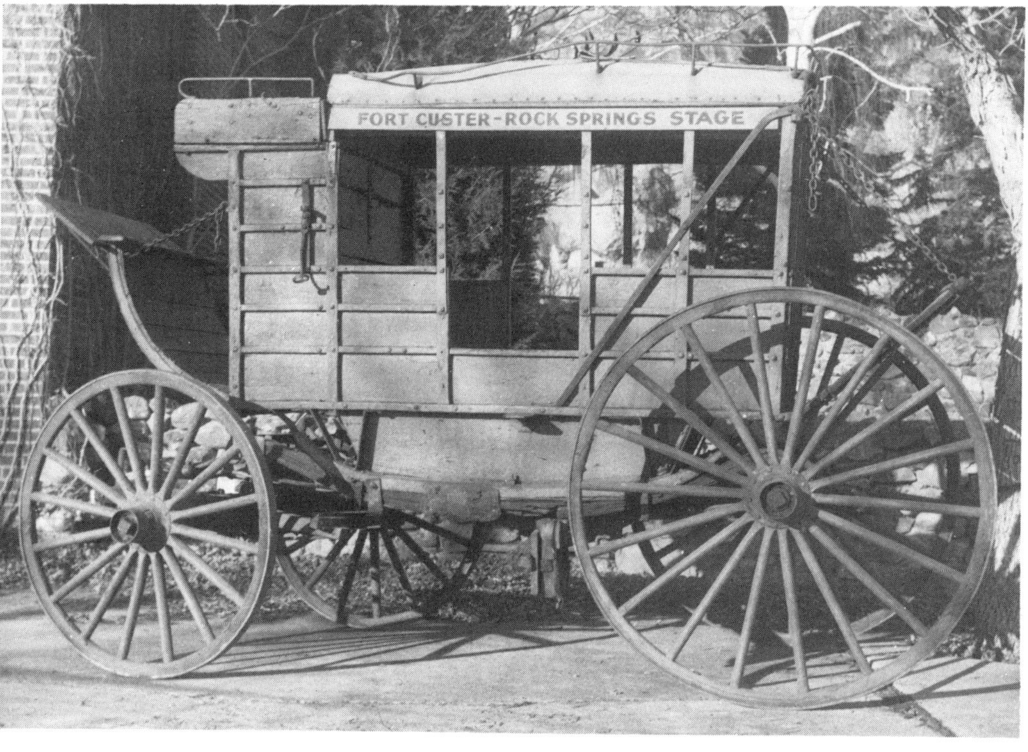
FORT CUSTER-ROCK SPRINGS STAGE

THE FORT CUSTER STAGE "RUNS FROM CUSTER STATION"
Courtesy, Mrs. Don C. Foote, "Treasures of the West," Billings, Montana.

These drivers are all Dicks. They are the old fellows who used to drive the Deadwood and Overland stages in the early days and they keenly feel the humiliation of their present position. To be compelled after such a glorious past, after having driven six- and eight-horse coaches through a land filled with gallant road agents, chivalrous horse thieves, and valiant Indians, after having been "held up" a dozen times, after having been through massacres, lynchings, cowboy fights, and all that – now in their old age, to come down to a miserable two-horse route through a settled country is almost more than they can bear. They sit on their lofty seats gloomy and taciturn. They rarely smile or talk. You just work hard if you hope to secure their favor or engage them in conversation. The only glimpse of sunlight they ever catch through the dun clouds that paper their sky is when a dude, an Englishman, or a fussy old lady, becomes the passenger. Then something like a smile touches up their darkly burned faces, and by the time a passenger, or what is left of him, has reached his destination, they are almost cheerful. The stages have no springs. The cushions are stuffed with flint. The trail is stony and crossed continually with gullies and deep buffalo trails. To one of these melancholy drivers, drawing his career to a disappointing close, nothing is so comfortable as to shoot a dudish tenderfoot through the stage window upon a jag of rocks below.

Observing that my driver was in a pensive humor I said nothing more to him than was necessary to procure permission to sit up there with him. We rode for 20 miles in dead silence, and at last when we neared the station at which we were to obtain dinner and a change of horses, he turned to me and said: "Pardner, I like you. When I first see you I thort I didn't. But I do! You're the fust man that ever rid on the top of my coach that didn't start for to tell me that gol derned story about Hank Monk and Horace Greeley!" The ice was broken and we continued fast friends to the end of the ride.

Wovoka and the Lame Deer Episode

From the Pioneer Press *and reprinted in the* Billings Gazette *of May 1, 1890, we read, in retrospect about the seeds of discontent that culminated in the Wounded Knee tragedy of December 1890. Major Henry Carroll's assignment to find out more about this matter certainly indicates that the army was interested in the phenomenon. Ultimately, the army confronted the worshippers at Wounded Knee in December of 1890.*

The new Indian religion offered hope and what nation or people can survive without hope?

General [Thomas H.] Ruger of the Department of Dakota, U.S.A., yesterday received letter of Major [Henry] Carroll, of Fort Custer, Montana, stating that the Indians of the Tongue River Agency were greatly excited over the expected appearance of a Savior. This is a peculiar case, and presents many strange and interesting features. The accounts that can be gathered of this coming of an Indian Christ are very fragmentary, but the belief is thoroughly ground in the minds of the Indians and under the leadership of their medicine men they have worked up quite a religious revival and are confidently waiting the appearance of their savior.

Some time ago the Indian interpreter at the Cheyenne and Arrapahoe Agency in the Indian Territory wrote in a personal letter to the interpreter at the Tongue River Agency that: "Cheyennes and Arrapahoes here are greatly excited about a Christ coming in among some of the northern tribes of Indians. The Arrapahoes have been getting letters from Northern Arrapahoes in regard to it. My friends here wish me to ask what there is about it and what do you know about it? They sent two of their young men to the Shoshone Agency in Idaho a month and a half ago to find out all about it but these two have not returned yet."

The Tongue River interpreter made an investigation among the Indians there and reports as follows: "That this Christ is in the mountains; that he wants all the Indians to come to him, that he will put them behind him, and having all the whites before him, will roll the world over on them (the whites) and destroy them; that he is a white man. The above has been told by Indians at the Shoshone Agency. In addition the Indians say that this Christ showed some Indian scars on his hands and feet and a spear wound in his side; that he wants all the Indians to come there, giving up firearms and using only bows and spears; that he is to roll the world over on the whites in case they abuse the Indians. Where this white man lives the sun is very close, and the earth is so hot it burns their feet. No grass grows there."

General Ruger says that it is not unlikely this report originated from the teachings of missionaries among the Indians, which they have mixed up with their mythology. The Indian medicine men have all taken up the new religion and are making themselves very popular. One of the difficult things to explain, however, is the wide distribution of the myth, which seems to have been brought out independently at two places, over a thousand miles apart. In order to prevent trouble which might arise from some white man pretending to be the Christ going among the Indians and making trouble, General Ruger has detailed Major Carroll, of Fort Custer, to proceed to the Tongue River Agency at once and thoroughly sift the matter to the bottom, if possible.

Major Carroll discovered that there was substance in the report of increased Indian religious activity. It seems that Porcupine, a Cheyenne, was a principal delegate from his tribe to Walker Lake, Nevada, where he learned from Wovoka a new dance – the Ghost Dance. Porcupine believed strongly in the sacredness of the Messiah (Wovoka) and his message, and proved to be a convincing disciple of the new found Messiah.

American Horse, a prominent Cheyenne, was in the crowd when Porcupine delivered the message of the Messiah to the Cheyennes at the Tongue River Reservation. Fraser Pakes, in his excellent article in the English Westerners *10th Anniversary Publication of 1964 entitled "The Lame Deer Incident: 1890" wonders, "were Head Chief and Young Mule present at Porcupine's discourse on the Ghost Dance when the tribe learned that Wovoka, the Messiah, had prophesied that 'certain things' would come to pass in September 1890."* [46]

[46] Fraser Pakes, "The Lame Deer Incident: 1890," in English Westerners' *10th Anniversary Publication – 1964*, p. 50.

Head Chief and Young Mule's[47] crime is documented fully in Pakes' account of this highly emotional action. The following story from the Billings Gazette *of September 18, 1890, records the coroner's verdict regarding the death of rancher Hugh Boyle at the hands of the two young Cheyenne braves.*

The coroner of Custer County held an inquest on the body of Hugh Boyle, the latest victim of Tongue River Cheyennes at the agency at Lame Deer last week. All the Cheyennes except the guilty two were at the agency and none are armed except the squad of Indian police who are scouting the country in search of the two murderers. From the evidence it appears that Head Chief, one of the murderers of the boy, communicated the fact to American Horse, who found the body and informed Acting Agent [James] Cooper of the confession. Testimony was given by military officers on duty in that section and by agency employees, all briefly as to the disappearance, identity and finding of the body. American Horse gave the testimony which incriminates Head Chief and Young Mule, and the tribe seem anxious to have the murderers arrested and punished. The coroners jury brought in the following verdict:

> An inquisition holden at Tongue River Agency on the Lame Deer in the County of Custer, state of Montana, the 12th day of September, A. D. 1890, before me Harold Brown, justice of the peace, acting coroner of said county, upon the body of Hugh Boyle, there lying dead, by the jurors

---

[47] James King of Lame Deer, Montana, in an interview regarding this event, constantly referred to Young Mule as Young Donkey. Mr. King is a Cheyenne Indian who is concerned about preserving Cheyenne culture and tradition, and is much involved in activities on the reservation that help to do just that.

whose names are here unto subscribed. The said jurors upon their oaths do say that Hugh Boyle came to his death by gunshot wounds, one in the head and one in the right breast, with felonious and fiendish intent, perpetrated by two Cheyenne Indians, Head Chief and Young Mule. The jury desire to express their highest commendation for the prompt and energetic action taken by Special Agent Cooper in trying to capture the murderers, and trust that the end may soon be attained, and the perpetrators of this devilish deed brought to speedy justice.

Troops from Fort Custer were at a mini-fort named Camp Crook, near Lame Deer. For once the army was in the right place at the right time and responded affirmatively to the news of the two Cheyenne Indians' decision to confront the United States Army in a duel.

Major Henry Carroll, 1st Cavalry, ordered Lieutenant Samuel C. Robertson of G Troop to go to the agency to protect the people, while Troop D, under the command of Lieutenant Barber and Troop E with Lieutenant John Pitcher would be held in reserve.

It is indeed fortunate that Lieutenant Robertson was also a gifted writer, and he recorded the following action in at least two different forms.[48]

Robertson's account in the Harper's Weekly *of October 18, 1890, is one of the very few accounts of western adventures that can qualify as pure literature. We know from subsequent articles in the* Billings Gazette, *that Lieutenant Robertson and frontier photographer O. S. Goff were collaborating on a picture story of the Indian as a soldier.*[49] *Robertson's untimely*

---

[48] In addition to the article quoted here, Robertson wrote "The Rush to Death," for *Harper's Weekly,* Oct. 18, 1890.

[49] No record, pictorial or otherwise, of this joint venture has been found by the present editor. Perhaps the work was just speculation on both of their parts.

death in 1893 deprived us of an articulate recorder of the western scene circa 1890.

What follows is a rare account by Robertson of the death of Head Chief and Young Mule, whom he surprisingly does not name. This story appeared in the September 27, 1890, edition of the Weekly Yellowstone Journal and Livestock Reporter *and was entitled, "How They Died":*

There have been few more romantic episodes in Indian annals than the killing of the two Cheyenne murderers of young Boyle at Camp Crook, Montana. The Indians, tiring of hiding in the hills and knowing that retribution was certain, determined to sell their lives as dearly as possible in preference to terminating their existence at the end of a halter. The following letter from Lieutenant S. C. Robertson, who was in command of the troops drawn up to receive the attack, to a friend in St. Paul, gives a graphic account of the scene as noted by an interested eye:

About 3 P.M., hearing the sound of "Boots and Saddles" suddenly given in camp, I sent hastily for G Troop's herd and reported with the other officers to the battalion commander for instructions. The latter explained that he had just returned from the agency, where the father of one of the young Cheyennes told him that the fugitives were in the hills near by; that they had sent in word that they were tired of hiding and that they intended to attack the agency and camp without delay and die in fair fight. They were known to be well armed and the message they had sent was equivalent to a challenge to the troops to come out and fight them.

The battalion commander instructed me to take my troop and make such disposition near the agency as would insure protection to the agent and his employees there. I was told the D and E troops would be held for future disposition.

LAME DEER EPISODE

I got out of camp as rapidly as possible and on arriving at the agency posted a guard around it. The rest of my men I moved up the road along which the two young braves announced they would arrive, and disposed them, some mounted and others on foot, at available points in the valley. The road I thus picketed is the Tongue River road east of the agency. Brave Wolf, a Cheyenne chief, was with me, and after my dispositions were made, in reply to my questions as to whether the two would really be mad enough to carry out their threats, he expressed his firm conviction that they would and that they would make a desperate fight when they appeared. On looking about me, the scene I beheld was certainly remarkable. During the excitement following the murder of young Boyle, the Indians had been assembled by Agent Cooper from all parts of the reservation and put in camp about the agency. As my troop took position these Indians left their tepees and in a few minutes nearly the whole Cheyenne tribe was assembled in groups on the neighboring hills awaiting in awe-stricken silence the tragedy that was about to take place in the valley below. The pony herds and squaws occupied the ridges further back across the Lame Deer. The two murderers had invited their people to come out and see how bravely they could die, and the deliberateness of their preparation for the scene to follow had about it all the flavor of a gladiatorial contest pre-arranged with careful regard to all the professional details.

The young men's parents were among the spectators, and, fearing the influence of the scene upon them and some of the younger Indians, I took measures to protect myself from any possible advance from their direction upon my rear. I had not waited more than a few minutes in my position when the two actors, for whose appearance every eye had been watching, rode out from a clump of timber across the valley about a rifle shot away. Through my glasses I could see that they were well mounted and in full war costume, one of them wearing a magnificent war bonnet. Riding their ponies up a steep incline they reached the top of the ridge north of the valley in which we were, and here circling their horses and chanting their war song, they opened fire upon my men. I crossed the valley promptly, dismounted my men and advanced up the ridge against them. Seeing this they took position in the rocks above and gave me a lively skirmish for a few minutes. During this, E Troop, Lieutenants Pitcher and Barber, appeared on the hills I had just left on the south edge of the valley. Seeing its position I left a part of my men to occupy the Indians with their fire, and with the remainder rode rapidly around the ridge to their rear, climbed the hill, dismounted and drove the Indians into the valley toward "E." One of them crossed it mounted, and with most reckless daring charged the line of "E" Troop on the heights. Lieutenant Pitcher tells me that his fire as he advanced was remarkably rapid, but strange to say he inflicted no damage beyond wounding three horses. He rode entirely through "E's" line, but fell with several pistol balls in his body, one of them through his brain. The second Indian took refuge in the creek bed in the valley, and from his concealed position there kept up a fire for fifteen or twenty minutes before he could be killed. I directed some of my men to keep up a plunging fire upon him from the hills, while with others I made a circuit and advanced upon him up the coulee. When within a few yards of him it was discovered that he was dead, having undoubtedly been killed by "G" Troop sharpshooters from the hills, "E" Troop not firing for fear of shooting my men. There was no casualty among the troops.

Owing to the inaccessibility and rapid moving of these Indians along the ridges, and the concealment of one of them in the cut mentioned, the affair lasted fully an hour. The bodies of the dead Cheyennes were taken charge of by their relatives, the squaws and young girls flocking from their camp to view them, and filling the valley with their songs and lamentations. Fearing the presence of my troop in this excited crowd might bring about some further clash, I left a guard of six men at the agency and returned with the rest of my troop to camp.

Throughout this affair the Indian police and headmen behaved most admirably, and to them is most probably

TROOP G, FIRST CAVALRY AT FORT CUSTER
". . . ordered Lieutenant S. C. Robertson of G Troop
to go to the agency to protect the people . . ."
T. N. Barnard photo. Courtesy, Montana Historical Society, Helena.

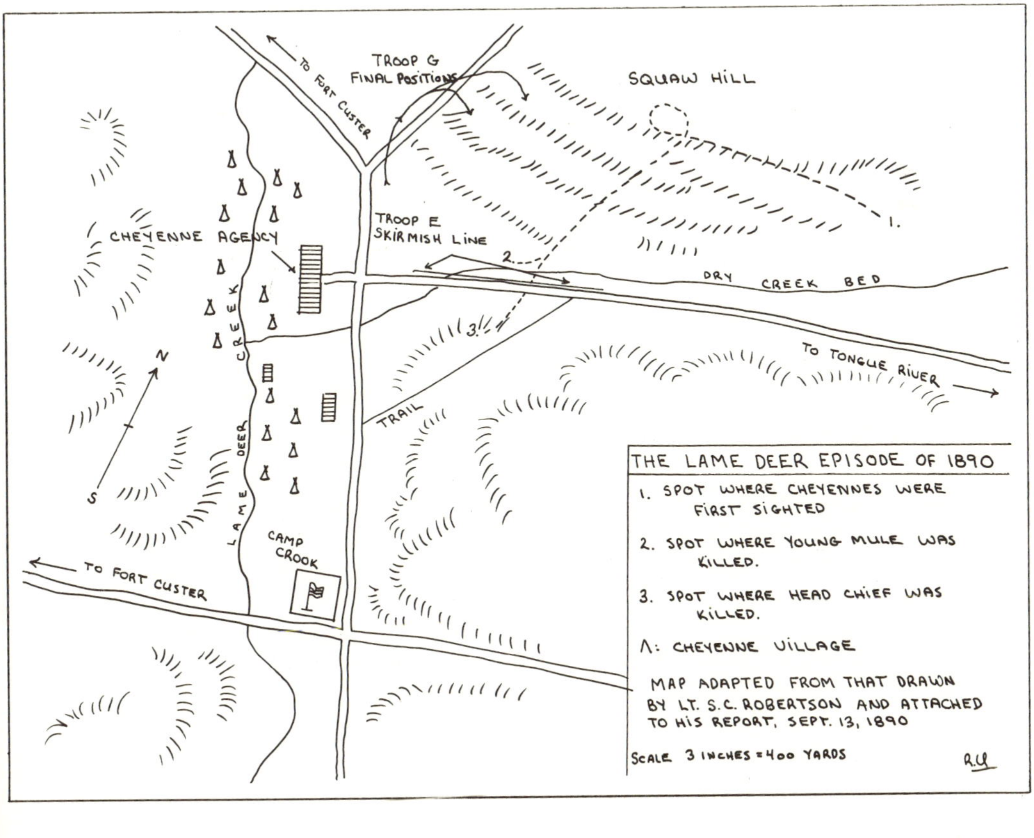

due the remarkable sight of scores of Cheyenne braves – many of them fierce warriors of other days – witnessing not unmoved, but without interference, the killing by troops of two of their tribe.

The young Cheyennes killed were only about eighteen years of age, but they seemed perfectly devoid of fear, and the audacity they displayed in this desperate attack upon two troops of cavalry was probably never surpassed in the records of Indian bravery.

Perhaps the most famous passage from Robertson's Harper's Magazine *article of October 18, 1890, is worth repeating here. His description of finding the body of Young Mule is an example of excellent first person reporting that is sorely lacking in his time and ours:*

Crawling through the bush toward him, we suddenly discovered him dead, and we were almost startled at the weird beauty of the picture he made as he lay in his vivid color of costume and painted face, his red blood dyeing the yellow of the Autumn leaves on which he fell.

In the hills and valleys near Lame Deer, Montana on the Tongue River Indian Reservation this dramatic event is documented by stone monuments that were placed by unknown persons at certain positions on the field of action. To the rapidly diminishing circle of knowledgeable people these stones tell the story of the courageous action by Head Chief and Young Mule.[50] It is quite possible that unless action is taken by the Cheyenne leaders of today, these important and historical places may be lost forever.[51]

---

[50] Margot Liberty, "I Will Play with the Soldiers," in *Montana, the Magazine of Western History*, vol. XIV, no. 4 (Autumn 1964), pp. 16–26.

[51] Perhaps, in a sense, this might not be a wholly undesirable eventuality. In the next issue of *Montana, the Magazine of Western History,* vol. xv, no. 1 (Winter 1965), Margot Liberty's exciting story prompted a letter from Father Peter J. Powell, director of American Indian work for the Episcopal Diocese of Chicago, and the founder and director of St. Augustine's Center. Father Powell's latest contribution is the two volume work, *Sweet Medicine,* a comprehensive record of the unique ceremonies of the Northern Cheyennes. Father Powell writes, "There is a sequel to the story . . . I visited Head Chief's grave on several occasions – the last some two and a half years ago. Later that same summer, certain Eastern collectors were shown the burial. One of them departed, carrying Head Chief's skull, as well as some of the objects interred with him. When news of this reached the Cheyennes in general and Head Chief's family in particular, they were more than upset. I happened to know one of the persons in the party who had taken the remains . . . I sent the individual a message, asking for the return of the bones, and offered to see that they were re-buried in their proper grave . . . Within a few days, a package arrived. In it was the skull of Head Chief – the bullet hole clearly visible in it. In separate packages were his breastplate and the German silver cross he had worn, also the bridle of the horse shot beside his grave . . . Once more Head Chief will rest in the pine covered hills of the people and land he died for in honor."

Crow Celebrations at the Custer Battlefield

The Fort Custer Monthly Post Returns and Record of Events for the month of December 1890 and January 1891 show that the First Cavalry was involved, while not in a major way, in the action at Wounded Knee.

Lieutenant Colonel Abraham K. Arnold and Major Henry Carroll, while on detached service from Fort Custer, led units, in addition to their own First Cavalry troops, from Fort Keogh and Fort Abraham Lincoln to form a second line of defense across southern North Dakota in case the Sioux should attempt to escape in that direction.

This strategy proved unnecessary and the First Cavalry returned to Fort Custer in February of 1891.

After the fight at Wounded Knee, duty at Fort Custer settled down to a dull routine interrupted only by the creativity of individuals of the command and the area. The fourth of July of 1890 provided the opportunity to stage a celebration. The Custer Battlefield was selected as the site.

The entire Crow tribe was assembled, and over four hundred lodges were camped around a hollow square at the foot of the hill on which stands the Custer monument. The program consisted of a grand procession, a sham battle and festive dancing. The performance was organized by Crow Agency Indian Agent Major Wyman and was described in the newspaper as a scene of "wild barbaric splendor." [52]

The event was so successful that it was scheduled again for the following July 4 in 1891.

In the July 9, 1891, issue of the Billings Gazette *an account of this celebration was recorded probably by a writer named H. L. Knight, under the heading – "Absorakys Celebrate."*

Mr. Knight's description of the trail to Fort Custer could be followed today and the same comments could be made. His recording of the state of once proud Fort Custer indicates a possible policy of benign neglect by the Federal Government.

Mr. Knight comments, as everyone that visits the Custer Battlefield does, on the Custer fight and the various participants thereof. His acoustical adventures are highly interesting to Custer fight fans, but can be refuted by many, including the writer, who can state the opposite results. Mr. Knight's informative and detailed story follows:

From Billings to the Crow Agency is sixty-five miles, but that did not hinder a number of our people from taking the trip to see Major Wyman's wards celebrate the 115th anniversary of the declaration of American Independence in their own peculiar manner. . .

Crossing the Yellowstone at Kennedy's Ferry, the Pryor Creek divide with its dangerous passes, steep

---

[52]News item from the Billings (Mont.) *Gazette,* July 10, 1890.

hills, and beaver slides is finally overcome and the creek forded. Indian Creek is followed up, leaving Pryor Creek to the right, and for a number of miles the road is good, an easy grade leading to the divide between Spring Creek and Pryor through grass clothed hills and a rolling country. Spring Creek soon shows up and clusters and groves of willow, ash and box elder begin to thicken. A good camping place is about half way between Billings and Fort Custer, 26 miles from town, and which can be easily reached in four hours. The water in the creek is pure and cold and countless springs add their flow to the babbling brook, each one apparently cooler, clearer and more refreshing than the other. Of course the grass is thick and high and wild flowers and vines luxuriant in growth throughout all this lovely valley. Fat cattle are seen in the distance lazily cropping the buffalo grass, which is here belly deep, and a few bunches of frisking ponies may be seen standing side by side, brushing from each other the pestiferous insects. The serpent in this Eden is the pest just referred to – creeping things are not nearly so exasperating as those which creep and fly and buzz and bite, setting at naught the mosquito netting which is indispensable on a camping trip at this season of the year. "The bed bug has no wings at all but gets there just the same" is true enough except in camp life, as some of the party will vouch who attempted to refresh themselves by one night indoors at the Fort Custer Hotel.

But we are still a long and weary way from the Crow Agency and ten miles more takes us out of the grassy valley of springs over onto Fly Creek – well named – and the tiresome part of the journey begins after the Big Horn divide is reached. Far off in the dim distances Fort Custer is outlined against the horizon and the winding of the wagon road can be traced for miles and miles ahead. Prairie-dog towns begin to thicken and green timber is no more seen except in the valley of the Little Horn, many miles ahead. Nine-mile Hole Creek, a succession of pools of brackish alkali water, is followed until the Big Horn is in sight, then a few miles across the wide fertile plain and noonday camp is made under the frowning bluffs of the Big Horn, near enough to hear the noises in the military post of Fort Custer and close enough to the ferry to watch our turn to cross.

The Big Horn River having been crossed, the steep approach to the post occupies the attention of the tourists and when the summit is reached all are prepared to see a neat and well kept fort, with nicely appointed building and evidenced as civilization, but in the weather-stained, unpainted barracks, rubbish-covered parade grounds and dilapidated officers' quarters, a gate unhinged here and a decrepit shutter creaking and rattling on one hinge at the next place, the future developments in the post appear questionable.

The dilapidated post leaves a depressing feeling upon every visitor. The writer would rather be flat broke and in Glendive than commanding officer at Fort Custer "only great in that strange spell – a name," as the late lamented Rienzi expresses it.

We are very close to the Crow Agency now, the Big Horn making an abrupt turn to the right at the junction of the Little Horn and we are making time on a fine road on the second bench above the beautiful valley. Across the river is the high range of hills where

FORGOTTEN FACES OF FORT CUSTER
These Troop M, First Cavalry, men's names were not recorded.
F. J. Haynes and O. S. Goff photos. Courtesy, May Klenck and Mabel Klenck Nelson, Billings, Montana.

Custer made his last fight in June 1876, and the granite shaft is discernible where he made his final stand and was killed, together with his whole command by the ambushed Sioux.

To digress from the subject in hand, briefly, it seems to the writer that Reno was unjustly censured and will never be set right before the country for his action, or rather inaction, at the time Custer with his whole command was massacred. It has been said, and generally accepted, that Reno must have been too cowardly to come to Custer's assistance, as being only four miles above and on the same side of the river he could certainly have heard the firing. The writer had a practical demonstration of this on July 4th, and is convinced that Major Reno could have heard no sound from the Custer field of slaughter on that bloody day under most favorable circumstances.

After visiting the battlefield the writer and a friend drove over the Custer trail upon which the ill fated command and Reno's men traveled from the Rosebud, noted the place where they separated, Custer following the divide leading down stream toward the junction of the two rivers and Reno following a high ridge pointing up stream, with the intention of fording the Little Horn should he be able to get to the river. The trail is plainly marked and we experienced no difficulty in following it to the place where the command stopped. Not half a mile from the Custer battlefield was an encampment of the Crow tribe and there the Fourth of July celebration was in progress at the time the writer reached the Reno camp. Though the wind was blowing strongly up the river direct to our location we could neither hear nor see any sign of the 2300 Crow Indians in the camp on the bottom nor could the slightest sound of the minute gun, a twelve pounder, which was being fired at regular intervals be heard by us, and we stood right on the spot where Reno's camp was made fourteen years ago. And more than this it was not until the hills had been left behind and we were nearly opposite the Crow camp that the cannon was heard by us. All this under the most favorable circumstances and who will ever say, especially in the light of Reno's declaration, substantiated by his troops that the wind was blowing down stream and away from him, that he could have possibly heard the noise of battle from the Custer field four miles away with a ridge of high hills between and a contrary wind. The cannonading of a man of war could not possibly have been heard, let alone the insignificant report of small arms, and Custer had no artillery.[53]

Mr. Knight, uncharacteristically, neglects to report on the July 4 celebration, which of course, was the purpose of his trip. This possible obsession to clear Reno and blame Custer, which incidentally is currently popular, seems to have replaced his journalistic duties.

On March 24, 1892, in a column headed "Junction Jottings," the Billings Gazette *reported that on Monday, March 21, 1892, orders went to Fort Custer stating that the First Cavalry would change stations with*

---

[53] Custer Battlefield Historian William B. Henry in 1969 initiated a firearms demonstration at the battlefield using weapons used in the Custer fight. The author, while visiting a point about two miles from the Custer monument (Sgt. Butler's marker) could plainly hear the single report of a Springfield 45-70 carbine that was being demonstrated by Mr. Henry near the spot where Custer fell.

the Tenth Cavalry now stationed in Arizona and Texas. This transfer to the southwest prompted many First Cavalry soldiers to take their discharge in Montana and settle in the Yellowstone Valley. The article indicated that "each regiment is to keep its horses and that means an overland trip. The First [Cavalry] is to march from Fort Custer not later than April 20, 1892."

The First Cavalry served during Fort Custer's most active period and contributed in a positive and meaningful way towards the settlement of the West. The influence of these hard riding soldiers and their devoted families is felt and seen in the Yellowstone Valley to this day.

PART THREE

The Twilight Years
1893–1898

FORT CUSTER ATOP THE BLUFFS OVERLOOKING THE BIG HORN RIVER
View looking north. The Little Big Horn flows in from the right beyond the fort and protruding hill.
Courtesy, Custer Battlefield Museum.

The Tenth Cavalry
"Buffalo Soldiers" Arrive

A news item from the Billings Gazette, *May 5, 1892:*

The sun baked troops of the Tenth Cavalry, fresh from the sand deserts and semi-tropical clime of the Gila River, in southern Arizona, shivered with every gust of wind that raced around the corners in Billings yesterday. The enlisted men are all Negroes and not at all pleased at the change from the sunny south to this northern latitude. A sergeant, with his teeth chattering as he talked, said, "Boss, is this what y' call summah, coudn hadly wear cotton shirt ten days ago at Fort Grant, Arizona Territory, diffunt heah, shuah."

The famous Tenth Cavalry, "the Buffalo Soldiers,"[54] *who were to win even more fame in the*

---

[54] William H. Leckie, in his *The Buffalo Soldiers,* p. 26n, states, "The origin of the term 'Buffalo Soldier' is uncertain, although the common explanation is that the Indian saw a similarity between the hair of the Negro soldier and that of the buffalo. The buffalo was a sacred animal to the Indian, and it is unlikely that he would so name an enemy if respect were lacking. It is a fair guess that the Negro trooper understood this and thus his willingness to accept the title." Dr. Leckie's excellent history does not include the 10th Cavalry's sojourn to Montana, and the material set forth in the present volume will make a useful supplementary study to *The Buffalo Soldiers.*

Spanish-American war, came to Fort Custer on May 5, 1892, after long service in the hot southwestern deserts.

On May 4, 1892, five troops of the Tenth U. S. Cavalry, A, B, E, G and K, together with camp equipage and supplies passed through Billings, Montana, on a special train of ten passenger coaches and twelve freight cars. The Tenth exchanged posts with the First Cavalry that was destined for Arizona. Additional Tenth Cavalry troops continued on to Fort Assinniboine (Troops C and F), Fort Keogh (Troop D), and Fort Buford, North Dakota (Troop H).[55]

Disembarking from the train at Custer, Montana, they marched a distance of thirty miles to the fort in a blizzard. The most serious troubles during their stay was with Coxey's Army and the American Railway Union strike, both in 1894.[56] *They helped round up the Coxeyite division from Butte at Forsyth, when the train the Coxeymen had seized was recaptured. During the summer, they did guard duty along the Northern Pacific Railway during the union's strike. Two of the troops, commanded by Captain [Robert D.] Read were encamped for a time on the outskirts of Billings, Montana.*

In the summer of 1896, the regiment aided in rounding up the Crees and escorting them back to the Canadian border where they were passed over to the Canadian troops. In the summer of 1897, three troops went to the Cheyenne Reservation and arrested several Indians who had killed a sheepherder and had frightened settlers with threats of war.

---

[55] News item in the *Billings Daily Gazette,* May 5, 1892.

[56] Thomas A. Clinch, "Coxey's Army in Montana," in *Montana, the Magazine of Western History,* vol. 15, no. 4 (Oct. 1965), pp. 2-11.

AN 1897 SNOW SCENE AT THE OFFICERS' QUARTERS, FORT CUSTER
During this period the 10th Cavalry and units of the 25th Infantry
were stationed at the fort.
Courtesy, The National Archives.

CAPTAIN ROBERT D. READ, TENTH CAVALRY
Two troops commanded by Read were encamped for a time
on the outskirts of Billings, Montana.
Courtesy, Custer Battlefield Museum.

The Tenth had many famous leaders that included former Fort Custer commanders Lieutenant Colonel George P. Buell, Colonel John W. Davidson, and Lieutenant Colonel Nathan Dudley. One of its lieutenants, John J. Pershing, though not serving at Fort Custer, rose to fame during World War I. Although Colonel J. K. Minser was in command of the regiment during most of its tour of duty in Montana, Lieutenant Colonel David Perry was usually in command of Fort Custer.

At the time the fort was abandoned in 1898 the regiment was in command of Colonel Guy T. Henry, one of the famous officers of the Spanish-American war who had had a stirring career on the plains.

Several accidental deaths occurred among the officers of the regiment near Fort Custer. Lieutenant Powhatan Clark, who had won the Congressional Medal of Honor for bringing in a wounded Negro corporal under fire in an Arizona campaign, was drowned in the Little Big Horn River in July 1893. The next February, Lieutenant Finley's leg was crushed when his horse fell during maneuvers at the fort, and failed to rally from the amputation.

Among the soldiers at Fort Custer with the Tenth, was Captain Horace W. Bivins, later of Billings, Montana, whose memories of his military duties are recounted later in this chapter. He was a non-commissioned officer at the time, and the regiment's leading marksman.

Several other of the Negro pioneers of the Billings area were at Fort Custer either as soldiers with the Tenth or in civilian capacities. Charles "Smokey" Wilson, who lived 60 years with the Crows, was interpreter for the Crow Scouts before going to Crow

Agency. John Lee, pioneer of Billings, and for many years steward at a downtown Billings private club, was, at one time, at Fort Custer.

A feature article that appeared in the March 3, 1935, Billings Gazette *and written by George Beebe, had as its subject a fascinating old Negro soldier who served with the Tenth Cavalry at Fort Custer. Mr. Beebe looks back upon the active, adventurous army career of Captain Bivins in the following story:*

CAPTAIN HORACE BIVINS

. . . It is a story of romance and bravery, a narrative of a loyal and trustworthy Negro who gave the best years of his life defending his country and was rewarded by frequent praise and numerous citations from the United States War Department.

When Captain Bivins decided on a military career he determined to make a record of which he would be proud in years to come. What he did in the army he did well. Captain Bivins has the distinction of having led the entire United States Army in marksmanship at various times, both with carbine and pistol.

By coincidence, he has 32 army medals, or an average of one for every year of military service. Among them is a citation star for operating a Hotchkiss mounting gun at the Battle of San Juan Hill – a gun which he maneuvered alone during much of the battle. The gun rebounded six or eight feet after each shot and Sergeant Bivins was obliged to pull it back in position, reload, get the range and fire, without assistance. He shot 72 shells in this manner.

Another honor that he holds – and one that has never been equaled – was the winning of five gold medals for expert marksmanship with a carbine and pistol in army competition in a single year, 1894.

So widespread was his fame as a marksman that in 1896 Colonel W. F. Cody offered him a position with his Buffalo Bill show, shooting against Ann Oakley, a crack shot with the outfit. The noted showman sought and obtained a furlough for Mr. Bivins and promised 100 dollars a month and expenses. But the soldier was in line to become an ordinance sergeant and he preferred the army routine to circus life.

. . . He served for a time at old Fort Custer, Fort Missoula and Fort Assinniboine as well as having won marksmanship contests at Fort Keogh near Miles City.

. . . In commenting on the Negro soldiers, Captain Bivins pointed out that there has always been a tendency on the part of some people to belittle the value of their service in time of war and realizing this, he said, the Negro has always attempted to justify the government's reliance upon him. In the Indian campaigns of the southwest, especially, the Negro soldiers endured many hardships and privations that the land might be safe for the white settlers.

On April 27, 1892, his regiment was ordered to Fort Custer to relieve the First Cavalry, arriving at Custer Junction, after passing through Billings on May 4. Detraining in unseasonal weather, the unit marched through a foot of snow next day to Fort Custer.

Soon after reaching the fort, the Tenth Cavalry was called out to quell a strike on the Northern Pacific Railroad. Troop G, of which Sergeant Bivins was a member, was stationed at Big Horn to guard the bridge at that place and several other troops were sent to Billings.

SERGEANT OF CROW SCOUTS
POSSIBLY JOHN WALLACE
The one-armed man is two
Whistle, survivor of the
Swordbearer fight.
Courtesy, Custer Battlefield Museum.

HORACE BIVINS, 10TH CAVALRY
A fascinating Negro soldier who
served at Fort Custer.
From H. V. Cashin *et al., Under Fire
with the Tenth U.S. Cavalry.*
Chicago, ca. 1902.

Soon afterward his troop was ordered to Custer Station to intercept a part of Coxey's army which had stolen a railroad train and was bound for Washington, D. C., but after riding all night from the fort and fording the Big Horn River, the troop arrived just a few minutes after the train had gone by. It was stopped at Forsyth and the men placed under arrest.

During their six years stay in Montana, however, the "Buffalo Soldiers," as the Indians referred to the Negro troopers, had few disorders. Once they were called out because of troubles with the Cheyennes in which a sheepherder was killed and they also helped to round up a band of Crees who came storming over the border of Canada.

The Tenth Cavalry remained at Fort Custer for four years and then marched overland by way of Billings and Lewistown to Fort Assinniboine, near Havre, in October 1896, remaining there until April 14, 1898, when war was declared with Spain.

During these years, Corporal Bivins was making an enviable record as a crack shot. One of the feats he performed was letting a bird fly from each hand and then taking up a rifle in each hand, killed them both in the order that they were given their freedom. Bivins won first prize in the regimental reunion held at Fort Custer in October 1892.

In the annual cavalry competition at Fort Keogh in 1892, 1893 and 1894, Mr. Bivins placed first each year. In October 1894, he was sent to participate in the army competition at Fort Sheridan, Illinois, representing the Department of Dakota. There he met the finest marksmen in the United States Army and there he won, with ease, the first gold medal which entitled him to the first rank in marksmanship and the best shot in the Army at that time. He scored 589 points out of a possible 800 and was announced as a "distinguished marksman" in General Orders.

Crow Scouts at Fort Custer

An article by W. H. Banfill appeared in the February 8, 1931, edition of the Billings Gazette, *giving an informative description of the organization of the Crow Indian Army Scouts.*

The author of the article takes us back to the campaign of 1876 and Lieutenant James Bradley's enlistment of the Crow Scouts at the original Crow Agency on the Stillwater River and proceeds to give a detailed account of the Crow Scouts' daily routine and history at Fort Custer.

. . . From the time of the Custer disaster, a band of Crow scouts was regularly attached to the Fort Custer command. About 1889 or perhaps a year or two later, a regular troop of cavalry was recruited from the Crow scouts and became Company L of the First Cavalry. After the First was replaced by the Tenth, the Indian troop remained at the fort for a year or two with the Negro outfit but was finally disbanded about 1893.

. . . The Crow troop was armed and dressed exactly the same as their white or Negro comrades. Lieutenant Robertson was in command during at least most of their enlistment. Lieutenants [Edmund S.]

Wright and [Second Lieutenant William H.] Osborne were also attached to the troop. The Crow soldiers were enlisted after the original Troops L and M of the First Cavalry had been disbanded. Troop L was at first skeletonized with white noncommissioned officers but they were soon replaced by Crow sergeants and corporals.

John Wallace was first sergeant of the troop. Frank Shane was another sergeant. Big Man was another noncommissioned officer of the troop. There are 14 or 15 other members of the troop still living on the Crow reservation.[57]

John Frost, the Baptist minister at Pryor, and for many years interpreter for Chief Plenty Coups, was a scout and interpreter for Troop L after his return from Carlisle. According to Mr. Frost, the troop experienced considerable difficulty at first because of necessity of translating the commands from English into Crow.

By the time the lieutenant's command had been transmitted by the corporals to their squads they were far behind the other troops in executing the formations. The problem was finally solved when the interpreter devised a series of short Crow words which would be understood by the soldiers and would stand for the whole command. To anyone who has heard the lengthy interpretations into Crow of what appear to be simple English sentences, the necessity of such short cuts will be manifest. Under the new system the Crows were finally able to go through the maneuvers at the same time as the other troops.

The families of the Crow troopers lived across the

---

[57] The article was written in 1931 and the participants therein are now deceased.

SIX CROW SCOUTS AT FORT CUSTER, 1897
To become a member of the troop was regarded as a high honor in the tribe.
Fred E. Miller photo. Courtesy, Smithsonian Institution, Anthropological Archives.

AN INTERIOR VIEW OF THE TWENTY-FIFTH INFANTRY BARRACKS
"Two companies . . . were among the commands sent
to the scene of hostilities."
Quartermaster General photo. Courtesy, The National Archives.

ravine from the fort grounds in what was known as the women's quarters. . .

Enlistment of Crow scouts dates back to the campaign of 1876 at which time Lieutenant [James] Bradley visited a Crow camp on the Stillwater River and induced Chief Blackfoot to allow about 30 of his young men to act as scouts in the campaign against the Sioux. Curley, who was generally regarded as the only survivor of the disaster, was one of the scouts. . .

When Fort Custer was established Lieutenant G. C. Doane was selected and surveyed the site, enlisted a band of Indian scouts, who served for a six month period. At times there were as many as 300 scouts in this service. Indian scouts performed an invaluable service in the campaigns of the 'sixties and 'seventies because of their knowledge of the country and of the ways of the hostile Indians.

After hostilities had ceased for a number of years, considerable difficulty was experienced by authorities in preventing horse-stealing raids by Indian bands and the scouts were employed in keeping these activities on the part of Piegans, Sioux and Cheyennes at a minimum. The scouters also served an effective purpose for furnishing an outlet for the restless spirits of the young Crows and for discouraging raids by Crows upon the horses of other tribes. Similar bands were recruited among the Cheyennes and Sioux after they had accepted the fact of their defeat.

The scouts were necessarily kept under very loose restraint. They had a camp at the foot of the hill at Fort Custer along the Little Big Horn. If they became dissatisfied they left the service without any formality.

It was felt at the time the troop was organized, that better service could be rendered by a small and select body under stricter rules. Scouts whose records were outstanding were given first opportunity to enlist in the troop. The men who were selected were all finely-developed men physically as well as of desirable character. To become a member of the troop came to be regarded as one of high honor in the tribe. Undoubtedly the Crow soldier, with a natural love of bright colors and the accoutrements of a warrior, greatly treasured the uniforms, which came to them when the troop was disbanded.

According to Mr. [Henry C.] Klenck (who was with the 1st Cavalry during its occupancy of Fort Custer and afterwards remained as quartermaster clerk at the post) the Crow troop was first drilled by Lieutenant [Edward W.] Casey at Fort Keogh.[58] At the time of the Wounded Knee trouble on the Standing Rock reservation, when Sitting Bull was killed in 1890-91, the First Cavalry and the two companies of the Twenty-fifth Infantry at Fort Custer were among the commands which were sent to the scene of hostilities, and there is little doubt but what the Crow troop was among the contingent. This was the last major Indian outbreak. . .

---

[58] Lieutenant Casey is well known for his excellent work in organizing his Cheyenne Indian scout troop. To this editor's knowledge, this is the first mention of Casey's help in the formation of the Crow Scouts at Fort Custer.

The Final Exodus and
Fort Custer's Last Stand

The need for Fort Custer had passed, and the fort was being phased out. The following brief news item from the Billings Gazette *tells of the final exodus:*

NOVEMBER 12, 1897. Two of the cavalry troops stationed at Fort Custer have been ordered transferred, one to Fort Keogh and the other to Camp Merritt. The soldiers will go overland.

NOVEMBER 19, 1897. Fort Custer as a military post is now but a reminiscence. The troops have all departed, with the exception of a detail of twenty soldiers, who, under command of Lieutenants Freeman and Hunt, have been ordered to remain at the abandoned fort and look after the vacant barracks until permanent arrangements are made for the care of the buildings and to protect them from vandal bands. The last of the departing troops arrived in Billings last night and left this afternoon by special train for Fort Harrison. They occupied four coaches, with ten freight cars loaded with accoutrements. They are colored soldiers, Companies A and D, the former in command of Captain Sanborn and the latter, owing to the absence on a recruiting expedition of Captain Sweet, in command of Lieutenant O'Neil. Troops A and C left Monday by overland route for Fort Keogh, while troop K, Captain Reade, Jr. [Robert D. Read] in command arrived overland today and will march to Fort Assinniboine by way of Lewistown.

FORT CUSTER'S LAST STAND

Whenever a military post is abandoned, whether in Europe, Korea or the plains of Montana, the economic conditions of the regions are dramatically altered. The civilian contracts to provide supplies for the military are terminated, thus causing unemployment, which in turn affects practically everything and everyone.[59]

By the same token, a new military post that is established can stimulate business by providing a need for various services and can even create whole towns.

The following series of editorials recount a rather belated effort on the part of the Billings Gazette *to attempt to persuade the government to rejuvenate Fort Custer to its former status, and reports the comic opera antics of the Sheridan, Wyoming, newspapers, the* Post *and the* Enterprise, *to influence Washington to establish a new post near Sheridan.*

On January 25, 1898, the following editorial appeared in the Billings Gazette.

The commander of the Department of the Dakota, in recommending the abandonment of Fort Custer

---

[59] The same situation is happening now in the 1970s due to the closing down or relocating of military installations and/or a lack of government contracts due to administrative economy measures.

as a military reservation presented two reasons why the step should be taken, both of which were equally absurd and fallacious. He contended, first, that the abolition of the post would be in the interest of economy in that the buildings were in such a dilapidated condition that it would require the expenditure of a quarter of a million dollars to make the necessary improvements, and secondly, that the health of the garrison was seriously threatened by reason of the contaminated source of the water supply. It is well to review the situation, even though the presentation of existing facts may have no weight with the War Department. Let us first refer briefly to the abandonment of the fort from the standpoint of economy, and see if it will not cost the government more in dollars and cents to carry out its plans than it would to have repaired the post and put it in as good condition as any of the old established western forts that are now occupied.

In addition to the expense incurred in transporting the troops to Forts Harrison, Assinniboine and Keogh, the War Department will have to pay a large sum in making available the quartermaster's supplies left behind. As these supplies are of no great value where they are, they must be transported either to market and sold at a sacrifice or taken to some other post for army consumption. From the fact that the department has already advertised for bids for loading the wood onto the cars, with a view of making it available at either Fort Keogh or Fort Harrison, it is undoubtedly the intention to divide the other supplies between these two posts. The *Gazette* has been to the pains to ascertain the nature and amount of supplies now at Fort Custer, and finds that they consist of 200,000 pounds of oats, 50,000 pounds of vegetables, 900 cords of wood, 300 tons of coal, 800 tons of hay and approximately 200,000 pounds of miscellaneous stores. It is estimated that it will cost $50,000 to transport these supplies to the nearest fort now under garrison and it is also estimated by competent contractors who are familiar with the condition of the fort barracks that this sum of money would be amply adequate to put the buildings in the very best of shape. As the abandonment of the post has not reduced the number of men or officers or resulted in any saving whatever, we fail to see wherein the economy lies.

The second reason that was urged in the report of the department commander is on a par with the first; if anything it is even more puerile, and contrary to the facts in the case. The mortuary reports furnished by Fort Custer since its establishment compare favorably with those of other posts, where no question has ever been raised as to impure water supply or bad sanitary condition. The water supply at Fort Custer is not only not contaminated, but it is abundant and never failing, and the man who asserts to the contrary makes a display of his ignorance in this regard. The War Department was falsely informed respecting this important matter, for the report submitted stated that the Little Horn River, which furnishes the Custer water supply, was contaminated from the offal of Indian camps and refuse of slaughter houses along the banks of the stream. The water of the Little Horn is undoubtedly impure at and just below the Crow Agency, but that it is contaminated in the vicinity of Fort Custer or even within a score of miles of the water works plant is not a fact. Crow Agency, where are congregated the Indians and located the slaughter houses, is forty two miles removed from Fort Custer and even if they were not half as far up the river the water of the beautiful winding stream which threads its way past the historic fort would still be as pure as any that ever leaped from Olympian heights or belched forth from creviced rock. It is a well-known fact that running water purifies itself within a distance of seven miles. The refuse of the Omaha slaughter and packing houses, the second largest in the United States, as well as the sewerage of the entire city finds its way into the Missouri River, and yet no complaints are entered about the contamination of the water source by the cities and towns farther down that sluggish stream. The fact of the matter is that the portion of the report which deals with the Fort Custer water supply is nothing but pure buncombe; it is as far from the truth as the statement that it would require an outlay of $250,000 to put the barracks in good condition.

In abandoning Fort Custer the War Department has deprived the Crows of a market for their agricultural products and rendered more difficult the task of making them self sustaining and curbing their savage nature. There is not a fort in the west where a cavalry post can be maintained as cheaply as at Fort Custer. Its abandonment was poor policy, not only from the standpoint of economy, but from every other standpoint, and its re-establishment ought to be ordered without delay. Though the troops have already been removed, we believe that if the situation were presented in its true light and an effort made by our representatives in congress to secure a revocation of the order, it could be accomplished even at this late date.

A new development was commented on by the Billings Gazette *editor on March 1, 1898. It was entitled:*

SHERIDAN TOO FAR AWAY

A delegation of seven prominent citizens of Sheridan, Wyoming, headed by Mayor Halbert, arrived in Washington yesterday to lobby for the establishment of a military post in northern Wyoming to take the place of the abandoned fort of Custer. The delegation is armed with documents and a petition which will be presented to the proper authorities, and every influence possible will be brought to bear in an effort to bring about the desired result. The people of Sheridan have been working in the strictest secrecy on this proposition for some time, but the *Sheridan Enterprise* unwittingly let the cat out of the bag by publishing the fact that the delegation left for Washington last Thursday, stating that it was "on a mission of vital importance to the business interests of Sheridan County" and that it hoped "to be enabled to furnish the full particulars" this week. The object became known in Billings on Sunday and realizing the importance of speedy action a message was immediately wired Senators Carter and Mantle, notifying them of the coming of the Sheridan delegation and remonstrating against the granting of the prayer of the petitioners from Wyoming. There is urgent need of a military post on or close to the Crow Reservation. Fort Custer should not have been abandoned, and we believe it would not have been vacated had the War Department been in possession of the true situation. The building of a new post would entail a needless expense, when Fort Custer can be repaired and put in the best possible shape for one-tenth the cost of constructing a new fort. Anyhow, the establishment of a post in Wyoming ought not to be seriously considered, and doubtless it will not be if our representatives in Washington will take the pains to secure and lay before the War Department the existing facts with reference to the urgent need for the reestablishment of the abandoned fort. If the Cheyennes are to be removed to the Crow Reservation, it would be little short of criminal neglect not to rehabilitate and regarrison Fort Custer. They are an ugly, vicious tribe, restless under restraint and liable to take the warpath at any time. If they are removed, the presence of troops at Fort Custer, in sight of the camps, would operate to hold in check the savages and if an uprising should take place it could be put down without subjecting the settlers to the ravages of a howling host of bloodthirsty reds.

The controversy continued in the Gazette *on March 8, 1898, in an editorial entitled:*

FORT CUSTER AGAIN

The *Sheridan Post* and the *Sheridan Enterprise* are having a tilt over an item which recently appeared in the latter newspaper about the departure for Washington of a delegation of prominent citizens. The *Post* charges the *Enterprise* with having given away secrets and thereby placed weapons in the hands of the people of Billings. As the *Gazetter* considers itself responsible for the dispute between its two contemporaries in Wyoming, it hastens to absolve the *Enterprise* from the charge preferred by the *Post*. It appears that the people of Sheridan have been working in secret for some time in the matter of securing the establishment at or near Sheridan of an army post to take the place of Fort Custer, recently abandoned by order of the War Department. So well was the secret guarded that the people of Billings, who desire the re-establishment of Custer as a military post, had no inkling of what was going on in Sheridan until after the departure of the delegation. Though the *Enterprise* mentioned the fact that the committee had left, the item was so worded that the *Gazetter* would never have suspected the mission of the delegation had we not received a tip through a source which we are not now at liberty to divulge. In fact the telegram sent to Senators Carter and Mantle, remonstrating against the establishment of a post in northern Wyoming, was indicted prior to the appearance of the *Enterprise* containing the item referred to, and when we stated that our contemporary had "let the cat out of the bag" we simply meant that it was the cause of confirming the knowledge of which the people of Billings were already in possession. We make this explanation in order that the *Enterprise* may not rest under the suspicion of having betrayed confidence.

The most cordial feeling has always existed between the people of Billings and those of Sheridan and we believe that the same friendly relations will continue, despite the efforts of our sister city to secure the establishment of a post in Sheridan County. In advocating the rehabilitation of Fort Custer in preference to the building of a new fort, The *Gazetter* is not actuated with a desire to injure Sheridan, but rather to promote what we believe to be the best interests of the War Department from the standpoint of economy, as well as for the protection of the settlers living on or contiguous to the Crow Reservation. We observe in the last issue of the *Enterprise* that a telegram has been received from the Sheridan lobby to the effect that the delegation is sanguine of ultimate success, and we also observe in a Washington special that Senator Warren of Wyoming is of the opinion that the "War Department will finally decide to establish a new military post east of the Big Horn in Wyoming or Montana." The dispatch also accredits Senator Warren with the statement that "it is not probable that Fort Custer will be re-established, because of the serious objections to the sanitary conditions there," and that "the most likely location is Sheridan. . ."

The Yellowstone Journal *of Miles City, Montana, couldn't resist commenting on the situation in an editorial that was reprinted in the* Billings Gazette *on March 8, 1898, titled:*

AN OUTSIDER'S VIEW

Billings will never rest easy until it gets Fort Custer re-established or a new post on the Crow Reservation contiguous to Alkali Flat. It cannot now understand how it was that Custer was wiped out, in the twinkling of an eye, and before the guardians of Billings prosperity were awakened to the consequences of the spoliation. We have always felt as if the Billingsites held Miles City in some degree responsible for the seizure, for the reasons that Fort Keogh was the residuary legatee of Fort Custer; but if any such suspicion exists it is erroneous, as the news of the evacuation was as much a surprise there as it was up the river.

However, this is a digression. What we intended to notice was the extreme alertness of the Billings people now in regard to the location of a new post. Sheridan, the little village on the northern border of Wyoming, has, it seems, been talking about military posts and quite recently it dispatched a special committee of leading citizens to Washington to depict the defenseless condition of northern Wyoming in general and Sheridan in particular on account of the evacuation of Fort Custer, and to paint in lurid hue the horrors of a raid by painted savages on the peaceful homes that are scattered along Big and Little Goose creeks. This thrilling narration was to be followed up by an appeal for the protection that would be afforded by the establishment of a military post in the vicinity of Sheridan. Of course the Sheridan people did not advertise their intentions in this regard far and wide. On the contrary, they conducted a rather still hunt, but after the Washington delegation had been finally and successfully loaded onto the cars, a Sheridan newspaper could not resist the temptation to "whoop" a little bit by referring to the departure of a number of eminent citizens "on a mission of vital importance to the business interests of Sheridan County." This caught the eagle eye of some Billings man, who sounded the alarm. An investigation was instituted at Sheridan and in a few hours the Billings sleuths had the whole story, with which they hastened to Billings. Then the wires began to sizzle with the vigor and frequency on the through service established for the occasion between Billings and Washington, and before the luckless but happy delegation from Sheridan had crossed the Missouri at Council Bluffs, the vantage ground they fondly hoped to occupy at Washington had been mined and torpedoed, the friendly ears they hoped to gain plugged with gun cotton, hearts of flesh and blood turned into marble, warm hands coated with ice, and friendly looks of recognition and welcome transformed into glassy stares.

That is the way Billings works when she has a job on hand. Everything is done with neatness and dispatch and when the job is over the guardians of Billings' welfare meet at the club and after a mild self congratulatory seance – during which a few "light ones" are absorbed into the system – they commend Alkali Flat to the tender mercy of Providence and go home – most of them.

The Spanish-American War burst upon the scene and rendered all arguments relative to Fort Custer academic. All soldiers were needed for the expected conflict. The remaining Fort Custer troops, all 20 of them, abandoned the fort on April 17, 1898.

The Gazette *reports the final departure and records the final skirmish in downtown Billings.*

Montana's colored regulars, the Twenty-fifth United States Infantry are off for the front. The two companies stationed at Fort Harrison proceeded over the Great Northern from Helena, while the four companies from Fort Missoula went over the Northern Pacific. The Missoula contingent passed through Billings early yesterday morning by special train, being joined here by the remnant left at Fort Custer at the time that post was abandoned. The companies comprising the Twenty-fifth will meet at St. Paul and proceed on to Chickamauga National Park, Tenn., and it is expected that they will be ordered to Key West at once, to be ready for transportation to Cuba and used as the nucleus of the invading army.

Last night while the members of the cavalry troop were participating in a practice skirmish around the city on the dead run, Lieutenant Bailey, with drawn sabre, at the head of the troop, collided, as he turned the corner of Montana Avenue and Twenty-Seventh Street, with a bicyclist. Both men were knocked down and the lieutenant's sabre caught the bicyclist in the ribs, but did not penetrate his heart. The officer was dazed by the force of the collision and when he came to, his first impression was that the troop had been attacked by a band of bloodthirsty Spaniards.

Dismantling the Fort

For five years the old fort stood abandoned atop the bluff attended only by a small custodial staff. On September 21, 1930, Major S. G. Reynolds commented on his part in the dismantling of Fort Custer. The Gazette *reports the story in this manner:*

Major S. G. Reynolds, who as Crow Indian Superintendent, was given charge of the dismantling of the fort when it was turned over to the Indian service by the War Department. In 1903, an appropriation of $10,000 was made for demolishing the fort and salvaging its material.

The work was done by the Crows and there were 250 Indians encamped at the fort for nearly three years while the work was being done. The work was directly under the charge of Clarence Brown. Sgt. John Wallace of the old Crow scouts and Robert Raises Up, an agency blacksmith, were assistants. "Old Frenchie," who had been a soldier at the post and later assistant custodian after the troops had been withdrawn, was the cook.

"Frenchie" was greatly afraid of ghosts which he declared were about the deserted post. There was a barbed wire entanglement along the top of the bluff

ABANDONED BUILDINGS AT FORT CUSTER
l. to r.: Guardhouse, warehouse, opera house, and officers' club.
F. J. Haynes photo. Courtesy, Custer Battlefield Museum.

THE ABANDONED FORT CUSTER HOSPITAL
F. J. Haynes photo. Courtesy, Custer Battlefield Museum.

THE WATER TOWER AT ABANDONED FORT CUSTER
"Conspicuous was the square water tank built of lumber."
Fred E. Miller photo. Courtesy, Smithsonian Institution, Anthropological Archives.

THE FORT CUSTER BAR
Courtesy, Mrs. Don C. Foote, "Treasures of the West," Billings, Montana.

behind the quarters. There was a tradition that some officer in his cups had stumbled to his death over the bluff and the wire had been placed there to prevent any repetition of the tragedy. In its 20 years of existence, the fort had seen other sudden deaths to furnish material for a lively imagination.

At the time of its dismantling, Fort Custer was considered a million dollar fort. French and German Army visitors had pronounced it the finest cavalry post in the world. The large plateau, stretching to the south, was without an obstacle to interfere with maneuvers.

The buildings were located in the common style about the square of the parade grounds. Conspicuous was the square-built water tank, built of lumber. There was water in every building. It was pumped from the river directly, through the water system as well as to the reserve tank. There was no sewage system but with the abundance of man power, adequate sanitation was obtained.

Connected with the water tower was the wagon and blacksmith shops of large proportions. Not far distant was a brick warehouse 150 feet long with a full basement, capable of storing an immense amount of supplies. The officer's club and the opera house were large frame structures. To one side was the guard house of brick and there was a frame hospital.

There were 15 to 20 double quarters for officers, each with a large fireplace and chimney. The barracks on another side of the quadrangle were substantially built. Wagon sheds and stables completed the ensemble.

In the center of the parade grounds was the flagstaff 105 feet high with a crow's nest for observations, 85

FORT CUSTER OFFICERS' QUARTERS DURING THE TWILIGHT YEARS
U.S. Signal Corps photo. Courtesy, The National Archives.

FORT CUSTER BARNS AFTER THE POST WAS ABANDONED
Many structures at the Crow Agency were built of
materials from the abandoned fort.
F. J. Haynes photo. Courtesy, Custer Battlefield Museum.

feet from the ground. There was also a beautiful grandstand on the parade grounds. Lighted oil lamps on posts were scattered over the grounds. Among the many articles stored at the fort were hundreds of camp candlesticks. Some of these were candelabra with five or six places for candles to be placed. There were also a large number of Dutch ovens of different sizes which were issued to the Indians.

The target range was beyond the fort quadrangle with the targets not far from the edge of the bluff. . . There were originally no embankments behind the targets but after the high powered Krag Jorgensens were adopted by the Army, the Indians started complaining that horses and cattle were being found killed several miles away across the river and they objected seriously to the guns that "shoot today; kill tomorrow." Banks were therefore thrown up behind the targets.

About a half mile south of the fort was the cemetery where a number of soldiers and members of their families were buried with perhaps some civilians. The soldiers' bodies were all moved to the national cemetery at the Custer Battlefield and the others were moved elsewhere, so that no trace of the burial grounds is left. About a mile south at the head of some of the coulees was the dumping grounds. Cartridges, buttons and similar relics are still picked up there.

The military reservation comprised an entire township. When it ceased to be used by the War Department the land reverted to the Crow Indians and individual allotments were made from it. The land on which Hardin (Mont.) was located was allotted as

THE FERRY BETWEEN THE FORT AND PRESENT HARDIN, MONTANA
An 1897 photo. The crossing was just below the present highway bridge.
Courtesy, Custer Battlefield Museum.

ENLISTED MEN'S BARRACKS AT FORT CUSTER
All the quarters for enlisted men faced west to the parade ground,
opposite the officers' quarters buildings.
U.S. Signal Corps photo. Courtesy, The National Archives.

deceased Indian land and then sold for townsite purposes.

The material from the fort was used for a variety of purposes. The brick from the guardhouse was used in the brick work and chimneys of the Indian flour mill at Crow Agency. The blacksmith and carpenter shop was built from the old opera house and the warehouse adjoining the mill from the barns and wagon sheds. The school barns and sheds at the agency school also came from Fort Custer. About 165 houses on the reservation and most of the material for barns and sheds on Individual Indian allotments came from the same source. The fireplace and chimney at the home of Plenty Coups at Pryor are from Fort Custer buildings.

When the fort was abandoned there was a carload or two of finely matched flooring, ceiling and siding with window sashes and glass. There also were hundreds of kegs of horseshoes and mule shoes. In the dispensary and hospital, there were large amounts of supplies as well as those for the veterinary department.

The original buildings were of cottonwood logs. Later pine was obtained from the Pine hills south of Pompey's Pillar and used for the framework of the buildings. The doors of the different buildings were of heavy material. Wrought iron nails were used and the bolts and ironwork were unusually heavy and substantial. One of the doors made a load in itself.

At one time while the Indians working on the tearing down of the buildings were away at a dance, teams of citizens' wagons came on the fort site and started, according to Major Reynolds, some salvaging on their own account. Their raid on the fort was discovered and a detachment of Indian police were sent to them and they were compelled to haul the stuff back to the agency. They were let off with a small fine and the warning that any further self-help activities would result in their being put off the reservation.[60]

---

[60] There still exists a feud between descendants of these citizens from the Fort Sarpy area who helped themselves to the Fort Custer remains and certain people that represented Major Reynolds' groups. Neither feuding party can recall now this incident that is the basis of their present disagreement.

PART FOUR

Pioneer Rememberings

Pioneer Rememberings

This final section is composed of old-timers' recollections of life at and around Fort Custer. While not always historically factual, they recount in detail, various activities reflecting the daily routine of life at the fort.

A careful reading of this section, combined with Parts One, Two and Three, will enable the reader to gain an accurate picture of the many aspects of life at old Fort Custer, Montana Territory.

CHARLES F. SCHNEIDER'S RECOLLECTIONS

Charles F. Schneider, the son of Bernard Schneider, an old soldier that was stationed at Forts Ellis and Custer, recalls some incidents that occurred while he was growing up on the frontier. The chief value, the reader will shortly realize, is the detail in which fort life is recounted.

The account of the trip from Fort Ellis to Fort Custer in 1885 is especially interesting.

His description of the layout of the fort is indispensable to the intellectually curious. One can compare his very graphic observations of the layout of Fort Custer to photographs of the place and can appreciate the high quality of Schneider's reporting.

His informative text describes everything from Fort Custer's plumbing and lighting system, to schools and stages, making this story invaluable to the student of life at forts on the western frontier.

Thomas B. Marquis writing in the June 7, 1934, issue of the Billings Gazette *recorded Charles F. Schneider's observations.*

. . . In the summer of 1885 all of the soldiers at Fort Ellis were ordered to move to Fort Custer. The move must have been made in the last part of the summer, for I remember the heavy smoke of a forest fire then raging in the Snowy Mountains. The smoke was not seen at Fort Ellis, but it came to notice on the upper Yellowstone, increasing as we traveled down that valley. The cavalry soldiers traveled on their horses, in a separate march, before the infantrymen and the properties started.

We boarded the train at Fort Ellis early in the morning. It was composed of mixed passenger and freight cars, mostly freight cars, I believe. Wagons, horses, mules, personal belongings, army property of all kinds were loaded into the freight cars in readiness before the people got on. We were all of one long summer day on the journey. The arrival at Custer Station was about at darkness. Tents were set up and the whole outfit camped there overnight.

Before sunrise the next morning we were on the march up the Big Horn valley or over the hills and valleys along the route southward. There were either three or four companies of infantry. All of the men were walking, and my father walked with them. . . The soldiers did not march in orderly array, but simply walked, each one according to his own step, but all kept in some sort of connection. They carried guns, belts and ammunition in the belts, but all the property was carried in the wagons. . .

. . . During the second day of march from Custer Station, a few antelope were seen. A couple of our soldiers got out after two of them. The men shot several bullets, but no hit was apparent and the two lively wild creatures scampered away out of sight. The rifles then in use were the 1873 Springfields, 45-caliber, using 75 grains of powder. These the men had were of the infantry model, having a longer barrel than the cavalry model. The infantry model was known as the "long Tom" and the cavalry model was known as the carbine. I do not know what make of revolver they had, but suppose it was the Colt, as that was the usual army revolver at that time.

The first Indians I ever saw came into our view as we approached the Big Horn River near Fort Custer. They were Crow men on their ponies, 15 or 20 of them, probably. They were near the ferry landing on the west side of the river. . .

The ferry crossing then was immediately below the present highway bridge. Sloping places for landing were scooped out of the banks, and the sloped excavation for that landing on the south side may still be seen. . . There was no bridge over the Big Horn at that time and no apparent expectation that a bridge ever would be built. . .

Our cavalcade, in sections were ferried across the river. As we got over the stream we continued on the way along the side of the hill and up to its plateau top at the southern part of the post. . .

Major Dudley was commanding officer of this post. It was larger than Fort Ellis, and there were more soldiers here. All of the quarters for enlisted men were on the opposite side of the parade ground, and their openings were on the west face. At the north of the parade ground was the hospital, the quarters for nurses and other hospital helpers, and perhaps other minor buildings. The hospital and the nurse quarters were the only brick buildings at the post. All of the other buildings were frame, or possibly a little of log structures. Along the entire front of the officer side of the post, where also was the headquarters office, was a brick sidewalk. Its course is easy to trace now, and there are yet several big stumps along there to show that in past times there was a row of fine cottonwood trees beside the brick sidewalk. There was no other well-built sidewalk about the post.

A mixture of post structures occupied land at the south part of the military assemblage. There was a post office, a sutler store, the guard house, the commissary supply house, the ordinance house, the blacksmith shop, the ice house, the corrals, stables, and whatever other like places were needed. The water reservoir was on the dirt bluff overlooking the Big Horn River and at a high point of course. Water was obtained from the Little Big Horn, much more clear than that which flowed in the Big Horn. The pump station for drawing the water supply was at the east edge of the plateau, out from the buildings at that side of the post. . .

Water faucets were located outside, here and there about the post. I do not know what houses may have had them inside, but there were none inside at our home, nor, I think at any of the other places where the enlisted men dwelt. There was a pipe and tap outside near our home and there we got our water. There were no fire plugs, no fire hose nor other fire fighting equipment except buckets. A part of the drilling of the men was as a bucket brigade. I remember one time seeing them in real action as such. A fire broke out in the quarters of one of the officers. The men lined up and passed buckets from various faucet taps to the fire center, and it soon was extinguished.

Candles, coal-oil lamps and lanterns provided our lights. Lanterns were most commonly in use. There were no outside lights as public or street lights. The fuel was wood, both at Ellis and at Custer. Contractors at Custer brought it, I think, from Pine Ridge, some miles north of the present Hardin. All of it was pine or fir. Cords of it, half a mile long, were stacked for the storage common supply. It appeared the lumber was brought from that same region.

A cannon shot in the morning and another in the evening signaled the beginning and the end of each day. Special salute firing was done on special occasions, including Fourth of July, Washington's birthday, and perhaps at other times. Then there were the bugle calls from time to time each day. I always liked to hear them. I conceived the idea of cultivating myself as a bugler. I got a battered old bugle, practiced with it and learned to make most of the calls. My ambition was stirred also by the drum major. He was a man of splendid physique. When he led the military band on the parade ground, clad in his gorgeous gilt-braid costume, wearing his tall fur hat with the chain under his chin and swinging his magnificent baton, I longed to grow up and become a drum major. But I never accomplished either of those boyhood dreams.

In later years my father often said that the reason he resigned from the army was a fear that his boys might become soldiers.

The row of quarters for non-commissioned officers, located behind the enlisted men's barracks, faced east. Our family home was in the house at the south end. Next to us was the drum major and his family. At the extreme north end of the row, near the hospital, was a Chinese laundry. . .

Mail stages went each way between Custer Station and Fort Custer every day. The stages were drawn by four horses, and passengers were carried. If officers had occasion to travel they used an ambulance with four mules to draw it. All of the heavy freighting was done by civilians. They used ox teams, no horses nor mules in that work, as I remember it. Each driver ordinarily had two or three wagons trailing together and drawn by from eight to 14 oxen. . .

There was no school except what might be carried on in short terms by a private teacher. We boys had plenty of play time in both summer and winter. In summer my father often took us down the hillside to paddle in the waters of the Little Big Horn. In winter we had sleds for coasting. Our coasting runs sometimes reached the Big Horn and out upon the ice at the ferry landing. . .

The money transactions there in those times were all in cash, silver or paper money, not much of gold, I think. The paymaster brought money on pay days for all of the soldiers and for all other post indebtedness. The base pay for an enlisted man was $13 a month. . .

I saw one man drummed out of the army – not simply dishonorably discharged, but ignominiously discharged on account of some serious offense. All of the troops at the post were in formation on the parade ground. The culprit was marched along in front of them. Immediately behind him were several soldiers with bayonets fixed and pointing toward him. Then came four drummers beating unison time on their snare drums. After the parade before the troops he was pursued by his compelling escort out from the post and to the Big Horn Ferry.

The Little Big Horn River at that time had its course along the base of the hill at the east side of the post. In later years the railroad workmen changed it to its present course on the opposite side of the valley, in order to avoid bridge building and possible washouts. The present main road, up the gulch to the golf course was at that time a special road, reserved for officers or important guests. The road used by freight wagons and for all other ordinary purposes was along the hillside to the southern part of the post area, where it turned to slope gradually to the top of the bench west of the pump station. . .

Father took our family on one trip to Custer Battlefield, in the summer of 1886, I believe. Two or three other soldiers and their families were with us. We went in army wagons. We started early in the morning and spent an entire long summer day going there, and back. The road then followed the bench southward all the way to Crow Agency, where it turned to the valley and across the Little Big Horn. There were but a few agency buildings and it appeared they were not arranged in any street order, the trader store being located about the middle of where a street might have been. On the battlefield there were no permanent markers, simply a few boards and stakes, and there was *no central monument*.⁶¹ The most notable features were some piles of horse bones, at the largest of which a flag on a staff was set in the midst of the pile.

Father's term of enlistment expired and we left Fort Custer in the early autumn of 1887. . . .

TRUMPETER OLSEN'S RECOLLECTIONS

This short article that appeared in the June 10, 1934, Billings Gazette *reported on the return to Montana of Anton "Kid" Olsen after an absence of forty-six years. A trumpeter at Fort Custer, Olsen relates what the trumpeter's job was like and also comments on the Swordbearer fight.*

. . . I have a picture taken of the 14 trumpeters at the fort in 1887 and I have often wondered what became of them all. McGovern was the chief trumpeter and the others were Penwell,⁶² Lilly, Kraus, McGuire, Lansendorfer, Sheffler, Hicks, Kaiser, Bouten, Deerholt, Oluck, Hinkley and myself.⁶³

You see, each company at the fort had two trum-

---

⁶¹ Charles Kuhlman, writing in his book, *Legend Into History,* quotes information stating that the monument was completed on July 29, *1881.* He states, "Lieutenant Charles Francis Roe, while stationed at Fort Custer, Montana Territory, in the spring and summer of *1881,* February to August 1881, hauled the three large pieces of granite weighing 14,000, 12,000 and 10,000 pounds from the bank of the Big Horn River to the Custer Battlefield and erected the Custer monument where it stands . . ." Schneider's statement that "there was no central monument," (you can hardly overlook 36,000 pounds of stone) is questionable. Pictures taken during the 10th Anniversary of the Custer Fight reveal, however faintly, the present monument.

⁶² Penwell was General Godfrey's orderly at the Custer Fight in 1876.

⁶³ The present editor has seen the picture and it is truly impressive to see the trumpeters in all their finery. The picture, however, is too poor to reproduce.

TRUMPETER KAISER
"Trumpeters were the best dressed men in camp."
Courtesy, Montana Historical Society.

THE MONUMENT ON THE CUSTER BATTLEFIELD
"Lt. Charles F. Roe . . . erected, in the spring and summer of 1881, the Monument where it now stands."
David F. Barry photo. Courtesy, Denver Public Library.

peters. Aside from the officers they were the best dressed men in camp. During the parades, musters and on pay day, the trumpeters would blossom out in full regalia.

Their importance, however, was chiefly confined to the field. Instead of attempting to shout his commands above the pounding of the horses hoofs, the officer of the cavalry would give the orders to the trumpeters and they would blow it. . .

Late in 1887, a medicine man named Swordbearer, alias Wraps-Up-His-Tail, aroused the Crows to take arms against the white man in order to regain their happy hunting grounds. The officers at Fort Custer instructed the Indians to turn Swordbearer over to them and when the red men refused the request, the attack started.

The skirmish was short, however, and the Indians were soon disorganized by the trained forces. Swordbearer was killed as he attempted to escape across the river. That battle was on November 5. . . We lost only one man in the combat.

SARAH THOMPSON'S RECOLLECTIONS

While many stories about the founding and activity of Fort Custer have been told by soldiers formerly stationed at the barracks, Mrs. Sarah Thompson is one of the few who has ever recalled experiences of the women living near the famous cantonment. Although inaccurate in some of the details dealing with the military, her story reflects a way of life that only a woman could relate.

On November 3, 1935, the Billings Gazette *printed the following story in which Mrs. Thompson tells of her arrival at Fort Custer and the highlights of her four years residence near the barracks:*

We arrived at Fort Custer on July 24 [1878] just as the sun was going down behind the barracks. The soldiers were on the parade grounds in drill formation and the band was playing. The sight was beautiful but we were tired after our eight weeks journey and lonesome in this strange wild land that was to be our home.

Our little band was "broke" and we couldn't have turned back toward the east no matter how strong the impulse to do so. Not being able to immediately locate Mr. Thompson's brother, we camped that first night where the Little Horn River and the Big Horn meet.

Crow Indians were camped all around us and we spent a very restless night. Next morning a resident of the fort, who knew we were looking for my husband's brother, informed us that most of the men at the post went by nicknames and he judged from our description that we were looking for a man called Whitehorse Jack.

The man's supposition proved to be right and soon we found Hiram's brother who took us at once to a cabin where we were to live. Fort Custer was attractive and there was a fascination in living in a new and unsettled country but I was afraid of the new surroundings, especially of Indians and strangers.

Our first home was across the river from the fort on the banks of the Big Horn, about where the town of Hardin now stands. . .

Wild game used to roam very close to the house and our meat storeroom always afforded a choice of buffalo, antelope, deer, bear and elk, besides beef and pork. Of the wild game, we greatly preferred buffalo.

I was an inexperienced cook at first, but my brother-in-law, who was an experienced camp cook, soon taught me the manner of cooking food correctly. I prepared meals for the woodchoppers employed by the government as well as put up lunches for their noon day meals.

The stage drivers took their meals at our place and left their horses in our barns. . . Two stages left each day, one for Custer and the other for Junction, each town being a distance of 50 miles from the fort. An overland stage also made our place a resting point. . .

The day in the Thompson homestead started at 4 o'clock in the morning and wasn't finished until 10 or 11 o'clock at night.

There were about 35 families of Crow Indians camped 150 yards from us, the men being scouts who were drawing small salaries from the government. They were extremely proud of their jobs but the bucks were very lazy. On cold days the bucks would not budge from their tepee, the squaws going out after wood to keep the fire going.

After we got settled, we used to charge a dollar a meal, putting everything on the table and letting the diners help themselves. Some of the Indian scouts from the camp near us used to eat with us occasionally and after eating their fill, would get up and go out and send someone else in. This fooled me for a long time as all Indians looked alike to me, but I finally caught on to their trick of feeding several for the price of one and put a stop to it. . .

The army paymaster visited Fort Custer only once every three months, paying off the soldiers and officers in gold and silver. Frequently the amount due the Thompson family from the garrison would be so heavy that I could not carry it home.

THE STEAMER "BATCHELOR" AT THE MOUTH OF THE YELLOWSTONE RIVER
"Our main supplies came up the river on the boat 'Batchelor'."
Stanley J. Morrow photo. Courtesy, W. H. Over Dakota Museum,
University of South Dakota, Vermillion.

THE LIVERY STABLE AT FORT CUSTER
"The day started at 4 a.m. and wasn't finished
until 10 or 11 o'clock at night."
Courtesy, Billings Public Library.

Our main supplies came up the river on the boat "Bachelor," which unloaded on the banks of the Big Horn close to our cabin. It was an exciting day when the boat arrived with the supplies for the fort and people dropped whatever work they were doing to watch the unloading. Often hams and bacon would be taken off the boat and piled on the ground in stacks 20 feet high. . .

The woodcutters and sawmill men at the fort were employed by the government and were not allowed to take or sell any of the lumber which they turned out. But occasionally some boards would slip away from them into the river and our men folks would get them as they floated by. From these boards we made a table or chair or whatever we needed in the way of furniture at that time. . .

From the butcher shop just across the river we could buy meat if there was any left after the post had been supplied.

We had to create all our amusement. Sometimes we would have a dance, one of the men playing the violin. There were many men, but few women to dance with them. The fall hunt for the winter's meat supply always was looked forward to.

At night we could always hear taps, and reveille in the morning. The soldiers were certainly a source of comfort to us, in view of the fact that many hostile Indians were still roaming Montana.

One cold day when the snow was blowing and drifting, the stage driver did not arrive on schedule. Next morning two men started for the stage station to inquire for him, but could not get through the storm. So Mr. Thompson finally put on snowshoes and went, ascertaining that the driver had left on schedule the previous day.

There was no doubt in anyone's mind but what he had frozen to death but later that day I noticed him drive up to our house on horseback and stand on the protected side of the building. After waiting awhile for him to come in, I went out and found him unconscious and tied in the saddle.

I pried him off the saddle, got him into the house and packed him in snow. I then searched through the bunkhouses and found a bottle of whisky for him. He later jokingly claimed that I kept him drunk until he got well. He remained with us, slowly convalescing for two months, after which he spent over eight months in the post hospital.

There were a couple of gardens near us, one at Fort Custer and one about three miles distant, the produce used almost exclusively for the soldiers and officers, but we managed to secure all the fresh vegetables we needed in season.

Money was easy to get in those days and equally easy to spend. There was no bank that civilians could use and we had to keep our money in sacks and cans underneath the floor of our cabin. I was cashier and the "bank" could be used by anyone who would furnish a can with his name written on it. Very often thousands of dollars were in these containers beneath the floor. Forty-five men besides ourselves took advantage of this novel way of storing money. . .

The freight outfits, along with an occasional trip up the Big Horn River by the steamboat "Josephine," hauled most of the freight for the post until the railroad came through.

General Hatch, who followed Davies [64] in command at Fort Custer, along with Mrs. Hatch was always very kind to me. According to army regulations at that time, soldiers were not allowed to associate with civilians, but frequently on leisurely horseback rides, the general and his wife would stop at our place for a meal. They were particularly fond of my sourdough bread.

Failing health compelled General Hatch to return before he had been long at the fort. He died two years later and was taken to West Point to be laid at rest. General Davies [Davidson] had stepped in a prairie dog hole and broke his leg, from which injury he never recovered, dying a few months later.[65]

We lived near Fort Custer for four years, 1878 to 1882, when we moved to Coulson.

There is very little at the present time to indicate the former location of Fort Custer, there being only a small marker placed there by the D.A.R.[66]

---

[64] Colonel John Wynn Davidson. Davidson was another of Fort Custer's commanders that distinguished himself in battle. During the Mexican War, Davidson served with Stephen Watts Kearney and Kit Carson in the Army of the West. Davidson served at Fort Tejon in California (near Bakersfield). During the Civil War he participated in the Virginia Peninsula Campaign with the Army of the Potomac. The action at Bayou Meto, which led to the capture of Little Rock prompted his promotion to General.

[65] An interview with Captain H. K. Davidson U.S.N., Ret., Colonel Davidson's grandson, revealed that on the 7th of February 1881, an officer had reported that the beef was fed on refuse forage from the stables, and he went, accompanied by Lieutenant Hoppin (his son-in-law) of the commissary, down to inspect the forage, and it being an intensely cold day, the horses were very restless, and the horse upon which General Davidson was riding gave a sudden spring and turned a somersault, precipitating him over an embankment twenty feet deep, which was covered with snow. The saddle struck him in the side and stomach, breaking two of his ribs, right side, which the doctors say caused cancer of the stomach, from the effects of which he died on June 26, 1881, at the Merchants Hotel in St. Paul, Minn.

[66] Daughters of the American Revolution.

THE MARKER AT THE SITE OF
FORT CUSTER PARADE GROUND
Maj. E. S. Luce photo.
Courtesy, Custer Battlefield Museum.

DENNY BURNS
FORT CUSTER FORAGE MASTER
". . . Col. Davidson went
down to inspect the
forage . . ."
Courtesy, Montana Historical Society.

Fort Custer was at one time valued at a million dollars. There was water in every building and many modern conveniences. About half a mile south of the fort was a cemetery where soldiers and civilians alike were buried. When the fort was abandoned all buried there were moved to the National Cemetery which now commemorates the scene of Custer's last fight.

EPILOGUE

The Search for
Fort Custer
1959–1971

The Search for Fort Custer

The road leading to what was once the finest cavalry post in the world is not marked.

The travelers, most likely either going to or coming from the Custer Battlefield, will not notice the narrow winding gravel road leading to the plateau that overlooks the junction of the Big Horn and Little Big Horn rivers.

Unless you have more than a passing interest in this area that is so rich in history, your car will flash by this road like it has a hundred other roads along your journey.

You are lucky if you are traveling with someone who at one time long ago lived at Fort Custer. I was lucky! My passenger, that typically hot July day in 1959 in Montana was Lillian Klenck Maynard, the daughter of Henry Carl Klenck, former Fort Custer soldier. Mr. Klenck's adventures challenge those of the legendary Jack Crabb and are recounted elsewhere in this book. (See Appendix D)

After leaving Hardin, Montana, traveling south on Highway 87, we crossed the bridge that spans the Big Horn River. Mrs. Maynard gently suggested that if we would turn right at the first road on the other side of the bridge and follow it to the top of the bluffs we would find the site of old Fort Custer, the place where she lived for three years as a child during the 1890s.

We sensed the excitement in Mrs. Maynard as we reached what used to be the parade ground and listened attentively as she described what she remembered of the old fort that she left almost sixty-five years before.

All that remained was a granite marker that the D.A.R. placed on the site back in 1930, depressions in the ground where various structures once stood, hundreds of square nails and the fading memories of the few remaining alumni of the grand old fort.

The site of the fort has been used as a golf course, an airport, and now is used periodically to graze cattle. The parade ground has never been plowed and with a map, it is quite easy to locate the site of most of the buildings that encircled it. Aerial photographs, taken in the spring, reveal, clearly, the outline of the parade ground and vicinity.

Who knows, for sure, what thoughts were in Mrs. Maynard's mind as we retraced our route back to the main highway – her for the last time, me for the first?

I felt a certain responsibility to her and to the others who spent portions of their lives at Fort Custer, to find out more about this forgotten spot.

References to Fort Custer are found in almost all books written about the Yellowstone Valley and its history; however, it almost invariably is a single statement of fact with reference to two forts which were constructed in 1877 and were called Big Horn Post #1, later Fort Keogh, and Big Horn Post #2 that was to become Fort Custer.

AERIAL VIEW OF THE SITE OF FORT CUSTER
The Little Big Horn joins the Big Horn River at lower right. At center left the parade ground outline shows, and depressions where many buildings once stood.
Courtesy, U.S. Department of Agriculture.

Aside from this casual reference the reader will be hard pressed to find much more on the subject. It seemed, for awhile, that the anonymous Fort Custer soldier was correct when he wrote,

> Like mimic shadows on a toyman's blind,
> We come and go, nor leave a trace behind.

Letters to various public and private institutions produced a collection of impressive pictures, proving that unlike the "mimic shadows on a toyman's blind," many photographers captured the shadows of the fort on film and left more than enough traces for the author to begin his search for old Fort Custer.

We discovered, in Hardin, Montana, Fred Weltner, who has a marvelous gun collection and is active, through the Big Horn County Historical Society, in preserving and recording the history of the area.

Return visits to the fort site were sometimes accompanied by Mr. Weltner. He provided many interesting sidelights that made each visit more exciting and meaningful.

He would find tiny Indian beads in the anthills and describe how the Indian women would do their beadwork as they watched the cavalry drill, and how, occasionally, a bead would fall to the ground only to be transported by some enterprising ant and become part of an anthill that survived the old fort.

Some actual buildings from the fort still exist, some intact and others as parts of new structures. The old fort's guardhouse was moved to Crow Agency where it rests today. The superintendent's home at Crow Agency is built from the bricks from Fort Custer.

A thrilling moment of my search for the story of

Fort Custer came while visiting a long time friend then living at Fort Smith, Montana. John Dracon (former Custer Battlefield seasonal ranger and now the administrator of a large federal project in progress on various Indian reservations of the area) casually asked if we would like to visit his friends, John and Dolly Lind, who live in a building that was formerly an officer's quarters at Fort Custer. Of course, we replied in the affirmative and proceeded to the nearby Lind residence.

John Lind proved to be informed on the local history that included such events and places as old Fort C.F. Smith, the Hayfield Fight, the Father De Smet tree and the Bozeman Trail. Mr. Lind's house was obviously a military structure with the only change from its Fort Custer days being the addition of electricity and plumbing.

The thick walls, the stairway paneling from the old steamboats, the old clock on the wall – it seemed authentic in every detail.

Mr. Lind purchased the house after World War II from some Indians who complained of ghosts being upstairs in one of the bedrooms. The Indians would not occupy that particular bedroom, and bullet holes in the ceiling indicate that other solutions were tried to rid the building of these unseen visitors.

Unexplained is how the building was transported the forty miles south to Fort Smith from Fort Custer. The architecture of the building suggests that it could not have been moved in sections. It was suggested that it may have been floated on the nearby Big Horn River. This is unlikely because the current runs the other way. One plausible explanation is that it was moved during the winter using various types of sleds. Whatever the answer, the building provided an interesting side light to the story of the fort.

A letter from Roy Marsh, owner of a truly impressive Indian museum in Pryor, Montana, informed me that, while in the course of remodeling the great Crow Chief Plenty Coups' home, it was necessary to dismantle the late chief's barn. Mr. Marsh knew that wood from old Fort Custer was used to make the barn many years ago. He saved some pieces for me and when I arrived in Pryor, Roy pointed out how the wood was sawed with an old circle saw by soldiers at the fort. Perhaps, as mentioned in Appendix A, this wood was originally used as a lodge pole in the Indian camp at the Custer Fight in 1876, before it became part of the fort.

The Fort Custer quest was not without its humorous moments. One time, while in Pryor, it was our good fortune to meet Plainfeather, the last of the old-time Crow Indians. Plainfeather was said to be about 107 years old at that time. We were saddened to learn of his death the following winter. In the Pryor General Store, with a young Crow girl as interpreter, we attempted to communicate with this representative of another age.

Even though the old warrior was stooped over and rested on his cane, we had to look up to see his face. He was dressed in typical reservation Crow fashion with his white shirt buttoned to the top and a black broad brimmed hat decorated only by a single white feather. His deeply lined, leather-like face revealed the weathering of 107 bitter cold winters and 107 blazing hot summers.

Our interpreter passed on our first question: "Plainfeather, they want to know what it was like when you were young." For fully ten minutes the old gentleman talked in the Crow language, accented by vigorous sign language symbols at what seemed to be the important points that he wished to stress.

We congratulated ourselves at this anthropological breakthrough. Imagine – two cultures, two eras meeting in the Pryor, Montana, General Store.

"What did he say? What did he say?" we asked, as Plainfeather finished speaking. Our young interpreter did not translate his answer. Finally she spoke.

"Plainfeather is ordering his groceries," she said, "he'll answer your questions later."

Whenever I start to take myself too seriously I try to remember my "interview" with Plainfeather in Pryor.

When Henry Carl Klenck was discharged from the 1st Cavalry in 1892, he stayed at Fort Custer in the quartermaster's department until the fort was abandoned in 1898. With the closing of the post, Mr. Klenck homesteaded a large farm on the Yellowstone River near Billings, Montana.

Henry Klenck died in February of 1935, but two of his six children, Mabel and May, are still living at the old Klenck farm. Lillian, Philip, Margaret and Frances have passed on. Mabel and Philip Klenck were both born at Fort Custer and we know that Lillian, while not born there, lived there as a child.

The farm has been reduced considerably in size as portions were sold from time to time to pay taxes and because it became too large for the children to handle.

The Klenck farm is located, appropriately enough,

MABEL KLENCK NELSON
At the site of the Post Hospital where she was born.
A photo in 1971.
From the author's collection.

LILLIAN KLENCK MAYNARD
A photo in 1914.
Courtesy, May Klenck and Mabel Klenck Nelson, Billings, Montana.

on Klenck Lane just outside Billings, Montana, in an area referred to by the citizens as Lockwood Flats.

In the summer of 1970, my wife Frances, a granddaughter of the old soldier, received an invitation from Mabel and May Klenck to come to dinner at the farm.

Everything that was consumed for dinner, that warm Montana evening, was raised or grown right there on the farm. As we sat outside amidst the old farm buildings we noticed the machinery, the men's work clothes and horses' riggings were in place as if waiting for Mr. Klenck and his son Philip to enter at any moment to begin labor in the fields. We talked about the old fort and its influence on the people gathered there that evening.

For that one short time things were as they once were. As at the fort in the 1880s and '90s, people were drawn together because of a desire to know each other better. Television was turned off and we gathered around the piano and sang songs that the Klenck family had not sung in sixty years; songs of old Fort Custer. It was that evening that the search for Fort Custer became something warm and personal, rather than just frozen images on film and paper.

I found Fort Custer. Not just the facts, but the feelings of the historic post.

Hank Maynard, grandson of Henry C. Klenck, First Cavalry, occasionally drives up atop the bluffs to the site of the old fort and stands in the quietness of the late afternoon while the heat of the day rises and turns the sunset into a golden spectacle. Hank says, "I can almost hear the strident call of the bugle that signals the cavalrymen to mount their horses, the silence is broken as the horses snort the dust from their nostrils. All eight companies are formed, Mr. Walker's band is mounted and is poised, ready to begin playing. In crisp military tones, the command is given. Pass in review!"

It's what you bring to something or someplace that makes the experience more meaningful.

Appendices

APPENDIX A

Fort Custer, Montana[67]

A United States military post, not fortified, located on the right bank of the Big Horn River, on a level plateau about 200 feet above the river, about one mile and a half above its junction with the Little Big Horn River, and about 222 east of Bozeman, Montana. Baker's battle-field on the Yellowstone, 48 miles distant.

HISTORY – Lieutenant General Philip H. Sheridan and Brigadier General Alfred H. Terry, United States Army, having in their reports to the Secretary of War for the year 1875, set forth the great importance and immediate necessity of the construction of military posts at certain points on the Yellowstone and Musselshell rivers, in Montana Territory, and in the Department of Dakota; the Secretary of War transmitted the same to Congress with his approval.

By act of Congress approved July 22, 1876, the sum of two hundred thousand dollars, or so much thereof as might be necessary, was appropriated for the construction of such military posts or depots, at such points as might be selected by the Secretary of War. Announced in General Orders, No. 65, Headquarters of the Army, Adjutant General's Office, July 22, 1876.

In accordance with the provisions of the above Act, the military authorities selected a suitable site on the east bank of the Big Horn River, about one mile and a half above its junction with the Little Horn River, to replace one of the posts previously dismantled in that region; a post was established thereon on July 4, 1877, by Company F, and detachments of the Eleventh Infantry, under the command of [Brevet] Brigadier General George P. Buell, Lieutenant Colonel, Eleventh Infantry, in compliance with Special Orders, No. 57, Headquarters Department of Dakota, May 10, 1877, and designated as "Post No. 2, Big Horn River."

---

[67] National Archives, Record Group 94.

The troops with a large number of mechanics, were set at work to construct the necessary buildings for the accommodation of the troops to constitute the garrison. The next day Lieutenant Colonel Michael V. Sheridan, Aide-de-Camp to the Lieutenant General of the Army, with Troop I, Seventh Cavalry as an escort, arrived at the post from the Custer Battlefield, with the remains of the officers killed in action June 25, 1876, and left with his charge en route to Bismarck, Dakota Territory, on July 7.

During the month of July the garrison was further strengthened by the arrival of companies B and C, Eleventh Infantry. The arrival of these troops made considerable difference in the building operations then being carried on at the post, and with their additional labor vigorous efforts were made to complete sufficient accommodations to shelter the garrison before the approaching winter should set in, which are generally very severe in this region.

General W. T. Sherman, Lieutenant General Philip H. Sheridan, and Brigadier General George Crook, accompanied by their staffs, and with suitable escorts arrived at the post during July; they were received with the usual honors and after a brief visit of one day departed for Bismarck. In August of this year Lieutenant General Sheridan, then commanding the Military Division of the Missouri, reported the following particulars regarding the construction of the "Post on the Big Horn River":

"General Buell has 100 mechanics at work, and expects 100 more; his three companies of infantry are assisting in the building operations. Two thousand cottonwood logs had been cut for projected buildings and the survey has been made. General Buell is determined to preserve the timber in the vicinity of the post, and has accordingly forbidden the cutting of timber within a radius of eight miles. The lodge poles left by the Sioux when they fled so precipitately after the fight with Custer, are being utilized in the construction of the barracks."

September 30, of the same year, Headquarters and Troops M, C, D and K, of the Second Cavalry, arrived from the Department of the Platte and took post. Before the close of the year, two double sets and one single set of infantry barracks, two double sets of cavalry barracks, band quarters, three storehouses, four cavalry stables, bakery, post headquarters, commanding officer's quarters, seven double sets of laundresses' quarters were completed and were at once occupied by the troops.

The designation of the post was changed to Fort Custer, pursuant to General Orders, No. 101, Headquarters of the Army, Adjutant General's Office, November 8, 1877, in honor to the memory of Brevet Major General George A. Custer, Lieutenant Colonel Seventh Cavalry, killed in action against hostile Sioux Indians in Montana Territory, on June 25, 1876.

. . . The allotment of one hundred thousand dollars authorized for the construction of the post, and ten thousand dollars for the erection of a hospital, from the sum of two hundred thousand dollars, appropriated by Act of Congress approved July 22, 1876, was expended by August 1878.

During 1891 one set of field officers' quarters, constructed of brick, and one set for Indian married soldiers, of frame, were completed.

The occupation of Fort Custer, Montana, has been continuous from its establishment. . . . The field artillery of the post consists of one 12-pounder brass Napoleon gun, two mountain Hotchkiss guns, one Gatling gun, and two 3-inch rifles; and present garrison of the headquarters and Troops A, B, E and G, Tenth Cavalry, Troop L, First Cavalry, and Companies A and D, Twenty-fifth Infantry, under the command of a field officer.

The Tenth Cavalry, the famous "Buffalo Soldiers," came to Fort Custer on May 5, 1892, after serving faithfully and well in the hot southwestern deserts.

The Tenth occupied the fort until the post was abandoned in April of 1898. The most serious troubles that the Tenth was involved in was with Coxey's Army and the American Railroad Strike, both in 1894.

With the advent of the Spanish-American War in 1898, the Tenth Cavalry was sent to Cuba where they distinguished themselves once again.

The post was abandoned at 4:30 P.M. on April 17, 1898. In 1903, 250 Crow Indians under the direction of the Crow Indian Agent at Crow Agency, Montana, began dismantling the old fort. It took them three years until 1906 to complete the job.

COMMUNICATION – Post office and telegraph station at the post daily mail. Nearest railway point, Custer Station on the Northern Pacific Railway, 29 miles distant. Daily stage and mail from Custer Station. The stage and mail route (tri-weekly) continues on to Rock Creek on the Union Pacific Railway. Stage and wagon roads to Custer Station and to Crow Indian Agency, 11 miles south, on Little Big Horn River, are passable at all seasons. The following are the distances from Fort Custer to the principal points of travel: Custer Station, on the Northern Pacific Railway, 29 miles; Billings, on same railway, 43 miles; Junction City, on the Yellowstone, opposite Terry's Landing, 30 miles; Dillon, Montana, on Utah and Northern Division Union Pacific Railway, via Custer Station and Bozeman, 365 miles; Bozeman, Montana, via Custer Station, 222 miles; same via Billings, 183 miles, (Bozeman Station, on the Northern Pacific Railway, to Fort Ellis, 2 miles); Helena, Montana, via Billings, 287 miles; Fort Maginnis, via Junction City, 140 miles; Benton, Montana, via Junction City, Fort Maginnis and road south of the Missouri River, 262 miles; Fort Keogh, Montana, via Custer Station, 121 miles; Bismarck, North Dakota, 422 miles; and Rock Creek, on Union Pacific Railway, 343 miles.

SUPPLIES – Quartermaster and subsistence stores are received from all supplying depots of the army, by rail at Custer Station, Montana, thence by contract wagons to the post. Water is pumped by steam engine from the Little Big Horn River, into a tank on the bluff near the post from which it is distributed by a system of iron pipes. Forage is furnished by contract. Up to the beginning of the year 1888, well-seasoned cottonwood of good quality was furnished, since that time pine has been furnished which is obtained about 16 miles from the post, being inferior to the cottonwood both in heating qualities and cleanliness. Six months' subsistence is kept on hand. The fall of the year is considered the best season for sending supplies to the post.

DESCRIPTION OF COUNTRY – The surrounding country is a rolling prairie, interspersed by the fertile valleys of the Big Horn and Little Horn Rivers and other streams. To the east and on the right banks of the Big Horn and Little Big Horn River, the country is very rugged; and to the west, on the left bank of the Big Horn River, it is a gradually-sloping and well-grassed prairie. Spurs of the Big Horn Mountains extend to near the southern and eastern boundaries of the reservation. They are the Big and Little Big Horn and Tallock's [Tullock's] Fork divides.

The Big Horn River runs west of the post from south to north and the Little Big Horn River is on the northeast side, making its junction with the Big Horn River north of the post. The Big Horn River cannot be forded from May to August inclusive, but the Little Big Horn River is fordable all the year round, except in the latter part of June and the beginning of July.

The soil of the river and creek bottoms is very productive; the post gardens have an area of forty acres under excellent cultivation, and yield good crops of all kinds of vegetables. The barren prairie land is covered with light, short and nutritious grass interspersed on the tablelands with prickly pear and sage. Excellent and abundant grazing is afforded to domestic animals.

Timber is found only in the river bottoms, and is mainly cottonwood; a few pines are found to the northeast and northwest, within ten miles, but not sufficient for any practical purposes. An abundance of pine grows on Pine Ridge, about twenty miles from the post, but not within the boundaries of the reservation.

There is a government sawmill at Bull Mountain, 25 miles northwest of the post, at which timber is sawed for use in construction and completion of buildings.

A very extensive deposit of coal has been discovered in the Wolf Mountains, a spur of the Big Horn range, six miles from the Little Big Horn River, 21 miles from the Crow Agency, and 32 miles from Fort Custer. This coal after a sufficient test has been pronounced excellent, being free from sulphur and a good welding fuel.

The only kind of stone found in the vicinity is sandstone, at a distance of five miles; it is slaty and not good for building purposes.

The annual mean temperature, 47; summer mean temperature, 70.2; and winter mean temperature, 25.8. Winters are very severe. The prevailing wind is from the southeast from July to September. The average monthly rainfall and melted snow, 1.64 inches. There are no malarial diseases, and the locality is very healthy.

No settlements are nearer than those in the Yellowstone Valley, and they are rapidly increasing. Junction City, about thirty-three miles distant, is the nearest settlement. There is a Justice of the Peace at the post and the nearest civil court is at Billings, Montana, 50 miles distant by wagon road. The post is considered healthy and its sanitary condition good.

RESERVATION - General Orders Nos. 1 and 2. Post No. 2, Big Horn River, Montana Territory, announced a post reservation 20 miles square at old Fort Smith, Montana Territory, and one 2 miles square, called the Limestone reservation; and by General Orders No. 78, Headquarters of the Army, Adjutant General's Office, August 1, 1879, the ground known as the Custer Battlefield, was announced as a National Cemetery of the fourth class. These orders were preliminary to a survey and declaration in due form by Executive Order.

By the President's Order, dated December 7, 1886, and announced in General Orders, No. 90, Headquarters of the Army, Adjutant General's Office, December 15, 1886, the following described tracts of land in the Territory of Montana, embraced within the limits of the Crow Indian Reservation created by treaty dated May 7, 1868; Executive Orders, dated, respectively, October 20, 1875, and March 8, 1876; and act of Congress approved July 10, 1882, were proclaimed military reservations in connection with the post of Fort Custer, viz:

1. Post Reservation. "Commencing at the center stone of the parade-ground of Fort Custer, Montana Territory, and running thence due south three (3) miles to the place of beginning on the southern boundary; thence due east three (3) miles; thence due north six (6) miles; thence due west six (6) miles; thence due south six (6) miles; thence due east three (3) miles to the place of beginning. Area, 36 square miles."

2. National Cemetery of Custer's Battlefield Reservation. "Commencing at a point 1,200 feet north 35 west of Custer's monument, and running thence north 55 east 1,200 feet; thence south 35 east one (1) miles; thence south 55 west to the right bank of the Little Big Horn River; thence along said right bank to the prolongation of the western boundary; thence along said prolongation to the place of beginning. Area, 1 square mile."

3. Limestone Reservation near old Fort C.F. Smith, Montana Territory. "Commencing at a point 1,772 feet due north and 700 feet due east of the site of the flag staff of the old post of Fort C. F. Smith, and running thence due south one (1) mile and 5,206 feet; thence due west two (2) miles; thence due north one (1) mile and 4,470 feet to midstream of the Big Horn River; thence down said mid-stream to its intersection with the prolongation of the eastern boundary; thence along said prolongation to the place of beginning. Area, 3.48 square miles." Total area, 40.48 square miles.

Provision was made that certain Indian families, about thirteen (13) in number, who have received allotments of land within the limits of the Post Reservation (No. 1) "Shall not be disturbed, but shall be allowed to remain where they are now located, and to retain their present allotments of land, and be permitted the free and unrestricted enjoyment thereof, unless they shall voluntarily release or abandon the same."

Act of Congress approved February 23, 1889, granted a right of way to the Big Horn Southern Railroad Company, across the Fort Custer Military Reservation upon such a line, in the vicinity of the Big Horn and Little Big Horn Rivers, as might be approved by the Secretary of War; Provided, That the said right of way granted should not exceed one hundred feet in width, except where side-tracks, spurs, turn-tables, and station are located or to be located; and at such point the right of way should not exceed two hundred feet on each side of the main track and not exceeding two thousand feet in length.

JURISDICTION. Cession by the Constitution of Montana.

BUILDINGS.[68] From report of annual inspection of public buildings at Fort Custer, Montana, on March 31, 1892.

No. 6. Commanding Officer's Quarters, frame, single set, 1½ stories, size 42 by 36 feet, four rooms on each floor; "L" to same embracing kitchen, pantry, closets, with attic chamber; size 20 by 16 feet. Porch in front.

No. 1 to 5, and 7 to 11. Officers' Quarters, frame, ten double sets 1½ stories, size 48 feet by 46 feet 6 inches, six rooms on first and 4 rooms on second floor; "L" to same, size 34 by 14 feet, embracing two kitchens, with pantries, closets and attic chambers. Porch in front.

No. 12. Officers' Quarters, frame, single set, one story; size 44 feet 6 inches by 14 feet 6 inches, four rooms; 2 "L"s to same, size 14 by 12 feet and 16 by 12 feet respectively, one room each. Porch in front.

No. 13.** Officers' Mess, frame, single set, one story, size 61 by 16 feet, three rooms; 4 "L"s containing one room each, 16 by 9, 16 by 10, 16 by 18 and 16 by 18 feet respectively. Porch in front.

No. 14.** Officers' Club, frame, single set, one story, size 42 by 25 feet, three rooms with addition 20 by 16 feet, one room. Porch in front.

No. 15.* Headquarters Building, offices, frame, 1 story, 42 by 38 feet, four rooms; 2 "L"s, one room each, 18 by 15 feet, and addition 15 by 12 feet, one room.

No. 16. Guardhouse, frame, one story, 70 by 26 feet, three rooms; "L", 30 by 15 feet, four cells. Porch in front.

No. 17. Band Quarters, frame, one story, 80 by 20 feet, one squad room, and two small store rooms; 2 "L"s, 26 by 16 and

---

[68] The accompanying plat of the fort is based on the "Inspection of Public Buildings, 1892, at Fort Custer" in the National Archives. Plats were also available for July 1, 1878 (courtesy of Floyd Warren of Hardin, Mont.); for March 1883 (courtesy of Custer Battlefield Museum); and for Aug. 31, 1889 (courtesy of Montana Historical Society). A comparison of these plats indicates approximate dates of construction of some of the buildings. These are believed to be as indicated thus in the above tabulation: *built after 1878; **built after 1883; ***built after 1889. No date determination was possible for building nos. 16, 33, 34, 43, 63, 64, 65, 66, 80, 92, and 101. Buildings nos. 30, 31, 73, 84, and 87, or others in their locations, apparently changed usage over the years and are difficult to identify as to construction dates.

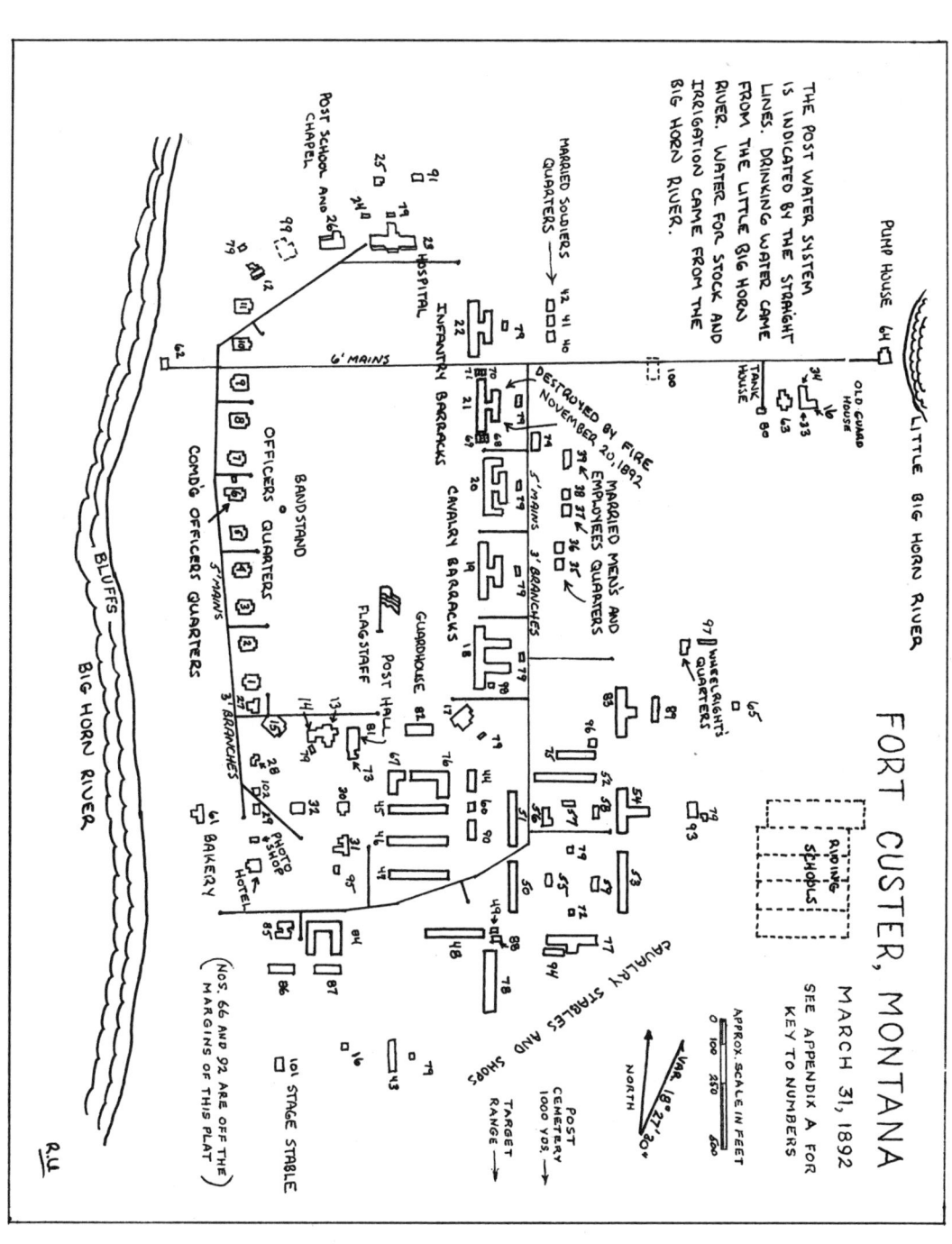

40 by 16 respectively, embracing non-commissioned officers' room, store room and dining room, with two additions, 26 by 16 and 25 by 22 feet respectively, kitchen and practice room. Porch in front.

No. 18. Cavalry Barracks, frame double set, one story, 230 by 30 feet, two squad rooms, orderly rooms and storerooms; 2 "L"'s, 100 by 30 feet, embracing two kitchens, mess halls, wash rooms, and additional squad rooms. Porch in front; cellar under each kitchen, 30 by 28 feet.

No. 19. Double Barracks, used as the Post Exchange, frame, one story, 232 by 25 feet, contains library, billiard room, card room, canteen and gymnasium. Back building, 126 by 24 feet, kitchen, storeroom and saloon, connected with main building by hall, 25 by 18 feet. Porch on front.

No. 20. Barracks, frame, double set, one story, 232 by 25 feet squad rooms, orderly rooms and storerooms, with two additions, 25 by 40 feet, additional squad room; and back building, 126 by 24 feet, contains mess halls, kitchen and storerooms connected with main building by hall 25 by 18 feet. Porch in front.

No. 21. Barracks, frame, double set, one story, 232 by 25 feet, squad rooms, orderly rooms, and storerooms; back building, 126 by 24 feet, contains mess halls, kitchens, storerooms and cooks' rooms connected with main building by hall 25 by 18 feet. Porch in front.

No. 22. Barracks, frame, double set, one story, same as No. 21.

No. 23. Post Hospital, frame, regulation; two wards of 12 beds each.

No. 24.* Dead House, frame, 27 feet 6 inches by 13 feet 6 inches.

No. 25. Quarters for Hospital Steward, frame, 30 by 18 feet, three rooms and kitchen.

No. 26. Post School and Chapel, frame, one story, 90 by 31 feet, comprising school room and chapel; addition to same, 14 by 10 feet, janitor's room.

No. 27.** Officers' Quarters, frame, single set, 42 by 16 feet, two rooms; addition 29 by 12 feet, two rooms. Porch in front.

No. 28.** Quarters for Non-Commissioned Staff Officers, frame single set, one story, 42 by 26 feet, three rooms and kitchen. Porch in front.

No. 29.** Quarters for Non-Commissioned Staff Officers, frame, single set, one story, 42 by 26 feet, three rooms and kitchen. Porch in front.

No. 30. Quarters for Non-Commissioned Staff Officers, frame, single set, one story, 30 by 18 feet, three rooms and kitchen. Porch in front.

No. 31. Quarters for Non-Commissioned Staff Officers, frame, double set, 47 by 19 feet, four rooms each; with two additions of one room each, 20 by 14 and 17 by 14 feet respectively. Porch in front.

No. 32.** Telegraph Office and Mechanics Shops, frame, 53 by 39 feet, six rooms. Porch in front.

No. 33. Blacksmith's and Wheelwright's Shops, frame, 60 by 25 feet, two rooms.

No. 34. Carpenter's Shop, frame, one story, 40 by 25 feet, one room.

No. 35 to 42. Quarters for Civilian employees, Hospital Matrons, Married Soldiers, frame, eight double sets, 40 by 16 feet, two rooms, additions, 28 by 11 feet.

No. 43. Quarters for Teamsters and Mess, log, one story, 113 by 24 feet, four rooms and kitchen.

No. 44.** Veterinary Hospital, frame, one story, 100 by 25 feet, contains 4 single stalls, 4 box stalls, dispensary and attendants' room.

No. 45. Old Quartermaster Storehouse, Clothing and Equipage, frame, one story, 215 by 25 feet, with cellar 65 by 25 feet.

No. 46. Old quartermaster Storehouse, Quartermaster's Stores, frame, one story, 215 by 25 feet, office and storage.

No. 47. Granary, frame, one story, 215 by 25 feet, storage with lean-to open wagon shed, 215 by 14 feet.

No. 48. Old Quartermaster Stables, frame, one story, 200 by 28 feet, capacity for 100 animals.

No. 49.** Quarters for Train Master, frame, one story, 16 by 12 feet, one room.

No. 50.* Cavalry Stables, frame, one story, 200 by 28 feet, with saddle room, grain room, tool room and farrier's room. Capacity for 60 animals.

No. 51.* Cavalry Stables, frame, one story, 205 by 31 feet, with saddle room, grain room, tool room and farrier's room. Capacity for 65 animals.

No. 52. Cavalry Stables, frame, one story, 207 feet 6 inches by 30 feet, with saddle room, grain room, tool room, and farrier's room. Capacity for 65 animals.

No. 53. Cavalry Stables, frame, one story, 230 by 32 feet, with saddle room, grain room, tool room, and farrier's room. Capacity for 66 animals.

No. 54. Cavalry Stables, frame, one story, 180 by 32 feet, with "L" 90 feet by 32 feet 6 inches, with saddle room. Capacity for 65 animals.

No. 55 to 59.** Troop Blacksmith's and Saddler's Shops, frame one story, 44 by 16, 36 by 16, 74 by 16, 48 by 32, and 60 by 32 feet respectively.

No. 60. Butcher's Shop, frame, one story, 16 by 16 feet.

No. 61. Post Bakery, frame, one story, 61 by 22 feet, contains 2 brick ovens, capacity 500 rations; L to same, 22 by 18 feet, contains proof rooms, and room for bakers.

No. 62, Old Tank House, frame, 20 by 20 feet, 40 feet high. Capacity 21,000 gallons.

No. 63. Steam Planing Mill, frame, one story, 36 by 36 feet; with additions 20 by 16 feet, and 10 by 10 feet respectively.

No. 64. Pump House, frame, one story, 32 by 14 feet, 2-25 Horse Power Boiler, and one Blake's Steam Pump No. 10. Ample capacity.

No. 65. Lime House, frame, one story, 18 by 18 feet.

No. 66. Magazine, brick, one story, 20 by 20 feet [not shown on plat].

No. 67.** Ordnance Building and Gun Shed, frame, 70 by 30 feet, contains office, ordnance sergeant's rooms; "L," gun shed, 30 by 30 feet, storage.

Nos. 68 to 72.** Stable Guardhouses, frame, five single sets one story, 18 by 16 feet, one room each.

No. 73. Old officer of the Guards Room, frame, one story, 18 by 16 feet. Porch in front.

No. 74.** Bath House, frame, one story, 72 by 26 feet, contains 15 bath tubs, supplied with hot and cold water.

No. 75.** Headquarters Stables, frame, one story, 150 by 52 feet, with saddle and grain rooms. Capacity for 50 animals.

No. 76.* Commissary Storehouse, brick, one story, 138 by 28 feet, has office issue room and storage; cellar under whole, L to same, 80 by 28 feet, storage.

APPENDIX A

No. 77. New Cavalry Stable, frame, one story, 190 by 32 feet with "L," 40 by 32 feet, with saddle, grain, tool and storerooms. Capacity for 68 animals.

No. 78.*** New Quartermaster's Stable, frame, one story, 225 by 24 feet. Capacity for 100 animals.

No. 79. Dry Earth Closets [approx. 12 locations].

No. 80. New Tank House.

No. 81. New Post Hall, frame, 100 by 40 feet.

No. 82. New Guardhouse, brick, 100 by 38 feet.

No. 83.*** New Cavalry Stables, frame, one story, 190 by 35 feet. Capacity for 60 animals.

No. 84. New Quartermaster's Storehouse, frame, one story, with 2 L's.

No. 85.** New Non-Commissioned Staff quarters, frame with L.

No. 86.** Quartermaster's Warehouse, West, log, 100 by 25 feet.

No. 87. Quartermaster's Warehouse, East, log, 100 by 25 feet.

No. 88.*** Post Saddler's Shop, frame, 30 by 25 feet.

No. 89.*** Troop Blacksmith's and Saddler's Shops, frame, one story, 100 by 20 feet.

No. 90.** Coal Shed, frame, one story, 100 by 20 feet.

No. 91.*** Hospital Stable, frame, 40 by 20 feet; capacity for four animals.

No. 92. Range House, frame, 20 by 20 feet [not shown on plat].

No. 93.** Quartermaster's Civilian Employees Quarters, frame, 60 by 25 feet.

No. 94.*** Wagon Shed, frame, 100 by 15 feet.

No. 95.*** Quarters for Civilian Employees, frame, 25 by 15 ft.

No. 96.** Carriage House, feed shed, 40 by 20 feet.

No. 97.** Hose Carriage House, frame shed, 15 by 25 feet.

No. 98.** Hose Carriage House, frame, 29 by 20 feet.

No. 99. Field Officers' Quarters, not yet built.

No. 100. Barracks for Married Indian Soldiers, not yet built.

No. 101. Stage stable.

No. 102. Unidentified Post Trader building.

A post canteen (now Post Exchange) was established on receipt of General Orders, No. 75, Headquarters of the Army, Adjutant General's Office, series of 1889, to date February 1, 1889; previous to this time, dating from the fall of 1886, a canteen had been in operation at the post in a small way—being so conducted as to not infringe on the rights of the resident trader; it is properly supplied and conducted in accordance with existing rules and regulations. The following extracts from the reports of the commanding officer of the post, show how the operations of the canteen have progressed since its establishment:

"The report shows a very favorable condition of the canteen, and it is probably one of the best canteens in the army. It has greatly improved the discipline of this command, as shown by the Post Records, and at posts where I have observed the operations of canteens, in contra-distinction to the Post Traders establishment, it has decreased drunkenness more than 50 per cent. There is very rarely now a case of drunkenness, that can be traced to the canteen. . . This canteen has given great satisfaction to the officers and enlisted men of the post and through its instrumentality, all persons, whether enlisted men or officers, have been enabled to live with a greater degree of comfort and less expense than formerly." (January 20, 1890).

"This canteen has added largely to the comfort, contentment and discipline of this command; it has enabled officers and men to procure, at reasonable rates, supplies, either formerly unobtainable, or if obtainable only so, at exorbitant prices; and it has greatly decreased drunkenness, confinements and desertions." (May 12, 1890).

"It is, I believe, one of the best in the Army, and its condition reflects great credit on its management. It has greatly improved the discipline, comfort and contentment of this command and merits the continued support of the military authorities." (July 23, 1890).

"The workings of the canteen for the period embraced, have been very satisfactory in spite of the continued depletion of the strength of the garrison by the larger portion of the command being absent in the field. . . The effect of the canteen upon the discipline of the post has been excellent." (January 18, 1891).

"By the enclosed reports, it will be seen that the financial operations of the canteen have been very satisfactory, giving large returns to each organization composing it at the least expense. It enables the soldiers to live almost sumptuously, giving him a great and plentious variety of food. The effect upon the welfare and discipline of the command has been excellent. In fact there has been no bad infraction of the regulations since the Post Tradership here has been abolished, and the canteen established. Drunkenness, and the offenses incident to it (for nearly all could be traced directly or indirectly to it for nine-tenths of the men were tried) has virtually disappeared." (July 25, 1891.)

"As to the effect upon the welfare of my command, the canteen is a great success in every way over the old post trader system. Drunkenness has almost ceased and after a pay day it is found that it is not necessary to fill up the guardhouse with disorderly and drunken soldiers, as was the case under the old system." (January 10, 1892.)

"The Post Exchange has become a necessity here to both officers and men, it being the only medium through which supplies not furnished by the Government, can be procured at reasonable rates, as a co-operation business concern declaring as it does large monthly dividends, the Exchange must be considered a success." (July 27, 1892.)

There is a Post Chaplain at the post of the Lutheran denomination, who holds regularly every Sunday, three services, viz: Sunday school at 10 A.M.; Morning prayers at 11 A.M.; and Evening prayers at 7:45 P.M.; also on Wednesday evenings at 7:45 P.M. In addition to his other duties the chaplain keeps a record of marriages, baptismals and funeral services performed, and superintends the garrison schools.

The post cemetery is located about 1000 yards south of the post; it is properly fenced, well kept and has a natural sod. It contains 61 graves, which are properly cared for, and fairly numbered and marked. Trees and shrubbery are planted as far as possible. A record of interments is kept in the prescribed form.

The post hospital is of frame construction (regulation building), has two wards with capacity for 24 beds. The building is heated by wood stoves, has ridge ventilation in wards and natural ventilation elsewhere. The convalescents are afforded occupation and amusement by light work, reading, cards, and other games of skill. Two cows are kept for the benefit of the sick. The means for subduing fire are buckets filled with water, force pumps and hand grenades; there are also hydrants and ample water close at hand.

The library contains 1502 volumes and is open daily from 6 A.M. to 9 P.M. The enlisted men have free access to it when off duty, and are provided with four periodicals and twelve newspapers; also they have every possible facility afforded them for reading.

The magazine of brick and cement construction is located about a quarter of a mile from the garrison. It is well guarded, ventilated, and kept dry by being opened frequently in light dry weather; and of sufficient capacity for the needs of the garrison.

Precaution against fire is taken at the post by having always ready for instant use axes, barrels, fire buckets, hose carriages and hydrants; the steam pump can also be utilized in case of need and there is ample water at hand.

An officers' school or lyceum for the study of military subjects is maintained from November to April. The non-commissioned officers have during the same period troop and company schools in the new drill regulations superintended by respective commanders; they are also required to study and recite in Blunt's Small Arms Firing Regulations. A garrison school is maintained during the school term, taught by three enlisted men detailed as teachers and under supervision of the Post Chaplain. Average attendance of children, 78.

The target range is located south of the post and is in good condition. Preliminary drill, gallery, pistol, carbine, rifle, and skirmish is had during the proper seasons and conducted in accordance with Blunt's Small Arms Firing Regulations. The greatest distances that men obtained at target practice during the past season with the following is as follows: Pistol, 75 yards; carbine, 800 yards; and rifle, 1000 yards. An officer is always present at all the firings.

INDIANS. The strength and disposition of the neighboring Indian tribes are the Northern Cheyennes about 1400, and the Crows about 2400, peaceable.

APPENDIX B

Post Commanders – Fort Custer

7/4/77 – 3/11/79 LT. COL. GEORGE P. BUELL, 11th Inf.
   Interims: Lt. Col. Albert G. Brackett, 2nd Cav., 12/10-12/77; 2/23-24/78; 7/9-13/78; 8/31 – 9/13/78; 11/26-29/78; 1/21-25/79; 2/25-27/79
     Maj. David S. Gordon, 2nd Cav., 7/23-24/78; 10/23 – 11/25/78
     Capt. Erasmus C. Gilbreath, 11th Inf., 9/28 – 10/22/78

3/12 – 12/3/79 LT. COL. BRACKETT
   Interims: Maj. Gordon, 5/17-21/79; 9/2 – 10/25/79; 11/9 – 12/3/79
     Capt. George K. Sanderson, 11th Inf., 7/3 – 9/1/79
     Capt. Joseph Conrad, 11th Inf., 8/1-5/79
     Lt. Col. Edwin F. Townsend, 11th Inf., 10/26 – 11/8/79

12/4/79 – 12/19/81 COL. JOHN W. DAVIDSON, 2nd Cav.
   Interims: Lt. Col. Townsend, 2/6-18/80; 3/4-9/80; 3/21-25/80
     Maj. Gordon, 7/29 – 8/7/80
     Capt. Sanderson, 8/12 – 9/16/80; 10/5-16/80; 5/21 – 8/9/81; 11/28 – 12/4/81
     Maj. Eugene M. Baker, 2nd Cav., 2/8-22/81
     Capt. Edward J. Spaulding, 2nd Cav., 2/27-28/81
     Lt. Col. Andrew J. Alexander, 2nd Cav., 8/10 – 12/19/81

12/20/81 – 9/6/84 COL. JOHN P. HATCH, 2nd Cav.
   Interims: Lt. Col. Alexander, 2/7-15/83; 6/12 – 7/20/83
     Capt. Thomas G. Troxel, 17th Inf., 7/21-31/83; 5/28 – 7/15/84
     Maj. George B. Sanford, 1st Cav., 7/16 – 9/6/84

9/7/84 – 7/8/85 COL. CUVIER GROVER, 1st Cav.
   Interims: Maj. Sanford, 3/8 – 5/30/85
     Capt. James Jackson, 1st Cav., 6/1 – 7/8/85

7/9/85 – 3/15/89   Col. Nathan A. M. Dudley, 1st Cav.
  Interims: Maj. Henry Carroll, 1st Cav., 10/17-28/85; 9/28 –
    10/4/86; 1/30 – 3/15/89
  Capt. Moses Harris, 1st Cav., 1/7-17/86
  Capt. Albert G. Forse, 1st Cav., 7/9-12/87
  Maj. John M. Hamilton, 1st Cav., 7/13 – 8/27/87
  Lt. Col. Abraham K. Arnold, 1st Cav., 8/28 – 9/6/87; 9/17-
    23/88

3/16 – 9/15/89   Lt. Col. Arnold
  Interim: Capt. John W. French, 25th Inf., 8/15 – 9/15/89

9/16/89 – 9/14/90   Col. James S. Brisbin, 1st Cav.
  Interims: Maj. Carroll, 11/25-28/89; 12/9-13/89
  Lt. Col. Arnold, 1/23 – 2/6/90

9/15/90 – 5/4/92   Col. Arnold (promoted, Col., 2/7/91)
  Interims: Maj. Charles D. Viele, 1st Cav., 12/18-31/90
    Capt. French, 1/1 – 2/8/91
    Lt. Col. John A. Wilcox, 1st Cav., 7/27 – 8/28/91; 12/9-15/91
    Capt. Owen J. Sweet, 25th Inf., 4/27 – 5/4/92

5/5/92 – 1/18/97   Lt. Col. David Perry, 10th Cav.
  Interims: Capt. Thomas Lebo, 10th Cav., 9/8-12/92
    Maj. Stevens T. Norvell, 10th Cav., 9/13-18/92; 5/8 –
      6/23/93; 8/24-31/94; 12/6-9/94; 1/11 – 4/8/95; 10/10-
      17/95; 3/31 – 4/4/96; 4/13-15/96; 8/1/96 – 1/18/97
    Capt. Washington I. Sanborn, 25th Inf., 4/5-12/96; 5/3-
      5/96; 12/6-12/96
    Capt. Charles L. Cooper, 10th Cav., 9/26 – 10/10/96

1/19 – 11/19/97   Lt. Col. Aaron S. Daggett, 25th Inf.
  Interim: Maj. Norvell, 8/25 – 9/8/97

11/20/97 – 4:30 p.m. 4/17/98   Lt. Samuel D. Freeman, 10th
  Cav.

APPENDIX C

Units Stationed at Fort Custer

11th Infantry, Troops B,C,F and H. July 4, 1877 – July 31, 1882

2nd Cavalry, Troops C,D,K and M. September 30, 1877 – May 1884

17th Infantry, Troops J and K. July 29, 1882 – July 10, 1886

5th Infantry, Troops E and K. June 25, 1882 – August 29, 1886

1st Cavalry, Troops B,D,E,G,K,L,M and Band. July 15, 1884 – April 27, 1892

3rd Infantry, Troops C and E. September 3, 1886 – May 18, 1888

25th Infantry, Troops A and D. June 10, 1888 – April 17, 1898

10th Cavalry, Troops A,B,E,G,K,L,M and Band. May 5, 1892 – November 1897

HENRY C. KLENCK
O. S. Goff photo. Courtesy, May Klenck and Mabel Klenck Nelson,
Billings, Montana.

APPENDIX D

Henry Klenck, Indian War Veteran[69]

Henry C. Klenck was born in Bremen, Germany, May 28, 1857. When but ten years old he arrived in New York where he attended the public schools, then called the old grammar school, No. 4.

In 1876 Mr. Klenck enlisted in the 2nd U.S. Cavalry and was sent to Jefferson Barracks then to Fort Snelling, Minnesota. He left Fort Abraham Lincoln, North Dakota, to come to Montana where his cavalry was ordered to the Custer Battlefield to relieve Reno. The route traveled was through the Bad Lands of North Dakota and along the cow trails to Sand Rock Agency, Fort Meade, Sturgis and other minor points to the Little Big Horn, Custer's Battlefield. The cavalry arrived at the battlefield in time to bury the dead from the battle and the following account was given: "The bodies were so mutilated that they were only recognized by the numbers inside of the collar of the shirts. Several of the bodies had been stripped of most of their garments, but there was something in the makeup of an Indian that induced him to leave the shirts on the men. All of the dead had been scalped and their faces and bodies were disfigured above recognition. The soldiers dug small shallow holes with shovels and did the best they could with burial until lumber came, then small wooden headstones were put up. The cavalry remained in the field from July 15th to September 1st. The days were terribly hot at this time and the odor that came from the dead was suffocating. That was one of Reno's last commands when he left the battlefield to stay as far as possible away from the dead. All of the horses had been killed also and the stench that arose from them before they could get them buried can not be imagined. By the first day of August all of the men had been buried who were killed on the battlefield, but there were still several men missing. The general ordered

---

[69] From I. D. O'Donnell (ed.), *Montana Monographs – Pioneer Biographies.*

us to search the canyons from the battlefield. We did so and found seven of the men who had been wounded in the fracas and tried to crawl to camp for medical aid. On the way they had become exhausted and died on the wayside. We buried them where we found them and put headstones up to mark their graves but they have since been taken down."

From the Custer Battlefield Mr. Klenck was sent down to the N.P. Railroad prospective line to guard the engineers who were looking for a transcontinental line, later following the survey as far west as Fort Ellis in the Gallatin Valley. In 1882 he was transferred to Arizona to take part in the Apache Indian war led by Chief Geronimo. He was wounded here in 1883 while carrying dispatches to General Miles. Mr. Klenck was carrying the dispatch under his arm. There were two men in front of him and two in the rear about 150 yards behind him so as to guard. The Indians attacked them. Mr. Klenck was shot in the leg with an arrow head, and was also wounded in the arm. Two of the men were killed. At that time a heliograph was used to telegraph so Mr. Klenck telegraphed to his commander for help and an ambulance. The advance guard returned and almost annihilated the Indians then. The second lieutenant was in charge of the advance guard and he ordered Mr. Klenck to give up his dispatch since he was wounded. Henry refused and the officer placed him under arrest. When they got back to headquarters the general said that Mr. Klenck was right for not giving up his orders and in accordance the second lieutenant was placed under arrest. Shortly after this Mr. Klenck was honorably discharged.

Re-enlistment took place in 1886 in the First Cavalry and Mr. Klenck was sent against the Sioux and Cheyennes in 1890 and 1891. During his time he took part in six different engagements against the Indians. He was discharged again in 1892 and remained at Fort Custer as quartermaster clerk until Fort Custer was abandoned.

When Mr. Klenck first enlisted he wanted to see the west. He liked military duty and the life very much. Mr. Klenck later married and has six children according to birth: Lillian, Philip, Mabel, May Dewey, Margaret and Frances. . .

Bibliography
and Index

Bibliography

DOCUMENTARY SOURCES

CALIFORNIA: El Segundo Public Library.

COLORADO: Denver Public Library, Western History Department.

MONTANA: Big Horn County Library, Hardin; Parmly Billings Memorial Library, Billings; Custer Battlefield National Monument, Crow Agency; Eastern Montana College Library, Billings; Montana Historical Society, Helena.

OKLAHOMA: University of Oklahoma Library, Norman.

SOUTH DAKOTA: University of South Dakota Library, Vermillion.

WASHINGTON, D.C.: National Archives, Old Army Section, Record Group Number 94, Historical Files K-9, Fort Custer Monthly Post Returns and Record of Events; Smithsonian Institution; U.S. Army Signal Corps.

NEWSPAPERS AND SERIALS

MINNESOTA
  St. Paul, *Pioneer-Press,* Oct. and Nov. 1887

MISSOURI
  St. Joseph, *Winners of the West,* Apr. 1933, Oct. 1930
  St. Louis Globe-Democrat, Sept. 8, 1886

MONTANA
  Baker, *Fallon County Times,* July 10, 1931
  Billings Gazette, Apr. 1886 – Nov. 1935
  Fort Benton, *River Press,* Oct.-Nov. 1887

Great Falls, *Rocky Mountain Husbandman,* July 2, 1931
Hardin Tribune-Herald, July 17 and 24, 1931
Helena Independent, June 1886, Oct. and Nov. 1887
Miles City, *Weekly Yellowstone Journal and Livestock Reporter,* Sept. 27, 1890
Miles City, *Yellowstone Journal,* Oct. and Nov. 1887

NEW YORK
New York Tribune, Sept. 1890
Utica Sunday Tribune, May 1886

WYOMING
Sheridan Enterprise, Feb. and Mar. 1898
Sheridan Post, Feb. and Mar. 1898

BOOKS AND ARTICLES

Baldwin, Alice Blackwood. *Memoirs of the Late Frank D. Baldwin.* Los Angeles: Wetzel Publishing Co., 1929.

Billington, Ray Allen. *Soldier and Brave.* New York: Harper and Row, 1963.

Bonney, Orrin H., and Lorraine. *Battle Drums and Geysers: The Life and Journals of Lieutenant Gustavus Cheyney Doane, Soldier and Explorer of the Yellowstone and Snake River Regions.* Chicago: Swallow Press, Inc., 1970.

Brown, Mark H., and W.R. Felton. *The Frontier Years; L.A. Huffman, Photographer of the Plains.* New York: Henry Holt and Co., 1955.

Brown, Mark H. *The Plainsman of the Yellowstone.* New York: G. P. Putnam's Sons, 1961.

Bryan, Capt. Roger B. *An Average American Army Officer.* San Diego, Calif: Buck-Molina Co., 1914.

Burlingame, Merrill G. "The Influence of the Military in the Building of Montana," in *Pacific Northwest Quarterly,* vol. 29 (Apr. 1938), pp. 135-150.

Clinch, Thomas A. "Coxey's Army in Montana," in *Montana, the Magazine of Western History,* vol. 15, no. 4 (Oct. 1965), pp. 2-11.

DeBarthe, Joe. *Life and Adventures of Frank Grouard.* St. Joseph, Mo., 1894; reprint, Norman: Univ. of Okla. Press, 1958.

Ege, Robert. *Tell Baker To Strike Them Hard.* Bellevue, Nebr.: Old Army Press, 1970.

Frink, Maurice, with Casey Barthelmess. *Photographer on an Army Mule.* Norman: Univ. of Okla. Press, 1965.

Godfrey, Gen. Edward Settle. "Custer's Last Battle," *Century Magazine,* vol. 43, no. 3 (Jan. 1892), pp. 358-387.

Hamilton, W. T. *My Sixty Years on the Plains.* New York, 1905; reprints, 1909; Columbus, Ohio: Long's College Book Co., 1951.

Hanson, Joseph Mills. *The Conquest of the Missouri: Being the Story of the Life and Exploits of Captain Grant Marsh.* Chicago: A.C. McClurg and Co., 1909; and reprints.

Hart, Herbert M. *Old Forts of the Northwest.* Seattle: Superior Publishing Co., 1963.

Hayne, Coe. *Red Men on the Big Horn.* Philadelphia: Judson Press, 1930.

Hein, Lieut. Col. O. L. *Memories of Long Ago.* New York: G. P. Putnam's Sons, 1925.

Heitman, Francis B. *Historical Register and Dictionary of the United States Army, 1789 to 1903.* Vol. I. Washington: Government Printing Office, 1903; reprint, Urbana: Univ. of Ill. Press, 1965.

Hope, Lucy. *Around the Mouth of the Big Horn.* Billings, Mont.: privately printed, 1932.

Huggins, Capt. Eli. "Notes and Documents: Letters of an Army Captain on the Sioux Campaign of 1879-1880," in *Pacific Northwest Quarterly,* vol. 39 (Jan. 1948) pp. 39-64.

Hurt, Wesley R., and William E. Lass. *Frontier Photographer: Stanley J. Morrow's Dakota Years.* Lincoln: Univ. of Nebr. Press, and Univ. of So. Dak., 1956.

Jones, Agnes L. *Crow Country.* Billings, Montana: privately printed, no date.

Kuhlman, Charles. *Legend Into History.* Harrisburg, Pa: Stackpole Co., 1951.

Lass, William E. *A History of Steamboating on the Upper Missouri.* Lincoln: Univ. of Nebr. Press, 1962.

Leckie, William H. *The Buffalo Soldiers: A Narrative of the Negro Cavalry in the West.* Norman: Univ. of Okla. Press, 1967.

Liberty, Margot. "I Will Play with the Soldiers," *Montana, the Magazine of Western History,* vol. XIV, no. 4 (Autumn 1964), pp. 16-26.

Linderman, Frank B. *American: The Life Story of a Great Indian* (Plenty Coups). New York: World Book Co., 1930; and reprints. (English title "Plenty Coups")

Marquis, Thomas B. *Memoirs of a White Crow Indian* (Thomas H. Leforge). New York: Century Co., 1928.

Mattes, Merrill J. *Indians, Infants and Infantry: Andrew and Elizabeth Burt on the Frontier.* Denver: Old West Publishing Co., 1960.

McCracken, Harold. *The Frederick Remington Book.* New York: Doubleday and Co., 1947.

Miles, Gen. Nelson A. *Personal Recollections and Observations of General Nelson A. Miles.* New York: Werner Co., 1896.

Miller, Francis Trevelyan. *The Photographic History of the Civil War.* Vol. X. New York: Review of Reviews Co., 1911; reprinted N.Y., 1957.

Mooney, James. *The Ghost-Dance Religion and the Sioux Outbreak of 1890.* Chicago: Phoenix Books, Univ. of Chicago Press, 1965.

Nabokov, Peter. *Two Leggings: The Making of a Crow Warrior.* New York: Thomas Y. Crowell Co., 1967.

O'Donnell, I.D. (ed.). *Montana Monographs – Pioneer Biographies.* Billings, Mont: published privately, 1928-1929.

Pakes, Fraser. "The Lame Deer Incident: 1890," in *English Westerners' 10th Anniversary Publication – 1964,* p. 50.

Palladino, L.B., s.j. *Indian and White in the Northwest or a History of Catholicity in Montana.* Baltimore: John Murphy and Co., 1894; reprint, Lancaster, Pa., 1922.

Powell, Father Peter J. "Letter to Editor," in *Montana, the Magazine of Western History,* vol. XV, no. 1 (Winter 1965).

Powell, Peter J. *Sweet Medicine.* 2 vols. Norman: Univ. of Okla. Press, 1969.

Quaife, M. M. *Yellowstone Kelly: Memoirs of Luther S. Kelly.* New Haven: Yale Univ. Press, 1926.

Rasch, Philip J. "A Note on N.A.M. Dudley," in Westerners, Los Angeles Corral, *Brand Book, 1949,* pp. 207-214.

Remington, Frederic. *Pony Tracks.* New York, 1895, and various reprints; Norman: Univ. of Okla. Press, 1961.

Rickey, Don, Jr. *Forty Miles A Day On Beans and Hay.* Norman: Univ. of Okla. Press, 1963.

Rickey, Don, Jr. *History of Custer Battlefield.* Crow Agency, Mont: Custer Battlefield Historical and Museum Assn., 1967.

Robertson, Lieut. Samuel C. "How They Died," in *Weekly Yellowstone Journal and Livestock Reporter* (Miles City), Sept. 27, 1890.

Robertson, Lieut. Samuel C. "The Rush to Death," in *Harper's Weekly,* Oct. 18, 1890.

Scott, Hugh Lenox. *Some Memories of a Soldier.* New York: Century Co., 1928.

Sheridan, Gen. Philip H. *Personal Memoirs.* 2 vols. New York: 1888.

Sheridan, Lieut.-Gen. Philip H. *Record of Engagements with Hostile Indians within the Military Division of the Missouri from 1868 to 1882.* Bellevue, Nebr: Old Army Press, 1969.

Sherman, William T. *Memoirs of General W. T. Sherman.* New York: D. Appleton and Co., 1875.

Thorp, Raymond W., and Robert Bunker. *Crow Killer: The Saga of Liver-Eating Johnson.* Bloomington, Ind: Univ. of Indiana Press, 1958.

Tilden, Freeman. *Following the Frontier with F. Jay Haynes: Pioneer Photographer of the Old West.* New York: Alfred A. Knopf, 1964.

Wagner, Glendolin Damon, and Dr. William A. Allen. *Blankets and Moccasins, Plenty Coups and his People, the Crows.* Caldwell, Idaho: Caxton Printers, Ltd., 1936.

Wister, Owen. *Red Men and White.* New York: Harper and Bros., 1896; and reprints.

Wormser, Richard. *The Yellowlegs: The Story of the United States Cavalry.* Garden City, N.Y.: Doubleday and Co., 1966.

Index

Abbott, Sgt. Chas: 95
Absorakys: *see* Crow Indians
"Adams Ale": 82
Aleshire, Mr. ---: 170
Aleshire, Lt. James B: 75, 116, 150, 170
Alexander, Lt. Col. Andrew J: 289
Alyshire: *see* Aleshire
American Horse (Cheyenne Indian): 181-82
American Railway Union: strike, 202, 275
Ancient Order of Hibernians: 78
Antelope: *see* wild game
Apache Indians: 294
Arizona: 198, 202, 204, 294
Arkansas River: 29
Armstrong, Inspector Gen. Frank: 130, 135, 147, 166; estimates Crow strength, 131
Army Board for Corrections: 105 fn.
Army of the Potomac: 256 fn.
Army of the West: 256 fn.
Arnold, Lt. Col. Abraham K: 191, 290
Arrapahoe Agency: 180
Arrapahoes: 107, 180
Artillery: 52; *see also* Fourth
"Ashland": *see* steamboats

B. C. Club: 96
Bacon, Col. John M: 35
Bad Lands: of No. Dak., 293
Bailey, Lt. ---: 228
Baker, Maj. Eugene: 17, 31, 289

Baker's Battlefield: 273
Baldwin, Maj. Gen. Frank D: 17, 84, 109
Ball, Capt. ---: 31
Baltimore (Md.): 66
Band: 68, 77, 116, 135, 245, 251, 291; at Bannock campaign, 49; uniforms described, 75
Banfill, W.H: 13, 27, 211
Bank, The: Crow Indian, 148, 152-53
Bannock Indians: 131; campaign of 1878, 48-54; meeting with Miles and Buell, 52-53
Barber, Lt. ---: 183, 186
Barnard, T.N.: 187
Barry, David F: 16, 33, 109-11, 249
Barry, Kittie: 93
Barstow, Maj. C.H: 118, 159-60, 163
Barstow, Elizabeth W: 118; account of Swordbearer incident, 159-66
Barthelmess, Casey: 14
Barthelmess, Christian: 16
Bartlett, Maj. Chas. G: 28, 30, 32, 35
Basinski, ---: *see* Batzinski
Bataan: 151 fn.
"Batchelor, F.Y.": *see* steamboats
Battle of San Juan Hill: 205
Battle of the Little Big Horn: 15, 22, 28, 30, 102, 106, 112, 130 fn., 143-44, 155, 192, 197, 211, 244, 246, 248, 258, 266; tenth anniversary, 21, 72, 100-12, 248 fn; Godfrey's account, 103-05; Gall's account, 106-07

Batzinski, ---: merchant, 39
Bayou Meto: 256 fn.
Bear: *see* wild game
Bear Claw: Indian policeman, 156
Bear-in-the-Water: Crow Indian, 66
Bear Paw Mts: 48
Beebe, Geo. H: 13, 205
Beethoven: 15
Bennett, ---: Army officer, 28
Bennett, Capt. Andrew S: 52-53; killed, 50, 53
Bennett Creek: 52
Benteen, Fred Jr: 111
Benteen, Capt. Frederick: 72, 109-12; at Custer fight, 103-04
Benton (Mont.): 276
Berry: *see* Barry
Bertrand, ---: saloon operator, 172
Big Goose Creek: 226
Big Hail: Crow Indian, 148, 152-53
Big Horn (Mont.): 206
Big Horn Canyon: 56
Big Horn County Historical Society: 264
Big Horn County Library (Hardin, Mont.): 14
Big Horn Mts: 48, 55-56, 107, 277
Big Horn Post #1: 262
Big Horn Post #2: 18, 262, 278
Big Horn River: 18, 27-28, 32, 34-37, 41, 44, 46, 55-56, 58, 83, 91, 94, 123, 130, 133-34, 169, 174, 194, 200, 208, 225, 243, 248, 251, 254-55, 261, 263, 265, 273, 276-79
Big Horn Southern Railroad: 279
Big Man (Crow scout): 212
Billings (Mont.): 13-14, 37 fn., 50, 74-75, 118, 142, 170, 192-93, 201-06, 208, 217, 222-27, 267, 269, 276-77; Parmly Billings Mem'l. Library, 13
Billings (Mont.) *Gazette:* 13, 20, 27, 71, 89-90, 117-18, 129-30, 142, 158-59, 169, 174, 179, 182-83, 192, 197, 201, 205, 211, 217-18, 229, 242, 248, 250; "Ft. Custer News" in, 71-112; editorials in, 218-25
"Billy the Kid": *see* Bonney

Bismarck (Dak. Terr.): 28-30, 38-39, 110, 274, 276
Bivins, Capt. Horace W: 204, 207; military career, 205-09
Black Canyon: 56, 73
Black Hawk: Crow chief, 152
"Black Jack": *see* Pershing
Blackfoot, Chief: 214
Blackfoot Agency: 123
Blake, ---: rancher, 127
Blunt's Small Arms Firing Regulations: 288
Boettger, Dennis: 14
Boettger, Rudy: 14
Bonney, William H: 124 fn.
Booth, Mr. ---: 55
Borden, Lt. Geo: 74
Borup, Charley: 73, 92
Borup, Theodore: 113
Boston (Mass.): 55
Boulder (Colo.): 14
Bouten, Trumpeter: 248
Boy-That-Grabs: Indian policeman, 161
Boyle, Hugh: 184-85; murder of, 182-83
Bozeman (Mont.): 39, 74-75, 81, 273, 276
Bozeman Trail: 265; forts on, 23
Brackett, Lt. Col. Albert G: 289
Bradley, Lt. James: 211, 214; describes Custer dead, 105
Brave Wolf: Cheyenne chief, 185
Bravo, Art: 151 fn.
Bremen (Germany): 293
Brewer, Lt. ---: 111
Briggs, ---: rancher, 127
Brisbin, Col. James S: 17, 290
British America (Canada): 48
Broadwater, Gen. ---: 32, 34, 38; nickname "Broady," 34
Brown, Clarence: 229
Brown, Harold: 182
Brown, J.H: 170
Brownwood (Texas): 28
Brule Sioux: 107
Buchner, Quartermaster Sgt: 96
Budds, Commissary Sgt: 83

INDEX

Buell, Gen. Geo. P: 17-19, 28-29, 36, 42, 44 fn., 48, 204, 273-74, 289; involved in trial, 44; in Bannock campaign, 48-53
Buffalo: *see* wild game
Buffalo (Wyo.): 170
Buffalo Soldiers: *see* Tenth Cavalry
Bull Chief: Crow Indian, 161
Bull-Goes-A-Hunting: Crow Indian, 161
Bull Mts: 277
Bull Nose: Crow Indian, 161
Bull Train: 34
Bullwhackers: 41
Burns, Denny: 257
Burr, D.A: 171
Burry, ---: store proprietor, 47
Butler, Sgt. James: 197
Butte (Mont.): 75, 202
Byram, Lt. ---: 160

"Calamity Bill": 41-42
Calhoun, Lt. James: 106
Camp Crittenden: 107, 112
Camp Crook: 183-84
Camp Merritt: 217
Campbell, Asst. Surgeon: 31
Campbell, Hugh S: 140-42
Campbell, James: 133, 144, 147
Campbell, T: 171
Canada: 48, 208
Canyon Creek: 40
Carlisle (Penna.): 212
Carries-his-Food: Crow Indian, 148, 152-53
Carroll, Maj. Henry: 17, 179, 183, 191, 290; investigates Ghost Dance, 181
Carroll, James: 80
Carson, Kit: 256 fn.
Carter, Senator ---: 222, 224
Casey, Lt. Edward W: 215
Casper (Wyo.): 14
Cavalry: barracks, 282; *see also* Fourth; Ninth; Second; Seventh; Tenth
Cemetery: 94, 234, 287
Century Magazine: 17; Godfrey article in, 72

Cheestapah or Cheschapah: *see* Swordbearer
Cheyenne Agency: 128-29, 131, 180
Cheyenne Indians: 131-32, 142, 180, 208, 214, 223, 288, 294; at Custer fight, 106-107; refuse to aid Swordbearer, 132-33; Lame Deer episode, 179-89
Chicago (Ill.): 112
Chickamauga Nat'l Pk. (Tenn.): 228
Chipman, Lt. Col. H.R: 59, 68
Choisey, Capt. Geo. Louis: 30
Christ: 15; *also see* Wovoka
Civic Societies: 76, 78
Civil War: 22, 87, 256 fn.
Clark, Pvt. ---: 149
Clark, Lt. Powhatan: 204
Clark, William: 169, 173
Clark's Fork: 48-49, 52, 144
Clifford, Harry: 14
Cody, Col. W. F. (Buffalo Bill): 206
Colonel, Jack: 47
Columbus (Mont.): 61
Conrad, Capt. Joseph: 289
Cook: Chinese, 47
Cooper, Capt. Chas. L: 290
Cooper, James: 182-83, 185
Cooper, Myrtle: 13
Cordelling: *see* steamboats
Cornell University: 22
Cottonwood (Sioux chief): 143
Coulson (Mont.): 256
Council Bluffs (Iowa): 226
Countryman and Sons: 61-62
Cowboys: 62, 142, 176
Coxey's Army: 202, 208, 275
Crabb, Jack: 261
Crazy Head: Crow chief, 65, 141, 145, 147-48, 150, 152, 165; makes speech, 65-66
Cree Indians: 202, 208
Crimmins, Jerry: 171-72
Crook, Brig. Gen. Geo: 35, 274
Crow Agency (Mont.): 14, 16, 50, 61, 118-22, 130, 132, 138, 144, 147, 152, 155-56, 192-94, 220, 247, 264, 275-77; issue day at, 125-26; preparations for fight at, 146; on Stillwater River, 211; buildings at, 236

Crow Indian Army Scouts: 54, 138, 204, 207, 211, 213, 229, 252; enlistment of, 211, 214; disbanded, 211; become Company L, 211; language problems, 212

Crow Indians: 50, 54, 61, 64, 66, 117, 121-24, 127, 130, 133-34, 140-45, 221, 229, 234, 243, 250-52, 266, 288; capture horses on Bannock Campaign, 52, 54; treaty with, 64-65, 67; want equipment returned, 92; attack agency, 118-120, 122, 156, 159-61; visit Cheyenne Agency, 131-33; fight soldiers, 148-52; captured by soldiers, 152-54; police, 156; celebrate, 191-92, 196-97; as Army Scouts, 211-15; dismantle fort, 275

Crow Reservation: 64, 121, 170, 212, 222-23, 225, 278; grazing privileges on, 127-28

Cuba: 228

Cuesta-by-the-Sea (Calif.): 14

Cumin, Calvin: 14

Cummings, Pvt. ---: 76, 110 fn.

Curley: Indian scout, 110, 214

Custer, Lt. Col. Geo. A: 18, 28, 30-31, 42-44, 108-09, 196-97, 274; fort named after, 22, 275; expedition of, 100, 102-03; at Little Big Horn, 101-12

Custer, Capt. Tom: 105

Custer (Mont.): 37 fn., 96, 169, 202

Custer Battlefield (Mont.): 14, 42-44, 100, 103-04, 107, 112, 129-30, 134, 194, 196-97, 234, 247-48, 261, 274, 293, 294 fn.; monument on, 43, 73, 248-49, 279; bones not buried, 44; dead re-buried, 45, 105 fn., 258; 10th anniversary ceremonies at, 100-12, 248 fn.; relics on, 110; Crow celebrations at, 191-92, 196-97; becomes National Cemetery, 278-79

Custer County (Mont.): 182; coroners verdict at, 182-83

Custer Fight: *see* Battle of Little Big Horn

Custer Forwarding Co: 170, 175

Custer Monument: *see* Custer Battlefield

Custer Social Club: 78

Custer Station: 134, 174-75, 208, 242-43, 252, 276; buildings described, 170-71

Daggett, Lt. Col. Aaron S: 290

Dahlgren, Pvt. ---: 103

Dakota, Dept. of: 208, 218

Dakota, Territory of: 28, 179, 273

Dailey, W. J: 96

Dana, ---: rancher, 113, 116

Daughters of the American Revolution: 256 fn., 262

Davey Milk Ranch: 99

David's Island (N.Y.): 60

Davidson, Capt. H. Kenneth: 14, 62, 256 fn.

Davidson, Col. John W: 17, 62, 204, 256-57, 289; death of, 256 fn.

Davies, Gen. ---: *see* Davidson, J.

Dayton (Wyo.): 170

Deadwood Stage: 176

Deaf Bull: Crow chief, 134, 141, 145-46, 151-53; counsels Swordbearer, 164

Deer: *see* wild game

Deerholt, Trumpeter ---: 248

DeLong, Mr. ---: hotel keeper, 171

DeMores, Marquis: 93

Denison (Texas): 28

Denver (Colo.): Public Library: 14

Dewitt, J. S: 171-72

Diamond R (freighting company): 33, 34, 37

Dillon (Mont.): 276

Doane, Lt. Gustavus C: 16, 19, 31; selects site of Ft. Custer, 18, 214

Doctor of Alcantara: 75, 77

Dog-robber: 85

Dracon, John: 265

Drunkenness: 286-87

Dudley, Col. Nathan A.M: 17, 21, 72, 74, 94, 96, 101, 111, 116, 128-29, 136, 148, 204, 243, 290; interview with, 123-24; described, 124 fn.

"Dugan": *see* steamboats

Eastern Montana College: 13

Ebert, H: telegrapher, 96

Edgerly, Capt. W. S: 109, 112

INDEX 307

Edwards, Lt. F. A: 149
Eichborg, Julius: 75, 77
El Segundo (Calif.): 14
Eleventh Infantry: 30, 44-45, 59, 68, 289; Co. H, 27-29, 42, 50, 52, 59-60, 291; Co. A, 28-30; Co. G, 30; Co. B, 42, 274, 291; Co. C, 42, 274, 291; Co. F, 42, 273, 291
Elk: *see* wild game
Empire Hotel (Junction City): 171
Europe: 218

Fallon County *Times* (Baker, Mont.): 27
Father De Smet Tree: 265
Fifteenth Infantry: 59
Fifth Infantry: 30, 35, 49-50; Co. K, 109-10, 112, 291; Troop E, 291
Finley, Lt. ---: 204
Fire Bear: Indian policeman, 118, 156; kills Swordbearer, 156-59, 165
First Cavalry: 18, 20, 74-76, 79, 116, 137, 139, 206, 215, 267, 269, 289-90, 294; Co. B, 71, 76, 88-91, 93, 98, 291; Co. D, barracks burn, 74, 291; Troop M, 80, 98, 195; Troop M disbanded, 212, 291; Troop G, 92, 150, 183-84, 186-87, 291; Troop K, 92, 113, 149, 291; Troop E, 149, 183-84, 186, 291; at Swordbearer fight, 164; at Lame Deer episode, 183-87; Troop D, 183-84; at Wounded Knee, 191; transfers to Arizona, 197-98; Co. L, 211, 275, 291; band, 291
First Infantry: 30
Fish: *see* wild game
Fly Creek: 49, 193
Foote, Don: 14, 173-74
Foote, Stella (Mrs. Don C.): 14, 173-75, 231
Forse, Capt. Albert G: 290
Forsyth, Capt. ---: 31
Forsyth, Maj. Gen. Geo. A: 105 fn.
Forsyth (Mont.): 68, 202, 208; described, 57
Fort Abraham Lincoln: 28, 103, 191, 293
Fort Alexander: 169

Fort Assinniboine: 17, 202, 206, 208, 218-19
Fort Benton: 169; newspaper, 118
Fort Buford: 27, 57-59, 66, 68, 202
Fort Cass: 169
Fort Coeur d'Alene: 81
Fort Concho: 28
Fort Custer: 4, 13-15, 18, 20-21, 23, 27-33, 35-40, 42, 44-46, 48, 50, 52, 54-57, 59, 61-63, 66, 68, 71, 73, 81, 83, 90-91, 95, 99, 115, 118, 121, 123-24, 126, 128, 133, 137, 156, 160, 161-62, 169-70, 173, 179, 181, 187, 195, 197-98, 200, 202, 204-06, 208, 213, 215, 217-21, 223-27, 229-30, 237 fn., 241-43, 248, 250-53, 256, 261-62, 264-66, 269, 275-78, 280, 294; photographers at, 16; alumni of, 16-17; monthly post returns, 17, 22, 191; documental records described, 20 fn.; named after G.A. Custer, 22, 275; building of described, 60, 274-75; officers qtrs. at, 60, 63, 203, 232, 244, 280, 282; soldiers qtrs. at, 60, 99, 213, 232, 235, 244, 246, 274; hospital at, 60, 80, 230, 232, 236, 244, 246, 255, 268, 275, 282, 287-88; headquarters building at, 60, 244, 275, 280; log trains at, 60; sawmill at, 60, 254, 277; restaurants at, 71-72, 82; officers club, 72, 230, 232-33, 280; lectures at, 73-74; target ranges at, 74, 78, 87-91, 138, 234, 288; post library, 74-75, 282, 288; school at, 76, 114, 246, 282, 288; civic societies at, 76, 78; commissary bldg., 83, 284; gardens at, 84, 255, 277; post chapel at, 86, 114, 282, 287; weddings at, 93-94; Decoration Day at, 94; picnic near, 96-98; Custer fight survivors at, 100-12; grand ball at, 113-16; troops to Crow Agency, 120; appearance described, 135-38, 243-46; stagecoach at, 173-77, 276; troops at Lame Deer episode, 183-87; trip to described, 192-94; hotel at, 193; dilapidated condition of, 194; 10th Cavalry arrives at, 201-02; Crow scouts at, 211-15; established, 214,

Fort Custer: (contin.) 273; troops evacuated, 217; abandoned, 218-28, 275; dismantled, 229-37; guardhouse at, 230, 232, 236, 244, 264, 280, 284-85; warehouse at, 230, 232; opera house at, 230, 232, 236; water tower at, 231-32; bar at, 231; stables at, 232-33, 244, 253, 275, 283-85; flagstaff at, 232; cemetery at, 94, 234, 287; water system, 244-45; dishonorable discharge at, 247; trumpeters at, 248-50; marker at, 257; aerial view of, 263; history of, 273-75; money appropriated for construction, 273, 275; band qtrs., 274, 280; storehouses at, 274; bakery, 275, 284; commanding officers qtrs., 275, 280; laundresses' qtrs., 275; field officers qtrs., 275, 285; Indian married soldiers qtrs., 275, 285; communications at, 276; post office at, 276; telegraph station at, 276, 283; supplies, 276; description of country near, 276-77; temperature at, 277-78; justice of the peace at, 278; post reservation dimensions, 278; jurisdiction of, 279; bldgs. at, 280-85; officers' mess, 280; cavalry barracks, 282; post exchange, 282, 287; billiard room, 282; card room, 282; canteen at, 282, 286-87; gymnasium, 282; dead house at, 282; hospital steward qtrs., 282; non-commissioned officers qtrs., 283, 285; mechanics shops, 283; blacksmith's shops, 283-85; wheelwright's shops, 283; carpenter's shop, 283; qtrs. for civilian employees, 283, 285; qtrs. for teamsters, 283; veterinary hospital, 283; quartermaster storehouses, 283, 285; granary, 283; qtrs. for trainmaster, 283; saddler shop, 284-85; butcher shop, 284; old tank house, 284; steam planing mill, 284; pumphouse, 284; lime house, 284; magazine, 284, 288; ordnance bldg., 284; gun shed, 284; bath house, 284; dry earth closets, 285; new tank house, 285; new post hall, 285; coal shed, 285; range house, 285; wagon shed, 285; carriage house, 285; hose carriage house, 285; drunkenness at, 286-87; Indians near, 288; post commanders of, 289-90; units stationed at, 291

Fort Custer Comic Opera and Burlesque: 74-75, 78

"Fort Custer News": 20, 71, 74, 76, 78, 80-81, 84, 86-87, 91-92, 95, 98, 100-02, 107, 110; Pvt. Purvis writes, 71-112; final item of, 112

Fort Ellis: 31, 74-75, 81, 241-43, 245, 276, 294

Fort Grant: 201

Fort Harrison: 217, 219, 227

Fort Keogh: 16, 28-31, 35, 39-40, 44, 50, 57, 89, 128, 131, 191, 202, 206, 215, 217-19, 225, 262, 276; target practice at, 90-91; daily routine at, 91

Fort Laramie: 14

Fort Lowell: 72

Fort McKinney: 128, 133-34

Fort Maginnis: 128, 276

Fort Manuel Lisa: 169

Fort Meade: 293

Fort Missoula: 133-34, 206, 227

Fort Phil Kearny: 23

Fort Reno: 22-23

Fort Sarpy: 169, 237 fn.

Fort Sheridan: 208

Fort Smith (Mont.): 265

Fort C. F. Smith: 23, 55-56, 60, 265; limestone reservation at, 278-79

Fort Snelling: 76, 154, 293

Fort Stanton: 124 fn.

Fort Tejon: 256 fn.

Fort Van Buren: 169

Fort Walla Walla: 113

Fort Yates: 28, 37

Fortress Monroe: 79

Fourth Artillery: 76

Fourth Cavalry: 72, 112

Fowler, Lt. Joshua L: 44

Freeman, Lt. Samuel D: 217, 290

Freeze, Alys: 14

INDEX

French, Capt. John: 290
Fringe (Crow Indian): 161
Frink, Maurice: 14
Frith, Pvt. Henry A: 50-54
Frost, John: 212
Frushman, Mrs. ---: 93

Gall (Sioux Chief): 18, 72, 101-02, 108, 110-111, 117, 130, fn.; account of Custer fight, 106-07; refuses to aid Swordbearer, 143-44
Gallatin Valley: 294
Garretty, Capt. Frank D: 73, 116
Gatling gun: 275
General Store: 47
Geronimo, Chief: 294
Ghost Dance: 181
Gilbreath, Capt. Erasmus C: 27, 35, 54, 59, 169, 289; describes trip up Big Horn River, 32-35; establishes Terry's Landing, 37; handling of mail, 38-39; daughter born, 39; transferred to Ft. Custer, 42; visits Custer Battlefield, 42, 44; builds road, 44; in Bannock campaign, 48-50; return to Ft. Custer, 54-55; trip to Big Horn and Black canyons, 56; surveys road, 57; to Poplar River, 57; describes Forsyth (Mont.), 57; sights last buffalo herd, 59; appointed inspector of supplies, 61; trip to Crow Agency, 61-62; crosses Yellowstone River, 62-63; rewrites treaty with the Crows, 64-65; east to Baltimore, 66; leaves Ft. Custer, 66, 68; commands Ft. Buford, 68; promoted to Maj., 68; dies, 68
Gilbreath, Mrs. E.C: 34, 38, 48
Gibbon, Col. John: 104, 107
Gibson, Col. ---: 131
Gila River: 201
Gleason, Kittie: 93
Glendive (Mont.): 57, 59, 66, 68, 194
Glendive Hotel: 57
Glendora (Calif.): 14
Glenwood Cemetery (Wash., D.C.): 105 fn.

Glover, Col. Cuvier: 289
Godfrey, Gen. E. S: 17, 72, 100-02, 105, 108-09, 111-12, 248, fn.; account of Custer fight, 103-05
Goff, O.S: 16, 77, 83, 137, 139, 183, 195, 292
Gold: 42, 81
Gordon, Maj. David S: 289
Grand Army of the Republic (G.A.R.): 94; John Buford Post, 94-95
Grass, John: Sioux chief, 143
Grass Lodge: *see* Lodge Grass
Great Falls (Mont.): 27
Great Northern Railroad: 227
Greeley, Horace: 177
Griffin, ---: saloon operator, 172
Gros Ventres: 107, 138
Grugan, Lt. ---: 31
Guns: firing manual, 288; Gatling, 275; Napoleon, 275; target ranges, 74, 78, 87-91, 138, 234, 288; *see also* Hotchkiss

Halbert, Mayor: 222
Hall, Cpl. ---: 109
Hamilton, Lt. ---: 31
Hamilton, Maj. John M: 290
Hamilton, William (Bill): 17, 142-43
Hamilton (Mont.): 14, 155
Hardin (Mont.): 14, 234-35, 245, 251, 261, 264
Hardin (Mont.) *Tribune-Herald:* 27
Harman, ---: store clerk, 47
Harris, Capt. Moses: 74, 290
Hart, Joe: 52
Hatch, Col. John P: 17, 256, 289; wife of, 256
Havre (Mont.): 208
Hayfield Fight: 265
Haynes, F. Jay: 16, 195, 230, 233
He Knows His Coups: Crow Indian, 148, 153
Head Chief: Cheyenne Indian, 181-83; killed, 186, 188
Heffner, William H: 86, 93
Helena (Mont.): 14, 39, 75, 227, 276
Helena (Mont.) *Independent:* 110, 118

Henry, B. William, Jr: 14, 197 fn.
Henry, Col. Guy T: 204
Henry, Joseph: 76
Herrman, Emil: 93
Hersey, A.H: 110
Hicks, Trumpeter Geo: 72, 248; discharge of, 98-99
Hinkley, Trumpeter: 248
Hollywood: 71
Hoppin, Lt. Curtis B: 62, 256 fn.
Horses: 30, 52, 54, 75, 122, 148, 159; see also mules; ox teams
Hospitals: 282-83
Hotchkiss guns: 138, 141, 148, 150, 152, 205, 275
Howard, Gen. O.O: 40, 126; as special agent, 126
Huffman, L.A: 16, 33
Hunt, Lt. ---: 217
Huntley (Mont.): 52, 62

Indian Agency: see Crow Agency
Indian Christ: see Wovoka
Indian Creek: 192
Indian Dept: 121
Indian Police: 125, 146, 156, 158-59, 161, 182, 237
Indians: 22, 30, 38, 41-42, 49, 52-53, 58, 62, 65-66, 71, 73, 87, 101-02, 106, 110, 117, 120, 122-23, 125-26, 128-31, 133-34, 142-44, 146-47, 176, 179-81, 183, 220, 223, 234, 236, 251, 254, 264-65, 288, 294; captured on Bannock campaign, 54; mutilate bodies, 102, 107; at Custer fight, 103-04, 107; at Swordbearer incident, 147-52, 159-66; at Lame Deer episode, 179-89
Indian Savior: see Wovoka
Independent Order of Good Templars: 78
Infantry: see Eleventh; Fifteenth; Fifth; Ninth; Seventeenth; Seventh; Third; Twenty-fifth; Twenty-second
Interior Dept: 121, 127
Interior, Sec. of: 127

Jackson, Maj. James: 76, 289

Jackson, W. H: 31
Jefferson Barracks: 293
Jerome, Lt. ---: 31
Johnson, John (Liver-Eating): 16, 113, 115
Judge, Correspondent: 89-91
Judith Basin: 120
Junction City (Mont.): 73, 76, 114, 134-35, 169, 252, 276-77; established, 39; described, 171-72
Junction Ferry: 171
Junction Hotel: 171

Kaiser, Trumpeter: 248-49
Kansas: 41
Kearney, Stephen Watts: 256 fn.
Kelly, Yellowstone: 16
Kennard, Jack: 112
Kennedy's Ferry: 192
Keogh, Capt. Myles: 30 fn.; fort named after, 30; at Custer fight, 106
Key West (Fla.): 228
King, James: 14, 182 fn.
"Kitchen Belles": 84
Klenck, Frances: 267, 294
Klenck, Henry Carl: 13, 215, 261, 269, 292-94; children of, 13; at the farm of, 13, 267; discharged, 267; homesteads farm, 267; dies, 267; biography of, 293-94; describes Custer Battlefield, 293-94; in Arizona, 294
Klenck, Margaret: 267, 294
Klenck, May: 13, 195, 267-69, 294
Klenck, Philip: 267, 269, 294
Klenck Lane: 269
Knight, H. L: 13, 192, 196; describes trip to Ft. Custer, 192-94
Korea: 218
Kraus, Trumpeter: 248
Krieg, Fred: 14

Lake Park (Minn.): 13
Lamar, Secy. of Inter: 127
Lame Deer (Mont.): 14, 182-83, 188; episode at, 179-89
Lander (Wyo.): 170
Lansendorfer, Trumpeter: 248

INDEX

Lebo, Capt. Thomas: 290
Lechner, Val: 99
Lee, John: 205
Leforge, Tom: 16, 19; helps establish Ft. Custer, 18
LeMoy, Veterinarian: 98
Lewis and Clark expedition: 173
Lewistown (Mont.): 208, 218
Library: 74-75, 282, 288
Lilly, Trumpeter: 248
Lincoln County (New Mex.) War: 124 fn.
Lind, Dolly: 265
Lind, John: 265
Little Big Horn: see Battle of Little Big Horn
Little Big Horn River: 18, 56-57, 84, 101, 123, 129-30, 149, 155-56, 165 fn., 174, 194, 196, 200, 204, 214, 244, 246-47, 251, 261-62, 273, 276-77, 279; picnic near, 96; not contaminated, 220
Little Goose Creek: 226
Little Horn: see Little Big Horn
Little Rock (Ark.): 256 fn.
Little Rock: half-breed Indian, 49-50
Livingstone (Mont.): 74-75
Lockwood Flats: 269
Lodge Grass Creek: 134
Log trains: 60
Long Beach (Calif.): 14
Looks-with-his-Ear: Crow Indian, 148, 152-53
Luce, Maj. E. S: 257

McArthur, C.H: 171
McClernand, Lt. Edward J: 31
McCormick, Paul: 113, 115, 135, 167, 170-71
McCormick Ferry: 171
McDougall, Capt. T.M: 109, 111-12
McGovern, Chief Trumpeter: 248
McGuire, Trumpeter: 248
McHale, Edward: 73
McHale, Red: 96
McMannus, James: 172
McNutt, Jim: 113, 166
McNutts Ranch: 73

Mackinaw boats: 39-40
Macklin, Lt. James E: 35
Mad Deer (Sioux chief): 143
Maennerchor Club: 78, 80
Maloy, Pvt. ---: 149
Man-Who-Wraps-Up-His-Tail: see Swordbearer
Mann, Lt. ---: 111
Mantle, Senator: 222-24
Maow, Professor: 92, 95
Marquis, Dr. Thomas B: 13, 18-19, 139, 242
Marsh, Capt. Grant: 16, 32; stuck on the Big Horn River, 34
Marsh, Roy: 266
Martin, Dr. T: 172
Masonic Lodge: 78
Maynard, Hank: 14, 269-70
Maynard, Lillian Klenck: 13, 261, 267-68, 294
Mechanics: 29
Medicine Crow: Crow Indian, 161
Medicine Man, The: see Swordbearer
Medicine Tail: Crow Indian, 165
Meloy, Harriett C: 14
Merchant's Forwarding Co: 170
Merchants Hotel: 256 fn.
Messiah: see Wovoka
Mexican War: 256 fn.
Miler, Lt. ---: 148
Miles, Gen. Nelson A: 17, 28-29, 35, 294; in Bannock campaign, 49-54
Miles City (Mont.): 14, 16, 33, 40, 206, 225
Miles City (Mont.) *Journal:* 118; see also *Yellowstone Journal*
Miller, Fred: 16, 213, 231
Mills, Lt. Anson L: 74-75
Milwaukee (Wis.): 14
Minneapolis (Minn.): 76
Minneconjous: 107
Minser, Col. J. K: 204
Missouri, Kansas and Texas Railway: 28
Missouri, Military Div. of: 274
Missouri River: 27-29, 57, 120, 169, 221, 226, 276

"Modoc" (race horse): 75
Moffett, Pvt. Rolando: 59, 61; describes building of Ft. Custer, 60
Monk, Hank: 177
Montana: 15, 27, 40, 54, 58, 142, 155, 173-74, 182, 198, 201, 204, 208, 218, 225, 227, 254, 261, 269, 293
Montana Historical Society: 14
Montana, Territory of: 273, 275, 278
Moore, Billy: 80
Morrow, Stanley J: 16, 43, 45, 51, 253
Morton, Edward: 92
Moylan, Capt. Myles: 150
Mules: 49, 57, 60
Musselshell River: 273

Napier, Sir Chas: 102
Napoleon gun: 275
National Archives: 18, 20
National Indian War Veterans: 60
Negroes: see Tenth Cavalry
"Nellie Peck": see steamboats
Nelson, Mabel Klenck: 13, 195, 267-69, 294
New Mexico: 124 fn.
New Orleans: 29
Newman, Annie: 93
New York (N.Y.): 39, 58, 87, 293
New York *Tribune:* 174
Newspapers: 27
Nez Perce Indians: 40, 48
Nine-mile Hole Creek: 194
Ninth Cavalry: 164
Ninth Infantry: 68
North Dakota: 37, 191
North Hollywood (Calif.): 13
Northern Pacific Railway: 42, 57, 170, 174-75, 202, 206, 227, 276, 294
Norvell, Maj. Stevens T: 290
Norwood, Capt. Randolph: 36
Nurre, Patricia: 14

Oakley, Ann: 206
O'Donnell, I.D: 50
Officer's Literary Club: 78
Ogallalas: 107
Ogden (Utah): 39

Ohio: 65
"Old Frenchie" (cook): 229
Old Kearney (Crow chief): 147
O'Leary, Maurice J: 113
Olsen, Trumpeter Anton "Kid": 248; describes job, 248-50; at Swordbearer fight, 250
Oluck, Trumpeter: 248
Omaha (Neb.): 221
O'Neill, Lt. ---: 218
Opera house: 230, 232, 236
Orchestra: 86, 92-93, 116
Oregon horses: 30
Osborne, 2nd Lt. William H: 212
Osten, Geo: 14
Overland Stage: 176
Ox Team: 33, 34, 246; described, 40-41

Pah-ches-tab: see Swordbearer
Pakes, Fraser: 181-82
Pass Creek: 142
Paymaster: 86
Penwell, Trumpeter: 109, 248
Pepper, Tom: 112
Perkins, ---: band musician, 80
Perry, Lt. Col. David: 204, 290
Pershing, Gen. John J: 17, 204
Photographers: 16
Piegan Indians: 115, 118, 120, 123, 142, 214
Pilcher, Lt. James: 74
Pioneer Press (St. Paul, Minn.): 113, 118, 127, 179
Pirates of Penzance: 75
Pitcher, Lt. John: 183, 186
Plainfeather: Crow Indian, 266-67
Platte, Dept. of: 274
Plenty Coups, chief: 17-18, 67, 145, 212, 236, 266
Poe, Col. Orlando M: 35
Pompey's Pillar: 173, 236
Poplar River: 57, 59
Porcupine (Cheyenne Indian): 181
Portello, Col. ---: 111
Porter, Dr. H. R: 109, 111-12
Post Returns: see Ft. Custer
Powell, Father Peter J: 189 fn.

INDEX

Powers, Provost Sgt. Mickey: 73
Pretty Eagle: Crow chief, 134, 147-48, 163
Prospectors: 42
Pryor (Mont.): 212, 236; Indian museum at, 266; general store, 266-67
Pryor Creek: 130, 144, 192-93
Pryor Gap: 55
Pugh, Chas. W: 93
Purvis, Pvt. James O: 20, 71, 81, 86, 89, 91, 100, 103, 110, 112; nickname, 21, 71; character described, 21; discharged, 72, 112; re-enlists, 72, 112; writes Ft. Custer News, 73, 112; view on dogs and Indians, 73; on band, 75-76; on deserters, 76; on work and drill; post hospital, 80; on military and civil courts, 80-81; on restaurants, 82; on soldiers gardens, 84; on "dog-robbers," 85; describes church services, 86; letter to newspaper, 87-89; describes Decoration Day ceremony, 94; on summer uniforms, 95-96; on soldier's pensions, 98-100; reports 10th anniversary of Custer fight, 100-12; comments on Godfrey's speech, 101

Quartermaster Dept: 48, 116

Railroads: 28, 32, 39, 42, 57, 82, 170, 174-75, 202, 206, 227, 247, 276, 279, 294
Rain-in-the-Face (Sioux chief): 66
Raises Up, Robert: blacksmith, 229
Ralston, J. K: 14
Rattlesnakes: 36
Read, Lt. Ogden B: 37, 49; becomes Capt., 59
Read (Reade), Capt. Robt. D: 202-03, 218
Red Cherries (Cheyenne Indian): 131-33
Red Fish (Sioux chief): 143
Red Tomahawk (Indian policeman): 156 fn.
Remington, Frederic: 17, 119

Reno, Maj. Marcus: 30 fn., 72, 101-04, 108, 196-97, 293; at Custer fight, 101-08; reburied, 105 fn.
Reno Creek: 106
Reno Hill: 17
Reva, Lt. ---: 35
Reynolds, Mike: 14, 118; describes Swordbearer death, 156-58
Reynolds, Maj. S.G: 118, 155, 236-37 fn.; supervises dismantling of Ft. Custer, 229
Richardson, Irvin A: 47
Rienzi, ---: comment on fort, 194
River Press (Ft. Benton, Mont.): 118
Roahen, Ken: 14, 145
Robertson, Lt. Samuel C: 184, 187; account of Lame Deer episode, 183-88; commands Crow scouts, 211
Rock, The (Crow Indian): 148, 152
Rock Creek (Wyo.): 39, 174, 276
Rocky Mts: 48
Rocky Mountain *Husbandman* (Great Falls, Mont.): 27
Roe, Lt. Chas. F: 42, 44, 105; 248-49 fns.
"Rosebud": *see* steamboats
Rosebud Creek: 57, 133, 196
Rounder's Club: 114, 116
Ruger, Brig. Gen. Thomas H: 129-30, 142, 152, 179-81; issues ultimatum to Swordbearer, 147-48
Running Antelope (Sioux chief): 143
Ryan, 2nd Lt. G. L: 149

St. Joseph (Mo.): 60
St. Louis (Mo.): 28
St. Paul (Minn.): 114, 129, 184, 227, 256 fn.
St. Paul (Minn.) *Globe:* 111; see also *Pioneer Press*
Sanborn, Capt. Washington I: 217, 290
Sand Rock Agency: 293
Sanderson, Capt. Geo. K: 45, 105 fn., 289
Sanford, Maj. Geo. B: 289
Savior: *see* Wovoka
Sawmill: 60, 254, 277

Schneider, Bernard: 241
Schneider, Chas. F: 241-42, 248 fn.; trip to Ft. Custer, 242-43; describes Ft. Custer, 243-48
Schofield, Lt. ---: 31
Schwerin, Cpl. ---: 93
Scott, Gen. Hugh: 17
Second Cavalry: 30-31, 42, 44, 52, 62, 289, 293; Troop L, 36; headquarters, 42, 274; Troop M, 274, 291; Troop C, 274, 291; Troop D, 274, 291; Troop K, 274, 291
Self, Josephine: 13
Server, Fred: 171
Server Hotel: 171
Seventeenth Infantry: 116, 289; Troop J, 291; Troop K, 291
Seventh Cavalry: 17, 28, 35, 40, 72, 100, 102-03, 110, 164; Troop I, 30, 274; Troop L, 40; Co. K, 104
Seventh Infantry: 59
Shane, Frank: 212
Sheep, Mountain: see wild game
Sheffler, Trumpeter: 248
Sheridan, Lt. Col. Michael V: 274
Sheridan, Lt. Gen. Philip H: 16, 35, 274; report to Sec. of War, 15, 273
Sheridan (Wyo.): 218, 222-26
Sheridan *Enterprise* (Wyo.): 218, 222-23, 225
Sheridan *Post* (Wyo.): 218, 223
Sherman, Gen. William T: 16, 32, 35-36, 274
Shick, Hugh and Penny: 13
Shoshone Agency (Ida.): 180
Shoshone Indians: 131
"Silver City": see steamboats
Simpson, Cpl. ---: 149
Sioux Indians: 40, 56, 66, 122, 142-43, 191, 214, 274-75, 294; at Custer fight, 103, 106, 196
Sitting Bull: 18, 117, 156 fn., 215; at Custer fight, 104, 106; stimulates Crows to action, 131, 144
Slocum, Col. ---: 111
Snake Indians: 131

Snowy Mts: 242
Snyder, Maj. Simon: 148
Soubier, Cliff: 14
Spain: 208
Spanish-American War: 202, 204, 227, 275
Spaulding, Capt. Edward J: 289
Spear, Chas: 171
Sports: Crow Indian, 162
Spotted Rabbit (Crow Indian): 158
Spring Creek: 193
Stagecoaches: 38-39, 61-63, 246, 252, 254-55; ride on described, 173-77
Standgrebe, Christine: 93
Standing Rock Agency: 28, 37, 101, 143, 215
Steamboats: 22, 28-30, 36, 66, 265; cordelling and warping, 32; meals on, 34
Steamboats (by name): *Arkansas*, 36 fn.; *Ashland*, 29-30, 36 fn.; *F.Y. Batchelor*, 36 fn., 253-54; *Big Horn*, 36 fn.; *Caro*, 68; *Dugan*, 30, 36 fn.; *E. H. Durfee*, 36 fn.; *Fanchin*, 36 fn.; *Far West*, 36 fn.; *J. C. Fletcher*, 36 fn.; *Florence*, 36 fn.; *Fontanelle*, 36 fn.; *General Custer*, 36 fn.; *General Meade*, 36 fn.; *General Sherman*, 36 fn.; *Josephine*, 36 fn., 255; *Kendall*, 36 fn.; *Meyer*, 36 fn.; *Nellie Peck*, 28, 36 fn.; *Osceola*, 36 fn.; *Peninah*, 36 fn.; *J. H. Rankin*, 36 fn.; *Rosebud*, 32-34, notable gathering on, 35, 36 fn.; *Savanah*, 36 fn.; *Silver City*, 35, 36 fn.; *Tidal Wave*, 36 fn.; *Tiger*, 36 fn.; *Victory*, 36 fn.; *Weaver*, 36 fn.; *Western*, 36 fn.; *Yellowstone*, 36 fn.
Stevenson, M. Allie: 118; account of Swordbearer's death, 158
Steward, Tom: 159
Stewart, Esther: 14
Stillwater River: 49, 61, 211, 214
Sturgis, Gen. ---: 40
Sultz, ---: army officer, 28
Surveyors: 42
Sweet, Capt. Owen J: 218, 290

INDEX

Swordbearer: 18, 117, 123, 125-26, 128-31, 133-35, 142, 146-47, 207, 248, 250; leads horse stealing raid, 122, 148, 159; becomes prophet, 122; seeks Cheyenne aid, 131-33; possesses occult power, 138, 155, 162-63; gains prestige among Crows, 140-41; final fight with, 147-52; death of, 150, 155-59, 165-66, 250; legend of, 165-66

Target ranges: 74, 78, 87-91; at Ft. Keogh, 90
"Tattler" (race horse): 75
Teamsters: 41
Teeple, Cpl. ---: 76
Tenth Cavalry: 4, 16-17, 22, 198, 203, 205-08, 275, 290; arrives in Mont., 201-02, 206, 275; origin of nickname "Buffalo Soldiers," 201 fn.; Troop A, 202, 217-18, 275, 291; Troop B, 202, 275, 291; Troop E, 202, 275, 291; Troop G, 202, 206, 275, 291; Troop K, 202, 218, 291; Troop C, 202, 218; Troop F, 202; Troop D, 202, 217; Troop H, 202; actions described, 202; commanders of, 204; Troop L becomes Crow scouts, 211; Headquarters Co., 275; sent to Cuba, 275; Troop L, 291; Troop M, 291; band, 291
Terry, Dr. ---: 56
Terry, Brig. Gen. Alfred H: 32, 35, 42, 101-02; at Custer fight, 104-05, 107, 121; report to Sec. of War, 15, 273
Terry's Landing (Mont. Terr.): 27, 33, 36, 39, 46, 66, 169, 276; founded, 37; ferry described, 37-38; gold prospectors at, 42; railway surveyors at, 42
Texas: 28, 198
Third Infantry: Troop C, 291; Troop E, 291
Thompson, Capt. ---: 31
Thompson, H. C: interpreter, 131
Thompson, Hiram: 251, 254
Thompson, Sara: 250; recalls life at Ft. Custer, 251-58

Thompson, Whitehorse Jack: 251
Throssel, Richard: 145
Tingell, ---: news reporter, 111
Titus, Sgt. ---: 112
Tongue River: 133
Tongue River Agency (Mont.): 179-82
Townsend, Lt. Col. Edwin F: 289
Trout: see wild game
Troxel, Capt. Thomas G: 289
Trumpeters: 248-50
Tullock's Fork: 57, 277
Twenty-Fifth Infantry: 203, 213, 215, 227-28, 290; Co. A, 275, 291; Co. D, 275, 291
Twenty-second Infantry: 30
Two Leggings: Crow Indian, 18
Two Moon, Chief: 117; refuses to join Crows against whites, 132-33
Two Whistles: Crow Indian, 151 fn., 207; wounded, 158
Tyler, Capt. ---: 31

Uncapapa Sioux: 107
Union Pacific Railroad: 39, 174, 276
U. S. Army: see army; artillery; band; Dakota Dept.; infantry; cavalry; Missouri Div.; Post Returns; Platte Dept.; Quartermaster Dept.
U. S. departments: Indian, 121; Interior, 121, 127; War, 127, 129-30, 219-25, 229, 234
Upham, Capt. F. K: 150
Upton, Frances: 13, 269
Upton, Geo: 14
Upton, Hazel: 14
Utica (N.Y.) Sunday *Tribune*: 87, 89

Van Squall, ---: store employee, 47
Viele, Maj. Chas. D: 290
Virginia Military Institute: 22
Virginia Peninsula Campaign: 256 fn.

Wainwright, Gen. Jonathan: 151 fn.
Wainwright, Lt. Robt. P. P: 151 fn.
Walker, Bandmaster: 75, 77, 270
Walker Lake (Nev.): 181

Walker's Opera Co: 78
Wallace, Sgt. John: 207, 212, 229
Walsh, P. J: 14
War Dept: 127, 129-30, 219-25, 229, 234; Secretary of, 15, 273, 279
Warping: *see* steamboats
Warren, Senator: 225
Warren, Floyd: 14
Washington (D.C.): 20, 65, 79, 95, 105, 121, 124, 126, 147, 166, 208, 218, 222-23, 225-27
Weir, Lt. Thomas: 104
Weltner, Fred: 264
Wesendorf, Capt. Max: 149, 160
West Point: 22, 105, 256
White, Sgt. Maj. Henry: 79, 95
White Rain Mts: *see* Big Horn Mts.
White Swan: Crow Indian, 109
Whitewood, Physician: 31
Whitehorse Jack: *see* Thompson, W.
Whitney, Frank S: 171-72
Whitney, Lt. John: 35
Wilcox, Lt. Col. John A: 290
Wild game: 55, 251; elk, 37, 251; deer, 37, 44, 251; buffalo, 37, 44, 59, 251; mountain sheep, 37; trout, 44, 49, 55-56; antelope, 59, 243, 251; bear, 251
Willert, Jim: 14
Williams, W. L: 172
Williamson, Agent Henry E: 117-18, 120, 124-25, 140, 156, 158; Crow hostility towards, 127-28; resigns as Crow Indian agent, 166-67
Wills, Frank: 76
Wind River: 56
Winners of the West: 60, 113
Wilson, Chas. "Smokey": 204
Wolf Mts: 107, 277
Wounded Knee (So. Dak.): 117, 179, 191, 215
Wovoka: 179; described, 180-81
Wraps-Up-His-Tail: *see* Swordbearer
Wright, Lt. ---: 31
Wright, Lt. Edmund S: 211-12
Wyman, Maj. ---: 192
Wyoming: 123, 174, 222-26

Yankton (Dak. Terr.): 28
Yegen, Peter Jr: 14
Yellowstone Journal (Miles City, Mont.): 118, 131, 134, 138, 184; editorial in, 225-27
Yellowstone Park: 16, 37 fn.
Yellowstone River: 18, 27-30, 35-41, 48-49, 52, 57, 61-62, 68, 120, 169, 171, 174, 192, 253, 267, 273, 276; polution in, 37 fn.; soldiers drowned, 92
Yellowstone Valley (Mont.): 15, 22-23, 90, 198, 242, 262, 278
Youell, T. H: 170
Young Mule (Young Donkey): Cheyenne Indian, 181, 182, 183; killed, 186, 188